Sarmaha

INDIAN ADMINISTRATION THEN AND NOW

Indian Administration Then and Now

M. V. Raj Kumari

MANGLAM PUBLICATIONS
DELHI-110053 (INDIA)

Published by :
MANGLAM PUBLICATIONS
L-21/1, Street No. 5, Shivaji Marg, Near Kali Mandir,
J.P. Nagar, Kartar Nagar, West Ghonda, Delhi-110053
Phone : 011-22945677, (M.) 9968367559, 9868572512
E-mail: manglam.books2007@rediffmail.com
manglam.publications2007@rediffmail.com

Indian Administration: Then and Now

First Edition 2010

ISBN 978-93-80013-25-1

PRINTED IN INDIA

Published by Ravindra Kumar Yadav for Manglam Publications, Delhi-110053 Laser Typesetting at M. K. Graphics, Delhi- 53, Printed at Sachin Printers, Moujpur Delhi- 53

Preface

From an institutional perspective, governance involves creating capable political actors who understand how political institutions work and are able to deal effectively with them. Institutional governance involves building and supporting cultures of rights and rules that make possible the agreements represented in coalition understandings. It involves building and supporting identities, preferences, and resources that can make a polity possible. It is related to many institutions that are not suitable when the idea of governance is propagated. So we have to consider the institutional issue of local governance.

Local governance will influence the existing framework of local government. When the idea of governance is propagated, some mechanisms have to be adjusted. Such institutional reforms have to stress the relationship among local governments in a political system: on the one hand, it is a subordinated level expected to effectively implement the objectives of the higher levels of government; on the other hand, local government has to offer space for democratic choice for local actors in accordance with local preferences. These reflections point to institutional reforms in local government as one approach to solve government failures in participation, transparency, and effectiveness.

One way to guarantee efficiency is to monitor performance through continuous policy evaluation. Parts of these budget-oriented reforms are changes in the organizational structure, especially changes that seek to strike a new balance between the public and private sectors: in other words, the introduction of market-type mechanisms to public tasks. This has become a key part of management reform strategies: government positioning in a competitive environment.

— *Author*

Contents

1

Public Administration and Government Policy

Public administration can be broadly described as the study and implementation of policy. As a moral endeavour, public administration is linked to pursuing the public good through the creation of civil society and social justice. The adjective 'public' often denotes 'government', though it increasingly encompasses Non-governmental organizations such as those of civil society or any entity and its management not specifically acting in self-interest. The term public administration sometimes is taken to refer to bureaucracy (as in Federal Administration). Although used negatively, bureaucracy is needed to perform day-to-day functions of government. In truth, public administration and bureaucracy are in a sense, the same thing.

THE PRE-GENERATION

The pre-generation includes thinkers such as Plato, Aristotle and Machiavelli. Until the birth of the national state, the emphasis lay principally on the problems of moral and political nature, and on the organization of the public administration. The operation of this administration was a less urgent problem. Machiavelli wrote the book The Prince, which offered a guideline for European rulers. The operation of the administration, and not only the organization, also profited from the attention it received in this book.

From the 16th century, the national state was the reigning model of the administrative organization in Western Europe. These states needed an organization for the implementation of law and order and for setting up a defensive structure. The need for expert civil servants, with knowledge about taxes, statistics, administration and the military organization grew. In the 18th century the need for administrative expertise grew even further.

Therefore king Frederick William I of Prussia established professorates in Cameralism, an economic and social school of thought within 18th century Prussia to reform society, at the universities of Frankfurt an her Oder and Halle. The most well know professor of Cameralism was Johann Heinrich Gottlob Justi (1717-1771), who linked Cameralism and the idea of natural law with each other, but the leading Public Administration scholar at that time was Christian Wolff, who was not a Cameralist. Cameralism is a predecessor of the modern science of public administration.

The First Generation

Lorenz von Stein, since 1855 professor in Vienna, is considered the founder of the science of public administration. In the time of Von Stein the science of public administration was considered to be a form of administrative law, but Von Stein thought that opinion was too restrictive. His opinions were innovative in several respects:

- He considered the science of public administration a melting pot of several disciplines, like sociology, political sciences, administrative law and public finance. In the opinion of Von Stein the science of public administration was an integrating science.
- According to Von Stein the science of public administration was an interaction between theory and practice. He considered the public administration as leading practically, but the theory had to form the base.
- Von Stein thought that the science of public administration should strive to adopt a scientific method.

In the United States Woodrow Wilson was the first to consider the science of public administration important. Wilson was more influential to the science of public administration than Von Stein, primarily due to an article Wilson wrote in 1887 in which he argued in favour of four concepts:

- o Separation between politics and the public administration.
- o Consideration of the government from a commercial perspective.
- o Comparative analysis between political and private organizations and political schemes.
- o Reaching effective management by training civil servants and assess their quality.

The separation between politics and the public administration, which Wilson argued, has been the subject of fierce debates for a long time, and the different points of view on this subject differentiate periods in the science of public administration.

The Second Generation

The discussion about the separation between politics and the public administration as argued by Wilson continued to play an important role up to 1945. Luther Gulick and Lyndall Urwick were the founders of the Science of Administration. They integrated the ideas of earlier theorists like Henri Fayol into a comprehensive theory of administration. Gulick and Urwick believed that the thoughts of Fayol offered a systematic treatment of management, which was unique at that time. They believed that this could be applied as well for the management of companies as for administrative sciences. They did not want to separate the two disciplines, but believed a single Science of Administration, which exceeds the borders between the private and the public sector, could exist. Later on the Science of Administration would focus primarily on governmental organizations. The reasoning of the Science of Administration was largely borrowed from the fourteen principles of organization of Fayol.

The Third Generation

After 1945 the third generation arose which questioned the ideas of Wilson and the second generation. Initially the distinction between politics and the public administration was strongly relativized by the third generation, but the discussion would continue. Because of the unsuccessful American intervention in Vietnam and the Watergate scandal politics got discredited and in the eighties there was again a plea in favour of bureaucracy, especially in the United States. The public administration had to detach itself from politics.

After Louis Brownlow from the University of Chicago chaired the Hoover Commission on the Reorganization of Government, he founded Public Administration Service on the University of Chicago campus (at 1313 E. 60th Street). From 193 until the late 1970s PAS provided consulting services to governments at all levels: cities counties, states, the federal government and many foreign countries.

PUBLIC ADMINISTRATION AS AN ACADEMIC DISCIPLINE

A Public Administrator can fill many voids. The academic field evolved in the United States from both academic political science and law as a separate study in the 1910s. In Europe, notably England and Germany (Max Weber), it started as a separate scholarly field in the 1890s, but it was first taught in Continental universities in the 1720s. The Federalist Papers several times referred to the importance of good administration, and scholars such as John A. Rohr see a long history behind the constitutional legitimacy of government bureaucracy.

A few public administration theorists advocate a bright line differentiation of the professional field from related academic disciplines like political science and sociology. But, in general, the interdisciplinary nature of PA is acknowledged and it is viewed as a field of study rather than a discipline.

As a field, public administration can be compared to business administration, and the MPA viewed as similar to an MBA for those wishing to pursue governmental or non-profit careers. An MPA often entails substantial ethical and sociological aspects not usually found in business schools. There are derivative and related degrees that address public affairs, public policy, and the like. Differences often connote program emphases on policy analysis techniques or other topical focuses such as the study of international affairs as opposed to focuses on constitutional issues such as separation of powers, administrative law, problems of governance and power, and participatory democracy.

Public administration theory is the domain where discussions of the meaning and purpose of government, bureaucracy, budgets, governance, and public affairs take place in the field. In recent years, public administration theory has occasionally connoted a heavy orientation toward critical theory and postmodern philosophical notions of government, governance, and power, but many public administration scholars support a classic definition of the term which gives weight to constitutionality, service, bureaucratic forms of organization, and hierarchical government.

There is minor tradition that holds that the more specific term public management refers to ordinary, routine or typical management concerns, but in the context of achieving public good. Others see public management as a new, economically driven perspective on the operation of government. This latter view is often termed "new public management" by its advocates and can be seen as a reform attempt aimed at re-emphasizing the professional nature of the field versus its academic, moral or disciplinary characteristics.

Bureaucracy

Bureaucracy is a concept in sociology and political science referring to the way that the administrative execution and enforcement of legal rules are socially organized. This office organization is characterized by standardized procedure (rule-following), formal division of responsibility, hierarchy, and impersonal relationships.

Examples of everyday bureaucracies include governments, armed forces, corporations, hospitals, courts, ministries and schools. A few specific examples of bureaucracies are the Department of Motor Vehicles and the College Board.

Origin of the Concept

Bureaucracy is derived from the word bureau, used from the early 18th century in Western Europe not just to refer to a writing desk, but to an office, i.e. a workplace, where officials worked. The original French meaning of the word bureau was the baize used to cover desks. The term bureaucracy came into use shortly before the French Revolution of 1789, and from there rapidly spread to other countries. The Greek suffix-kratia or kratos-means "power" or "rule". Bureaucracy thus basically means office power or office rule, the rule of the officialdom.

In a letter of July 1, 1764, the French Baron de Grimm declared: "We are obsessed by the idea of regulation, and our Masters of Requests refuse to understand that there is an infinity of things in a great state with which a government should not concern itself." Jean Claude Marie Vincent de Gournay sometimes used to say, "We have an illness in France which bids fair to play havoc with us; this illness is called bureaumania." Sometimes he used to invent a fourth or fifth form of government under the heading of "bureaucracy". In another letter of July 15, 1765 Baron Grimm wrote also, "The real spirit of the laws in France is that bureaucracy of which the late Monsieur de Gournay used to complain so greatly; here the offices, clerks, secretaries, inspectors and intendants are not appointed to benefit the public interest, indeed the public interest appears to have been established so that offices might exist." This quote refers to a traditional controversy about bureaucracy, namely the perversion of means and ends so that means become ends in themselves, and the greater good is lost sight of; as a corollary, the substitution of sectional interests for the general interest. The suggestion here is that, left uncontrolled, the bureaucracy will become increasingly self-serving and corrupt, rather than serving society.

However, bureaucracy existed long before words and theories were devised to describe it in detail. The Chinese Song dynasty (960 AD) for example constructed a centralized bureaucracy staffed with civilian scholar-officials. This system of rule led to a much greater concentration of power in the hands of the emperor and his palace bureaucracy than was achieved in previous dynasties. The first occurrence of this was in Ancient China, during the Wang dynasty in 380 BC.

Karl Marx and Bureaucracy

In Karl Marx's theory of historical materialism, the historical origin of bureaucracy is to be found in four sources: religion, the formation of the state, commerce and technology. Thus, the earliest bureaucracies consisted of castes of religious clergy, officials and scribes operating various rituals, and armed functionaries specifically delegated to keep order. In the historical transition from primitive egalitarian communities to a civil society divided into social classes and estates, occurring from about 10,000 years ago, authority is increasingly centralized in, and enforced by a state apparatus existing separately from society. This state formulates, imposes and enforces laws, and levies taxes, giving rise to an officialdom enacting these functions. Thus, the state mediates in conflicts among the people and keeps those conflicts within acceptable bounds; it also organises the defence of territory. Most importantly, the right of ordinary people to carry and use weapons of force becomes increasingly restricted; forcing other people to do things becomes increasingly the legal right of the state authorities only.

But the growth of trade and commerce adds a new, distinctive dimension to bureaucracy, insofar as it requires the keeping of accounts and the processing/recording of transactions, as well as the enforcement of legal rules governing trade. If resources are increasingly distributed by prices in markets, this requires extensive and complex systems of record-keeping, management and calculation, conforming to legal standards. Eventually, this means that the total amount of work involved in commercial administration outgrows the total amount of work involved in government administration. In modern capitalist society, private sector bureaucracy is larger than government bureaucracy, if measured by the number of administrative workers in the division of labour as a whole. Some corporations nowadays have a turnover larger than the national income of whole countries, with large administrations supervising operations.

A fourth source of bureaucracy Marxists have commented on inheres in the technologies of mass production, which require many standardised routines and procedures to be performed. Even if mechanisation replaces people with machinery, people are still necessary to design, control, supervise and operate the machinery. The technologies chosen may not be the ones that are best for everybody, but which create incomes for a particular class of people or maintain their power. This type of bureaucracy is nowadays often called a technocracy, which owes its power to control over specialised technical knowledge or control over critical information.

In Marx's theory, bureaucracy rarely creates new wealth by itself, but rather controls, coordinates and governs the production, distribution and consumption of wealth. The bureaucracy as a social stratum derives its income from the appropriation of part of the social surplus product of human labour. Wealth is appropriated by the bureaucracy by law through fees, taxes, levies, tributes, licensing etc.

Bureaucracy is therefore always a cost to society, but this cost may be accepted insofar as it makes social order possible, and maintains it by enforcing the rule of law. Nevertheless there are constant conflicts about this cost, because it has the big effect on the distribution of incomes; all producers will try to get the maximum return from what they produce, and minimise administrative costs. Typically, in epochs of strong economic growth, bureaucracies proliferate; when economic growth declines, a fight breaks out to cut back bureaucratic costs.

Whether or not a bureaucracy as a social stratum can become a genuine ruling class depends greatly on the prevailing property relations and the mode of production of wealth. In capitalist society, the state typically lacks an independent economic base, finances many activities on credit, and is heavily dependent on levying taxes as a source of income. Therefore, its power is limited by the costs which private owners of the productive assets will tolerate. If, however, the state owns the means of production itself, defended by military power, the state bureaucracy can become much more powerful, and act as a ruling class or power elite. Because in that case, it directly controls the sources of new wealth, and manages or distributes the social product. This is the subject of Marxist theories of bureaucratic collectivism.

Marx himself however never theorised this possibility in detail, and it has been the subject of much controversy among Marxists. The core organisational issue in these disputes concerns the degree to which the administrative allocation of resources by government authorities and the market allocation of resources can achieve the social goal of creating a more free, just and prosperous society. Which decisions should be made by whom, at what level, so that an optimal allocation of resources results? This is just as much a moral-political issue as an economic issue.

Central to the Marxian concept of socialism is the idea of workers' self-management, which assumes the internalisation of a morality and self-discipline among people that would make bureaucratic supervision and control redundant, together with a drastic reorganisation of the division of labour in society. Bureaucracies emerge to mediate conflicts of interest on the basis of laws, but if those conflicts of interest disappear (because resources are allocated directly in a fair way), bureaucracies would also be redundant.

Marx's critics are however skeptical of the feasibility of this kind of socialism, given the continuing need for administration and the rule of law, as well as the propensity of people to put their own self-interest before the communal interest. That is, the argument is that self-interest and the communal interest might never coincide, or, at any rate, can always diverge significantly.

Max Weber on Bureaucracy

Max Weber has probably been one of the most influential users of the word in its social science sense. He is well-known for his study of bureaucratization of society; many aspects of modern public administration go back to him; a classic, hierarchically organized civil service of the continental type is- if basically mistakenly - called "Weberian civil service".

However, contrary to popular belief, "bureaucracy" was an English word before Weber; the Oxford English Dictionary cites usage in several different years between 1818 and 1860, prior to Weber's birth in 1864. Weber described the ideal type bureaucracy in positive terms, considering it to be a more rational and efficient form of organization than the alternatives that preceded it, which he characterized as charismatic domination and traditional domination. According to his terminology, bureaucracy is part of legal domination. However, he also emphasized that bureaucracy becomes inefficient when a decision must be adopted to an individual case.

According to Weber, the attributes of modern bureaucracy include its impersonality, concentration of the means of administration, a levelling effect on social and economic differences and implementation of a system of authority that is practically indestructible.

Weber's analysis of bureaucracy concerns:

- o the historical and administrative reasons for the process of bureaucratization (especially in the Western civilisation)
- o the impact of the rule of law upon the functioning of bureaucratic organisations
- o the typical personal orientation and occupational position of a bureaucratic officials as a status group
- o the most important attributes and consequences of bureaucracy in the modern world

A bureaucratic organization is governed by the following seven principles:

1. official business is conducted on a continuous basis
2. official business is conducted with strict accordance to the following rules:
   a. the duty of each official to do certain types of work is delimited in terms of impersonal criteria
   b. the official is given the authority necessary to carry out his assigned functions
   c. the means of coercion at his disposal are strictly limited and conditions of their use strictly defined
3. every official's responsibilities and authority are part of a vertical hierarchy of authority, with respective rights of supervision and appeal
4. officials do not own the resources necessary for the performance of their assigned functions but are accountable for their use of these resources
5. official and private business and income are strictly separated
6. offices cannot be appropriated by their incumbents (inherited, sold, etc.)

7. official business is conducted on the basis of written documents

A bureaucratic official:

- o is personally free and appointed to his position on the basis of conduct
- o exercises the authority delegated to him in accordance with impersonal rules, and his loyalty is enlisted on behalf of the faithful execution of his official duties
- o appointment and job placement are dependent upon his technical qualifications
- o administrative work is a full-time occupation
- o work is rewarded by a regular salary and prospects of advancement in a lifetime career

An official must exercise his judgment and his skills, but his duty is to place these at the service of a higher authority; ultimately he is responsible only for the impartial execution of assigned tasks and must sacrifice his personal judgment if it runs counter to his official duties. Weber's work has been continued by many, like Robert Michels with his Iron Law of Oligarchy.

Street-level Bureaucracy

Street-level bureaucracy is a term used to refer to a public agency employee who actually performs the actions that implement laws.

Examples of Street-level Bureaucrats

Street-level bureaucrats include police officers, firefighters, and others who "walk the streets" with regular citizens, and provide services to protect, as well as uphold the laws.

SYSTEM ADMINISTRATOR

A system administrator, or sysadmin, is a person employed to maintain, and operate a computer system or network for a company or other organization. System administrators are often members of an information technology department.

The duties of a system administrator are wide-ranging, and vary widely from one organization to another. Sysadmins are usually charged with installing, supporting, and maintaining servers or other computer systems, and planning for and responding to service outages and other problems. Other duties may include scripting or light programming, project management for systems-related projects, supervising or training computer operators, and being the equivalent of a handyman for computer problems beyond the knowledge of technical support staff.

Skills

The subject matter of systems administration includes computer systems and the ways people use them in an organization. This entails a knowledge of operating systems and applications, as well as hardware and software troubleshooting, but also knowledge of the purposes for which people in the organization use the computers. However, perhaps the most important skill to a system administrator is problem solving-frequently under various sorts of constraints and stress. The sysadmin is on call when a computer system goes down or malfunctions, and must be able to quickly and correctly diagnose what is wrong and how best to fix it. System administrators are not software engineers or developers. It is not usually within their duties to design or write new applications software. However, sysadmins must understand the behaviour of software in order to deploy it and to troubleshoot problems, and generally know several programming languages used for scripting or automation of routine tasks.

Particularly when dealing with Internet-facing or business-critical systems, a sysadmin must have a strong grasp of computer security. This includes not merely deploying software patches, but also preventing break-ins and other security problems with preventative measures. In some organizations, computer security administration is a separate role responsible for overall security and the upkeep of firewalls and intrusion detection systems, but all sysadmins are generally responsible for the security of the systems in their keep.

Related Fields

Many organizations staff other jobs related to systems administration. In a larger company, these may all be separate positions within a computer support or Information Services (IS) department. In a smaller group they may be shared by a few sysadmins, or even a single person.

- o A database administrator (DBA) maintains a database system, and is responsible for the integrity of the data and the efficiency and performance of the system.
- o A network administrator maintains network infrastructure such as switches and routers, and diagnoses problems with these or with the behaviour of network-attached computers.
- o A security administrator is a specialist in computer and network security, including the administration of security devices such as firewalls, as well as consulting on general security measures.
- o Technical support staff respond to individual users' difficulties with computer systems, provide instructions and sometimes training, and diagnose and solve common problems.
- o A computer operator performs routine maintenance and upkeep, such as changing backup tapes or replacing failed drives in a RAID array. Such tasks usually require physical presence in the room with the computer; and while less skilled than sysadmin tasks require a similar level of trust, since the operator has access to possibly sensitive data.

In some organizations, a person may begin as a member of technical support staff or a computer operator, then gain experience on the job to be promoted to a sysadmin position and afterwards an IT Manager.

Training

Unlike many other professions, there is no single path to becoming a system administrator. Few colleges or universities have specific programs for system administration, so many system administrators have a degree in generic fields: computer science, computer engineering, information system management, or even a trade school program. As of 2006, only four U.S. Universities, Rochester Institute of Technology, Tufts, Florida State University,

Miller-Motte Technical College in AAS in Microcomputer Applications Systems Network Engineer and Michigan Tech have postgraduate programs in system administration. In Europe, Norway, there is a special English-taught MSc programme organized by Oslo University College in cooperation with Oslo University, named "Masters programme in Network and System Administration". The founder of the programme is the creator of avenging, Mark Burgess. In addition, because of the practical nature of systems administration and the easy availability of open-source server software, many systems administrators enter the field self-taught.

Generally, a prospective administrator will be required to have some experience with the computer system he or she is expected to manage. In some cases, candidates are expected to possess industry certifications such as the Microsoft MCSA or Red Hat RHCE. At the same time, some employers consider reliance on such certifications to be a sign of a poor candidate, or 'paper cert'-someone who has trade-school "book learning" rather than formal theoretical knowledge or hard practical experience.

Sometimes, almost exclusively in smaller sites, the role of system administrator may be given to a skilled user in addition to or in replacement of his or her duties.

Duties of a System Administrator

A system administrator's responsibilities typically include:

- o Morning checks of systems/software.
- o Performing backups of data.
- o Applying operating system updates, and configuration changes.
- o Installing and configuring new hardware/software.
- o Adding/deleting/creating/modifying user account information, resetting passwords, etc.
- o Answering technical queries.
- o Responsibility for security.
- o Responsibility for documenting the configuration of the system.

- o Troubleshooting any reported problems.
- o System performance tuning.
- o Keeping the network up and running.

In larger organizations, some tasks listed above may be divided among different system administrators or members of different organizational groups. For example, a dedicated individual may apply all system upgrades, a Quality Assurance (QA) team may perform testing and validation, and one or more technical writers may be responsible for all technical documentation written for a company. In smaller organizations, the system administrator can also perform any number of duties elsewhere associated with other fields:

- o Technical support
- o Database administrator (DBA)
- o Network administrator/analyst/specialist
- o Application analyst
- o Security administrator
- o Programmer

System administrators, in larger organizations, also tend not to be system architects, system engineers, or system designers, however, like many roles in this field, demarcations between systems administration and these other roles are often not well defined in smaller organizations. However, even in larger organizations, senior systems administrators often have skills in these other areas as a result of their working experience.

In smaller organizations, IT/computing specialities are less often discerned in detail, and the term "system administrator" is used in a rather generic way - they are the people who know how the computer systems work and can respond when something fails.

Public Policy

Public policy is a course of action or inaction chosen by public authorities to address a problem. Public policy is expressed in the body of laws, regulations, decisions and actions of government. Policy analysis may be used to formulate public policy and to evaluate its effectiveness. Many public policy analysts earn Ph.D., Master of Public Policy and Master of Public Administration degrees in public policy schools, while others earn specialized degrees, such as an M.Ed for specializing in educational policy or an MSW for specializing in social welfare policy.

Various Definitions

According to William Jenkins in Policy Analysis: A Political and Organizational Perspective (1978), a Public Policy is 'a set of interrelated decisions taken by a political actor or group of actors concerning the selection of goals and the means of achieving them within a specified situation where those decisions should, in principle, be within the power of those actors to achieve'. Thus, Jenkins understands Public Policy making to be a process, and not simply a choice. According to Thomas A. Birkland in An Introduction to the Policy Process (2001), there is a lack of a consensus on the definition of public policy. Birkland outlines a few definitions of public policy:

- Clarke E. Cochran, et al.: "The term public policy always refers to the actions of government and the intentions that determine those actions".
- Clarke E. Cochran, et al.: "Public policy is the outcome of the struggle in government over who gets what".
- Thomas Dye: Public policy is "Whatever governments choose to do or not do".
- Charles L. Cochran and Eloise F. Malone: "Public policy consists of political decisions for implementing programs to achieve societal goals".
- B. Guy Peters: "Stated most simply, public policy is the sum of government activities, whether acting directly or through agents, as it has an influence on the life of citizens".

Birkland indicates that the elements common to all definitions of public policy are as follows (p. 20):

- The policy is made in the name of the "public".
- Policy is generally made or initiated by government.
- Policy is interpreted and implemented by public and private actors.

- o Policy is what the government intends to do.
- o Policy is what the government chooses not to do.

History of Public Policy

According to Birkland: While the study of politics has a long history, the systematic study of public policy, on the other hand, can be said to be a twentieth century creation. It dates, according to Daniel McCool, to 1922, when political scientist Charles Merriam sought to connect the theory and practices of politics to understanding the actual activities of government, that is public policy."

Types of Public Policy

Domestic Policy

In government, domestic policy is the counterpart of foreign policy; it consists of all government policy decisions, programs, and actions that primarily deal with internal matters, as opposed to relations with other nation-states. Major areas of domestic policy include tax policy, social security and welfare programs, environmental laws, and regulations on businesses and their practices.

Education Policy

Education policy refers to the collection of laws or rules that govern the operation of education systems. It seeks to answer questions about the purpose of education, the objectives (societal and personal) that it is designed to attain, the methods for attaining them and the tools for measuring their success or failure.

Education being an activity that impacts upon people of all ages, Education policy may be broken down into policy as regards preschool provision, schooling, adult education and training, university education, and so on.

Examples of areas subject to debate in education policy, specifically from the field of schools, include school size, class size, school choice, school privatization, tracking, teacher education and certification, teacher pay, teaching methods, curricular content, graduation requirements, school infrastructure investment, and the values that schools are expected to uphold and model. Education policy analysis is the scholarly study of education policy. Research intended to inform education policy is carried out in a wide variety of institutions and in many academic disciplines. Important researchers are affiliated with departments of psychology, economics, sociology, and human development, in addition to schools and departments of education or public policy. Examples of education policy analysis may be found in such academic journals as Education Policy Analysis Archives.

Energy Policy

Energy policy is the manner a given entity (often governmental) has decided to address issues of energy production, distribution and consumption. The attributes of energy policy may include legislation, international treaties, incentives to investment, guidelines for energy conservation, taxation and other public policy techniques.

National Energy Policy

Measures used to Produce an Energy Policy

A national energy policy is comprised by set of measures involving that country's laws, treaties and agency directives. The energy policy of a sovereign nation may include one or more of the following measures:

- statement of national policy regarding energy generation, transmission and usage
- legislation on commercial energy activities (trading, transport, storage, etc.)
- legislation affecting energy use, such as efficiency standards, emission standards
- instructions for state owned energy sector assets and organizations
- active participation in, coordination of and incentives for mineral fuels exploration (see geological survey) and other energy-related research and development
- fiscal policies related to energy products and services (taxes, exemptions, subsidies...

- o international policy measures such as:
- o international energy sector treaties and alliances,
- o general international trade agreements,
- o special relations with energy-rich countries, including military presence and/or domination.

Frequently the dominant issue of energy policy is the risk of supply-demand mismatch. Current energy policies also address environmental issues. Some governments state explicit energy policy, but, declared or not, each government practices some type of energy policy.

Factors within an Energy Policy

There are a number of elements that are naturally contained in a national energy policy, regardless of which of the above measures was used to arrive at the resultant policy. The chief elements intrinsic to an energy policy are:

- o What is the extent of energy self-sufficiency for this nation
- o Where future energy sources will derive
- o How future energy will be consumed (e.g. among sectors)
- o What fraction of the population will be acceptable to endure energy poverty
- o What are the goals for future energy intensity, ratio of energy consumed to GDP
- o What is the reliability standard for distribution reliability
- o What environmental externalities are acceptable and are forecast
- o What form of "portable energy" is forecast (e.g. sources of fuel for motor vehicles)
- o How will energy efficient hardware (e.g. hybrid vehicles, household appliances) be encouraged
- o How can the national policy drive province, state and municipal functions
- o What specific mechanisms (e.g. taxes, incentives, manufacturing standards) are in place to implement the total policy

State, Province or Municipal Energy Policy

Even within a state it is proper to talk about energy policies in plural. Influential entities, such as municipal or regional governments and energy industries, will each exercise policy. Policy measures available to these entities are lesser in sovereignty, but may be equally important to national measures.

In fact, there are certain activities vital to energy policy which realistically cannot be administered at the national level, such as monitoring energy conservation practices in the process of building construction, which is normally controlled by state-regional and municipal building codes (although can appear basic federal legislation).

Environmental Policy

Environmental policy may refer to either the private sector or the public sector. In the public sector it generally refers to a government's use and creation of the laws, regulations, and other policy mechanisms concerning environmental issues and sustainability. In the private sector it usually refers to the compliance with those tools, or the independent development of self-regulation and rule-making that may go beyond what is required by governments.

The environmental issues generally addressed include air and water pollution, solid waste management, ecosystem management, maintenance of biodiversity, the protection of natural resources, wildlife and endangered species. Policies concerning energy or regulation of toxic substances like pesticides and many types of industrial waste are included in the topic of environmental policy.

Environmental Preservation

Environmental preservation is the act of maintaining the natural state of a particular habitat. In terms of policy making this often means setting aside areas as nature reserves (otherwise known as wildlife reserves). These areas usually restrict or prohibit activities that may cause damage to habitat or wildlife. Such activities may include: logging, hunting, fishing, mining and so on. A government's environmental policy will determine which areas are protected and how.

Foreign Policy

A country's foreign policy is a set of political goals that seeks to outline how that particular country will interact with other countries of the world and, to a lesser extent, non-state actors. Foreign policies generally are designed to help protect a country's national interests, national security, ideological goals, and economic prosperity. This can occur as a result of peaceful cooperation with other nations, or through aggression, war, and exploitation. It may be assumed that foreign policy is as ancient as the human society itself. The twentieth century saw a rapid rise in the importance of foreign policy, with virtually every nation in the world now being able to interact with one another in some diplomatic form.

Nominally, creating foreign policy is usually the job of the head of government and the foreign minister (or equivalent). In some countries the legislature also has considerable oversight. As an exception, in France and in Finland it is the head of state who is responsible for foreign policy, while the head of government mainly deals with internal policy.

In fact, foreign policy is a product of pressure from various groups and classes, political as well as economic. In many countries, foreign policy ranks high on the list of factors that influence public opinion.

International Relations

International relations have been studied and analysed for centuries, and can partially explain the foreign policy of particular states. However note that International Relations Theory tries to explain the interaction in the international system between all states (and possibly non-state actors) and does not take into account the specific characteristics of particular states. The sub-discipline that specialises in the study of foreign policy is known as foreign policy analysis (FPA).

The Politics Series

International relations (IR), a branch of political science, is the study of foreign affairs of and relations among states within the international system, including the roles of states, intergovernmental organizations (IGOs), non-governmental organizations (NGOs), and multinational corporations (MNCs). It is both an academic and public policy field, and can be either positive or normative as it both seeks to analyse as well as formulate foreign policy. Apart from political science, IR draws upon such diverse fields as economics, history, law, philosophy, geography, sociology, anthropology, psychology, and cultural studies. It involves a diverse range of issues, from globalization and its impacts on societies and state sovereignty to ecological sustainability, nuclear proliferation, nationalism, economic development, terrorism, organized crime, human security, and human rights.

The International System

The history of international relations is often traced back to the Peace of Westphalia of 1648, where the modern state system was developed. Prior to this, the European medieval organization of political authority was based on a vaguely hierarchical religious order. Westphalia instituted the notion of sovereignty, which essentially meant that rulers, or sovereigns, would recognize no internal equals within a defined territory, and no external superiors. Classical Greek and Roman authority at times resembled the Westphalian system, but both lacked the notion of sovereignty. Westphalia encouraged the rise of the nation-state and the institutionalization of diplomacy and armies. This particular European system was exported to the Americas, Africa, and Asia via colonialism and the "standards of civilization". The contemporary international system was finally established through decolonization during the Cold War. However, this is somewhat over-simplified. While the nation-state system is considered "modern", many states have not incorporated the system and are termed "pre-modern". Further, a handful of states have moved beyond the nation-state system and can be considered "post-modern". The ability of contemporary IR discourse to explain the relations of these different types of states is disputed.

INTERNATIONAL RELATIONS THEORY

What is explicitly recognized as international relations theory was not developed until after World War I, and is dealt with in more detail below. IR theory, however, has a long tradition of drawing on the work of other social sciences. The use of capitalizations of the 'I' and 'R' in International Relations aims to distinguish the academic discipline of International Relations from the phenomena of international relations. Many cite Thucydides' History of the Peloponnesian War as the inspiration for realist theory, with Hobbes' Leviathan and Machiavelli's The Prince providing further elaboration. Similarly, liberalism draws upon the work of Kant and Rousseau, with the work of the former often being cited as the first elaboration of Democratic Peace Theory. Though contemporary human rights is considerably different than the type of rights envisioned under natural law, Francisco de Vitoria, Hugo Grotius and John Locke offered the first accounts of universal entitlement to certain rights on the basis of common humanity. In the twentieth century, in addition to contemporary theories of liberal internationalism, Marxism has been a durable foundation of international relations.

The Study of IR

Initially, international relations as a distinct field of study was almost entirely British-centred. In 1919, the first Chair in International Politics established at the University of Wales, Aberystwyth, from an endowment given by David Davies, became the first academic position dedicated to IR. In the early 1920s, the London School of Economics' department of International Relations was founded at the behest of Nobel Peace Prize winner Phillip Noel-Baker. While schools dedicated to the study of IR have been founded in Asia and South America, IR as a discipline remains to be studied chiefly in Europe and North America.

Epistemology and IR Theory

IR theories can be roughly divided into one of two epistemological camps: "positivist" and "post-positivist". Positivist theories aim to replicate the methods of the natural sciences by analysing the impact of material forces. They typically focus on features of international relations such as state interactions, size of military forces, balance of powers etc. Post-positivist epistemology rejects the idea that the social world can be studied in an objective and value-free way. It rejects the central ideas of neo-realism/liberalism, such as rational choice theory, on the grounds that the scientific method cannot be applied to the social world and that a 'science' of IR is impossible.

A key difference between the two positions is that while positivist theories, such as neo-realism, offer causal explanations (such as why and how power is exercised) post-positivist theories focus instead on constitutive questions, for instance what is meant by 'power'; what makes it up, how it is experienced and how it is reproduced. Often, post-positivist theories explicitly promote a normative approach to IR, by considering ethics. This is something which has often been ignored under 'traditional' IR as positivist theories make a distinction between 'facts' and normative judgments, or 'values'.

During the late 1980s/1990 debate between positivists and post-positivists became the dominant debate and has been described as constituting the Third "Great Debate" (Lapid 1989).

Positivist Theories

Liberalism/Idealism/Liberal Internationalism

Liberalism arose after World War I in response to the inability of states to control and limit war in their international relations. Early adherents include Woodrow Wilson and Norman Angell, who argued variously that states mutually gained from cooperation and that war was so destructive to be essentially futile. Liberalism was not recognized as a coherent theory as such until it was collectively and derisively termed idealism by E. H. Carr.

Realism

Realism was a response to liberalism that chiefly denies that states seek to cooperate. Early realists such as E.H. Carr and Hans Morgenthau argued that states are self-interested, power-seeking rational actors. Any cooperation between states is explained as purely incidental. Realists saw World War II as the vindication of their theory. It should be noted that classical writers such as Thucydides, Machiavelli, and Hobbes are often cited as the "founding fathers" of realism by contemporary self-described realists. However, while their work may support realist doctrine, it is not likely that they would have classified themselves as realists (in this sense of the term).

Neorealism

Neorealism is largely the work of Kenneth Waltz (who actually called his theory "structural realism"). While retaining the empirical observations of realism, that international relations are characterized by antagonistic interstate relations, neorealists point to the anarchic structure of the international system as the cause. They reject explanations that take account of states' domestic characteristics. States are compelled by relative gains and balance against concentration of power. Unlike realism, neo-realism seeks to be scientific and more positivist.

Neoliberalism

Neoliberalism seeks to update liberalism by accepting the neorealist presumption that states are the key actors in international relations, but still maintains that non-state actors (NSAs) and intergovernmental organizations (IGOs) matter. Proponents such as Joseph Nye argue that states will cooperate irrespective of relative gains, and are thus concerned with absolute gains. The growing interdependence throughout the Cold War through international institutions means that neo-liberalism is also called liberal institutionalism. This also means that nations are, in essence, free to make their own choices as to how they will go about conducting policy without any international organizations blocking a nation's right to sovereignty. Neoliberalism also contains an economic theory that is based the use of open and free markets with little, if any, government intervention to prevent monopolies and other conglomerates from forming.

POST-POSITIVIST/REFLECTIVIST THEORIES

International Society Theory (the English School)

International society theory, also called the English School, focuses on the shared norms and values of states and how they regulate international relations. Examples of such norms include diplomacy, order, and international law. Unlike neo-realism, it is not necessarily positivist. Theorists have focused particularly on humanitarian intervention, and are subdivided between solidarists, who tend to advocate it more, and pluralists, who place greater value in order and sovereignty. Nicholas Wheeler is a prominent solidarist, while Hedley Bull is perhaps the best known pluralist.

Social Constructivism

Social Constructivism encompasses a broad range of theories that aim to address questions of ontology, such as the Structure and agency debate, as well as questions of epistemology, such as the "material/ideational" debate that concerns the relative role of material forces versus ideas. Constructivism is not a theory of IR, for example in the manner of neo-realism, but instead is a social theory.

Constructivism in IR can be divided into what Hopf (1998) calls 'conventional' and 'critical' constructivism. Common to all varieties of constructivism is an interest in the role that ideational forces play. The most famous constructivist scholar, Alexander Wendt noted in a 1992 article in International Organization (later followed up by a book, Social Theory of International Politics (1999)), that "anarchy is what states make of it". By this he means that the anarchical structure that neo-realists claim governs state interaction is in fact a phenomenon that is socially constructed and reproduced by states. For example, if the system is dominated by states that see anarchy as a life or death situation (what Wendt terms a "Hobbesian" anarchy) then the system will be characterised by warfare. If on the other hand anarchy is seen as restricted (a "Lockean" anarchy) then a more peaceful system will exist. Anarchy in this view is constituted by state interaction, rather than accepted as a natural and immutable feature of international life as viewed by neo-realist IR scholars.

Critics, however, abound from both sides of the epistemological divide: Post-positivists say the focus on the state at the expense of ethnicity/race/class/gender makes social constructivism yet another positivist theory. The use of implicit rational choice theory by Wendt has also raised criticisms from scholars such as Steven Smith. Positivist scholars of (neo-) liberalism/realism hold that the theory forgoes too many positivist assumptions for it to be considered positivist.

Critical Theory

Critical international relations theory is the application of 'critical theory' to international relations. Proponents such as Andrew Linklater and Robert Cox focus on the need for human emancipation from States. Hence, it is "critical" of mainstream IR theories that tend to be state-centric.

Marxism

Marxist and Neo-Marxist theories of IR reject the realist/ liberal view of state conflict or cooperation; instead focusing on the economic and material aspects. It makes the assumption that the economy trumps other concerns; allowing for the elevation of class as the focus of study. Marxists view the international system as an integrated capitalist system in pursuit of capital accumulation. Thus, the period of colonialism brought in sources for raw materials and captive markets for exports, while decolonialization brought new opportunities in the form of dependence.

Linked in with Marxist theories is dependency theory which argues that developed countries, in their pursuit of power, penetrate developing states through political advisors, missionaries, experts and MNCs to integrate them into the integrated capitalist system in order to appropriate natural resources and foster dependence by developing countries on developed countries.

Marxist theories receive scant attention in the United States where no significant socialist party ever existed. It is more common in parts of Europe and is one of the most important theoretic contributions of Latin American academia, for example through Liberation theology.

Poststructuralist Theories

Poststructuralist theories of IR developed in the 1980s from post-modernist studies in political science. Post-structuralism explores the deconstruction of concepts traditionally not problematic in IR, such as 'power' and 'agency' and examines how the construction of these concepts shapes international relations. The examination of 'narratives' plays an important part in poststructuralist analysis, for example feminist poststructuralist work has examined the role that 'women' play in global society and how they are constructed in war as 'innocent' and 'civilians'.

Examples of post-positivist research include:

- o Feminisms ("gendering" war)
- o Post-colonialism (challenges the euro-centrism of IR)

Systemic Level Concepts

International relations is often viewed in terms of levels of analysis, the systemic level concepts are those broad concepts that define and shape an international milieu, characterised by Anarchy.

Power

The concept of Power in international relations can be described as the degree of resources, capabilities, and influence in international affairs. It is often divided up into the concepts of hard power and soft power, hard power relating to the use of force, and soft power commonly covering economics, diplomacy and cultural influence.

Polarity

Polarity in International Relations refers to the arrangement of power within the international system. The concept arose from bipolarity during the Cold War, with the international system dominated by the conflict between two superpowers, and has been applied retrospectively. Consequently, the international system prior to 1945 can be described as multi-polar, with power being shared among Great powers. The collapse of the Soviet Union in 1991 has lead to what some would call unipolarity, with the United States as a sole superpower. Several theories of international relations draw upon the idea of polarity.

The balance of power was a concept prevalent in Europe prior to the First World War, the thought being that by balancing power blocs it would create stability and prevent war. Theories of the balance of power gained prominence again during the Cold War, being a central mechanism of Kenneth Waltz's Neorealism. Here, the concepts of balancing (rising in power to counter another) and bandwagonning (siding with another) are developed. Hegemonic stability theory also draws upon the idea of Polarity, specifically the state of unipolarity. Hegemony is the preponderance of power at one pole in the international system, and the theory argues this is stable configuration because of mutual gains by both the dominant power and others in the international system. This is contrary to many Neorealist arguments, particularly made by Kenneth Waltz, stating that the end of the Cold War and the state of unipolarity is an unstable configuration that will inevitably change.

This can be expressed in Power transition theory, which states that it is likely that a great power would challenge a hegemon after a certain period, resulting in a major war. It suggests that while hegemony can control the occurence of wars, it also results in the creation of one. It's main proponent, A.F.K. Organski, argued this based on the occurence of previous wars during British, Portugese and Dutch hegemony.

Interdependence

Many advocate that the current international system is characterised by growing interdependence; the mutual responsibility and dependency on others. Advocates of this point to growing globalization, particularly with international economic interaction. The role of international institutions, and widespread acceptance of a number of operating principles in the international system, reinforces ideas that relations are characterised by interdependence.

Dependency

Dependency theory is a theory most commonly associated with Marxism, stating that a set of Core states exploit a set of weaker Periphery states for their prosperity. Various versions of the theory suggest that this is either an inevitability (standard dependency theory), or use the theory to highlight the necessity for change (Neo-Marxist).

Systemic tools of international relations:

- o Diplomacy is the practice of conducting negotiation between representatives of states. To an extent, all other tools of international relations can be considered the failure of diplomacy.

- o Sanctions are usually a first resort after the failure of diplomacy, and are one of the main tools used to enforce treaties. They can take the form of diplomatic or economic sanctions and involve the cutting of ties and imposition of barriers to communication or trade.
- o War, the use of force, is often thought of as the ultimate tool of international relations. A widely accepted definition is that given by Clausewitz, with war being "the continuation of politics by other means". There a growing study into 'new wars' involving actors other than states. The study of war in International Relations is covered by the disciplines of 'War Studies' and 'Strategic studies'.
- o The mobilization of international shame can also be thought of as a tool of International Relations. This is attempting to alter states actions through 'naming and shaming' at the international level. A prominent use of this would be the UN Commission on Human Rights 1235 procedure, which publicly exposes states human rights violations.

Unit-level Concepts in International Relations: As a level of analysis the unit level is often referred to as the state level, as it locates its explanation at the level of the state, rather than the international system.

Regime Type

It is often considered that a states regime type can dictate the way that a state interacts with others in the international system. Democratic Peace Theory is a theory that suggests that the nature of democracy means that democratic countries will not go to war with each other. The justifications for this are that democracies externalise their norms and only go to war for just causes, and that democracy encourages mutual trust and respect. Communism justifies a world revolution, which similarly would lead to peaceful coexistence, based on a proletarian global society.

Revisionism/Status Quo

States can be classified by whether they accept the international status quo, or are revisionist, i.e. want change. Revisionist states seek to fundamentally change the rules and practices of international relations, feeling disadvantaged by the status quo. They see the international system as a largely western creation which serves to reinforce current realities. China is an example of a state that has gone from being a revisionist state to one that is satisfied with the status quo, because the status quo is now beneficial to it.

Religion

It is often considered that religion can have an effect on the way a state acts within the international system. Religion is visible as an organising principle particularly for Islamic states, whereas secularism sits at the other end of the spectrum, with the separation of state and religion being responsible for the Liberal tradition.

Individual or Sub-unit Level Concepts

The level beneath the unit (state) level can be useful both for explaining factors in International Relations that other theories fail to explain, and for moving away from a state-centric view of international relations.

- o Psychological factors in International Relations-Evaluating psychological factors in international relations comes from the understanding that a state is not a 'black box' as proposed by Realism, and that there may be other influences on foreign policy decisions. Examining the role of personalities in the decision making process can have some explanatory power, as can the role of misperception between various actors. A prominent application of sub-unit level psychological factors in international relations is the concept of Groupthink, another is the propensity of policymakers to think in terms of analogies.
- o Bureaucratic politics-Looks at the role of the bureaucracy in decision making, and sees decisions as a result of bureaucratic infighting, and as having been shaped by various constraints.
- o Religious, Ethnic, and secessionist groups-Viewing these aspects of the sub-unit level has explanatory power with regards to ethnic conflicts, religious wars, and other actors do not consider themselves to fit with the defined state

boundaries. This is particularly useful in the context of the pre-modern world of weak states.

Consent of the Governed

"Consent of the governed" is a political theory that says a government's legitimacy and moral right to use state power is, or ought to be, derived from the people or society over which that power is exercised. This theory of "consent" is historically contrasted to the divine right of kings and has often been invoked against the legitimacy of colonialism.

Following John Locke's notion of a nation of "free and equal" citizens, the Founders of the United States believed that consent of the governed was the only legitimate basis upon which one "free and equal" citizen could exercise legal authority over another-otherwise neither equal could overcome the other. This phrase is often attributed to John Locke, but the idea was around much earlier. Consent of the governed appears in the Scottish Declaration of Arbroath (1320) which states that lord Robert, because of "Divine Providence" along with "the due consent and assent of us all, have made him our prince and king."

The United States was the first nation of modern times to break away from the colonial rule of a distant monarch by invoking "consent of the governed" as a right in the United States Declaration of Independence. Today, consent of the governed is a presumptive aspect of all democracies. Indeed, any government that cannot plausibly claim to rule by consent of the governed tends not to enjoy the benefit of the doubt about their legitimacy, either by their own people or the peoples of other nations.

A more theoretical, if less constrained, approach to the "consent" doctrine relies on the notion of a social contract between the government and the people. In a modern democracy, few, if any, of "the people" have an opportunity to actually consent to such a "contract." However, a proponent of government legitimacy under this theory would contend that each adult implicitly provides their consent by remaining in their country of birth versus emigrating, and those who immigrate indicate their consent by explicitly agreeing to abide by the constitutional or statutory laws of the country that allows their entry. By this logic, consent of the governed is a presumed fact for any government that does not restrict emigration.

A more satisfying particularization of consent of the governed is that it is obtained through the practice of regular elections that feature broad or universal suffrage (i.e., rights to vote). That some choose not to vote would not prevent the People as a whole, via majority rule, from establishing their consent via elections, just as the existence of Representatives elected by the People does not mean the laws approved by the Representatives are invalid. Under this approach, the government must come before the People for continuing authority at each election and establish through open and transparent checks and balances that it has achieved the right to exercise authority in a fair and incontestable manner. The Founders also thought consent of the governed to be conditional, in that there are certain things that the government just cannot do, when they are against the interests of the People themselves such that it could not be reasonably deemed that the People had consented to it.

Political Economy

Political economy was the original term for the study of production, the acts of buying and selling, and their relationships to laws, customs and government. It developed in the 18th century as the study of the economies of states (also known as polities, hence the word "political" in "political economy"). In contradistinction to the theory of the Physiocrats, in which land was seen as the source of all wealth, some political economists proposed the labour theory of value (first introduced by John Locke, developed by Adam Smith and later Karl Marx), according to which labour is the real source of value. Many political economists also attracted attention to the accelerating development of technology, whose role in economic and social relationships grew ever more important.

In late 19th century, the term "political economy" was generally superseded by the term economics, which was used by those seeking to place the study of economy on a mathematical and axiomatic basis, rather than studying the structural relationships within production and consumption.

In the present, political economy refers to a variety of different, but related, approaches to studying economic and political behaviour, which range from combining economics with other fields, to using different fundamental assumptions which challenge those of orthodox economics:

- o Political economy is most commonly used to refer to interdisciplinary studies that draw on economics, law and political science in order to understand how political institutions, the political environment and capitalism influence each other.
- o Within political science, the term refers to modern liberal, realist, Marxian, and constructivist theories concerning the relationship between economic and political power among states. This is also of concern to students of economic history and institutional economics.
- o Historians have employed the term to explore the various ways in the past that individuals or groups with common economic interests have utilized the political process to effect change over time that is beneficial to their interest.
- o "International political economy" (IPE) is an interdisciplinary field comprising a variety of approaches that are concerned with international trade and finance, and state policies that affect international trade, such as monetary and fiscal policy. In the U.S. these approaches are associated with the journal International Organization, which became the leading journal of international political economy in the 1970s under the editorship of Robert Keohane; subsequent editors Peter J. Katzenstein and Stephen Krasner. They are also associated with the journal The Review of International Political Economy (RIPE), which is edited by both British and U.S. scholars.
- o Economists often associate the term with approaches using game theory.
- o Others, especially anthropologists, sociologists and geographers, use the term "political economy" to refer to neo-Marxian approaches to development and underdevelopment set forth by Andre Gunder Frank and Immanuel Wallerstein.

History of the Term

The term political economy originally meant the study of the conditions under which production was organized in the nation-states of the new-born capitalist system. The term was first used in England in the 18th Century, to replace the earlier approach of the (French) physiocrats. The main exponents of Political Economy are Adam Smith, David Ricardo and Karl Marx. In 1805 Thomas Malthus became Britain's first professor of political economy at the East India Company College at Haileybury in Hertfordshire. The world's first professorship for political economy was established in 1763 at the University of Vienna, with Joseph von Sonnenfels as the first professor.

In America, political economy was first taught at the College of William and Mary in 1784; Adam Smith's Wealth of Nations was a required textbook. Glasgow University, where Smith held the chairs of Logic and Moral Philosophy, changed the name of its Department of Political Economy to the Department of Economics (ostensibly to avoid confusing prospective undergraduates) in academic year 1997-98, leaving the class of '98 as the last to graduate with a Scottish MA degree in Political Economy.

Scope of Political Economy

Political economy is centrally focused on the development of the polity. It pays particular attention to whether the polity is running a surplus or a deficit, since in the view of most political economy, any deficit must be met by selling assets, such as gold or other capital, to other polities-or by some form of borrowing or externalization.

Political economy, then, studies the mechanism of human activity in organizing material, and the mechanism of distributing the surplus or deficit that is the result of that activity. Note the difference between this paradigm and that of economics which sees human wants as unlimited, resources as generically scarce, historical context as not particularly important, and income distribution issues as less important than efficiency and growth. While for some there is no difference between the two terms, for others the difference is one of basic method. Economics studies trade-offs through measurable values, whereas political economy focuses on structural relationships. However, there is no generally accepted distinction between these terms and they are most often used on a case by case basis.

Disciplines which Relate to Political Economy

Because political economy is not a unified discipline, there are a variety of studies that use the term which have overlapping subject matter, but radically different viewpoints.

Sociology is the study of the effects of involvement in society on individuals as members groups, and how this changes their ability to function. Many sociologists begin from a framework of production determining relationship drawn from Karl Marx.

Anthropology often studies political economy by studying the relationship between the world capitalist system and local cultures. Psychology is frequently the fulcrum around which political economy centres, in that it deals with decision making, not as being a black box whose effects are seen only in price decisions, but as being a source of study, and therefore the assumptions in a model of political economy.

History since it documents change over time, is often used as a means of arguing in political economy, and often historical works have a framework of political economy which they assume or argue as the basis for the narrative structure.

Economics, because it studies activity and price relationships and the effects of scarcity, grew out of political economy. It is often used in political economy to argue policy effects and study the results of actions, and it is often in opposition to political economy, in that many, if not most, practicing economists see political economy as being a hindrance to the operation of economic forces. From the point of view of political economy, economics is a branch of the entire study, and economics has, at its basis, a theory of political economy which should be open to examination.

Law since it concerns the creation of policy, or the mediation of policy ends through political acts which have specific individual results, is seen, in political economy, as both political capital and social infrastructure, on one hand-and as the result of the sociology of a society on the other. Human Geography is concerned, amongst others, with economic and political processes with an emphasis on spatial and environmental aspects thereof.

Ecology is often involved in political economy, because human activity is one of the single largest effects on the environment, and because it is the suitability of the environment for human beings which is one of the central concerns of most human beings. The ecological effects of economic activity on the environment have spurred the creation of a great deal of research studying means of changing the incentives balance of the market economy. This work is particularly controversial in its interaction with economics, since it questions the fundamental econometric assumptions of market economics and their basic validity.

The Market

One of the central conflicts in political economy is, of course, the role and functioning of the market economy in society. It is here where the broad range of paradigmatic assumptions collide, and on particular issues, individuals and groups with widely differing views will find common intellectual and practical political cause. In the political world, the fulcrum is on the ownership of capital surplus and production.

In the context of political economy, capitalism takes on a very broad meaning: the focus of the state on the maintaining and creating of capital and the means of its utilization. Many paradigms use the word in a much narrower context to mean private ownership and the self-justifying results of market operation, and deny that any other use of the word is appropriate. However, the vast majority of governing and major opposition parties in the industrialized world see the maintaining of capital capability as an area for legitimate state interest, and therefore maintain that government intervention in the market to prevent its disintegration, and even to promote certain aspects of its advancement is a proper use of state power.

Socialism, viewed as a system of political economy, states that the forms of production (on which labour is dependent to sell to) should be maintained, or overseen, by political power, and generally state power, in order to give their benefits to the many rather than the few. Communism sees the necessity of social control over all surplus generating activity. Communist parties exist in most industrialized nations, while communist revolutionary movements are more common in less industrialized ones. Within the paradigm of communism there are a host of particular theories. Not all Marxist theories are communist, and not all communists are necessarily Marxist in their orientation.

Privatization Challenges for Good Governance

The quantitative dimensions of privatization provide an insight into the happenings and progress of privatization at the central and state levels. These dimensions vary between the central Government and the states and further between one state and another. Any study of privatization issues needs to begin with a discussion of the quantitative dimensions of privatization. The state-wide details of privatization of the state-level public enterprises (SLPEs) in India.

Common Features

The following are the main common features of the SLPE privatization practices in the various states:

(i) Most of the states explicitly or implicitly realized the need for privatization of the SLPEs. The fiscal crunch pressed them hard to go in for privatization.

(ii) Many states formulated a public enterprise policy to consider afresh the retention of their SLPE portfolio.

(iii) Some states set up a mechanism to deal with privatization of the SLPEs, whereas many others were still only beginning to give thought to this issue.

(iv) Manufacturing SLPEs were easier to privatize.

(v) The social safety net emerged as an important issue in the privatization exercise.

(vi) Trade sale was the preferred modality for the transfer of ownership.

Distinguishing Features

The following are the main distinguishing features among the states' privatization exercises:

(i) Whereas states such as Andhra Pradesh, Karnataka, Punjab, Maharashtra, Orissa, Uttar Pradesh, Manipur, and Assam showed a clear preference for privatization, states like West Bengal, Kerala, Tamil Nadu, Madhya Pradesh, and Meghalaya have preferred restructuring.

(ii) Punjab, Maharashtra, Karnataka, and Kerala set up privatization mechanisms through independent enactments. Rajasthan, Haryana, Madhya Pradesh, Orissa, Andhra Pradesh, Assam, and Tamil Nadu have either set up separate departments or used existing mechanisms to handle the issues related to privatization.

(iii) Andhra Pradesh, Orissa, Kerala, and Karnataka prepared programs for privatization of their SLPEs in different phases.

(iv) The privatization programs of Andhra Pradesh, Orissa and Uttar Pradesh received the support of the United Kingdom's Department for International Development (DFID) and have been carried out with the support of foreign consultants. The Madhya Pradesh and Gujarat programs received the support of the Asian Development Bank and have also been carried out with the support of foreign consultants.

Process of Privatization

The due diligence process for privatization of the central public enterprises (CPEs) and the SLPEs is as follows:

Step-1: The government gives its approval for the privatization/sale of an enterprise.

Step-2: The Department of Public Enterprise (DPE) invites "expressions of interest" (EoI) through open advertisement for the selection of an advisor to assist in implementing the disinvestment decisions. Concurrently, valuation of the SLPE is undertaken in accordance with the standard national and international practices.

Step-3: The Advisor or Advisors are appointed, with the approval of the Restructuring Committee.

Step-4: Advisors assist the DPE in issue of advertisement for EoI from prospective buyers.

Step-5: The prospective buyers are shortlisted, using the pre-qualification criteria set out in the EoI advertisement.

Step-6: An Information Memorandum is prepared by the Advisors, in consultation with the concerned SLPE; the memorandum is then given to the short-listed prospective bidders, after they enter into a confidentiality agreement.

Step-7: The draft sale agreement and other legal agreements are prepared by the Advisors and given to the short-listed bidders to elicit their response.

Step-8: The prospective bidders undertake due diligence of the SLPE and hold discussions with the Advisors, the government, and the Management of the SLPE for any clarification.

Step-9: Based on the response received from the prospective bidders, the draft sale agreement and other legal agreements are finalized, vetted by the Law Department, approved by the Cabinet Committee on Disinvestment (CCD) and then sent to the prospective bidders for the invitation of final binding bids (Technical & Financial).

Step-10: After examination, analysis, evaluation and further negotiation, if necessary, the recommendations of the Inter-Departmental Core Group are placed before the CCD for final decision regarding selection of the preferred bidder, signing of necessary legal agreements, and other ancillary issues. It is clear that the privatization process is very slow-moving and cumbersome.

The implementation mechanism is too complex at the central level, whereas some state governments have modified the mechanism adopted by the centre to their requirements, giving due consideration to factors such as transparency and speed. The cumbersome privatization process adopted by the central Government and the various state governments in India has delayed the implementation of privatization programs and undermined the revenue potential from privatization.

Comparative View: Centre vs. States

The following are the chief comparative features of privatization relating to CPEs and SLPEs.

(i) The disinvestment/privatization of CPEs began after the launching of the New Economic Policy in July 1991, whereas the states resorted to privatization of SLPEs much earlier, e.g., Allwyn Nissan in Andhra Pradesh, Uttar Pradesh Auto Tractors Limited in Uttar Pradesh, and Charge Chrome Plant in Orissa.

(ii) The states preferred trade sale as the modality of privatization, whereas the central Government preferred partial disinvestment and strategic sale.

(iii) The states tended to prefer an independent legislative act to execute privatization programs, while the central Government tended to use executive action.

(iv) The privatization exercise in the state governments is not target based, whereas the central Government laid down the targeted amounts of money to be mobilized through disinvestment/ privatization.

(v) The central Government prefers to use the term "disinvestment" to ward off any ideological/political problems, whereas the state governments do not avoid revealing their preference for privatization. However, some states, such as West Bengal, Kerala, and Tripura, have rejected the use of both privatization and disinvestment.

(vi) The privatization of SLPEs, except for the State Electricity Boards (SEBs), turned out to be an easier exercise than privatization of the CPEs because of their size and greater appeal.

(vii) The privatization of both CPEs and SLPEs was confounded by problems of transparency and valuation.

(viii) Both the speed and the mechanisms for privatization posed governance challenges at the central and state levels in socio-politico-administrative issues.

(ix) Cultural factors were also responsible for the success or failure of privatization.

Issues in Privatization

The privatization experiences of the central and state governments point out very clearly that effective governance could go a long way in speeding up the implementation of the privatization programs, which could yield considerable revenues for poverty alleviation programs. Mishra, Davies, and Bhat (2004) summarize below some important issues in privatization based on the privatization experience:

(i) It is easier to privatize smaller enterprises.

(ii) The manufacturing enterprises possess a greater appeal for privatization.

(iii) Effective due diligence expedites privatization.

(iv) The SLPEs organized under the Companies Act could be taken to market with greater ease and comfort than those organized as public corporations.

(v) Valuation should be considered an important element of the privatization process. The entire valuation exercise should be made transparent.

(vi) In the case of loss-making enterprises with multiple subsidiaries and product groups/strategic business units, restructuring should precede privatization.

(vii) It is always helpful to establish a dialogue with the employees before any action is initiated to privatize an enterprise.

(viii) Sole reliance should not be placed on any particular method of privatization. Depending on the nature of the SLPE and market conditions, a combination of methods of divesting the SLPEs should be employed to achieve the objectives of privatization.

Conclusion

Mishra and Kumari (2004) in their study on privatization of the SLPEs have observed that the central Government as well as most of the states explicitly or implicitly realize the need for privatization of the SLPEs to mobilize finances for poverty alleviation programs, implement the philosophy of rolling back the state, and diminish poverty levels through creation of larger number of jobs in the privatized public enterprise. However, whereas states such as Andhra Pradesh, Karnataka, Punjab, and Orissa show a clear preference for privatization, states like West

Bengal, Tripura, and Kerala indicated their disenchantment with the term "privatization" and opted for restructuring. The privatization patterns of the central and state governments differ in many areas, especially in relation to the method of sale. The central Government prefers partial disinvestment and strategic sale, while the state governments preferred to adopt the trade sale modality. The privatization experiences of the state governments point to a number of lessons to be learned for the future. Instead of depending on a specific modality, it would be beneficial to depend on a mix of methods. The smaller enterprises, specially those in manufacturing, should be preferred for privatization. Both the privatization process and privatization mechanism should be simplified. Governance dimensions, such as transparency and accountability, should have a trade-off against the efficiency and the speed dimensions. The matrix of interactions between poverty and privatization of enterprises very clearly shows healthy outcomes, dispelling the existing belief that privatization results in job losses.

Administrative Law

Administrative law (or regulatory law) is the body of law that arises from the activities of administrative agencies of government. Government agency action can include rulemaking, adjudication, or the enforcement of a specific regulatory agenda. Administrative law is considered a branch of public law. As a body of law, administrative law deals with the decision-making of administrative units of government (e.g., tribunals, boards or commissions) that are part of a national regulatory scheme in such areas as international trade, manufacturing, the environment, taxation, broadcasting, immigration and transport. Administrative law expanded greatly during the twentieth century, as legislative bodies worldwide created more government agencies to regulate the increasingly complex social, economic and political spheres of human interaction.

Administrative Law in Common Law Countries

Generally speaking, most countries that follow the principles of common law have developed procedures for judicial review that limit the reviewability of decisions made by administrative law bodies. Often these procedures are coupled with legislation or other common law doctrines that establish standards for proper rulemaking. Administrative law may also apply to review of decisions of so-called quasi-public bodies, such as non-profit corporations, disciplinary boards, and other decision-making bodies that effect the legal rights of members of a particular group or entity.

While administrative decision-making bodies are often controlled by larger governmental units, their decisions could be reviewed by a court of general jurisdiction under some principle of judicial review based upon due process (United States) or fundamental justice (Canada). Judicial review of administrative decision, it must be noted, is different from an appeal. When sitting in review of a decision, the Court will only look at the method in which the decision was arrived at, whereas in appeal the correctness of the decision itself will be under question. This difference is vital in appreciating administrative law in common law countries.

The scope of judicial review may be limited to certain questions of fairness, or whether the administrative action is ultra vires. In terms of ultra vires actions in the broad sense, a reviewing court may set aside an administrative decision if it is patently unreasonable (under Canadian law), Wednesbury unreasonable (under British law), or arbitrary and capricious (under U.S. Administrative Procedure Act and New York State law). Administrative law, as laid down by the Supreme Court in India, has also recognized two more grounds of judicial review which were recognized but not applied by English Courts viz. legitimate expectation and proportionality.

The powers to review administrative decisions are usually established by statute, but were originally developed from the royal prerogative writs of English law, such as the writ of mandamus and the writ of certiorari. In certain Common Law jurisdictions, such as India or Pakistan, the power to pass such writs is a Constitutionally guaranteed power. This power is seen as fundamental to the power of judicial review and an aspect of the independent judiciary.

2

Administrative Discretion and Representative

Much has been said about the public service lately. Most of the time, the opinions tend to be negative. Wasteful, inefficient, arrogant, unresponsive, impersonal, autocratic, and undemocratic are among the harsher criticisms thrown at the bureaucracy. Yet, despite these criticisms, the public service plays essential roles in implementing and enforcing government policies. Many people whose lives have been affected by government agencies though a variety of policies in areas such as income redistribution, environmental protection, crime prevention, and health care management realize the importance of those agencies.

However, when government becomes too big and too powerful, it poses a threat to democracy. Thus, when Kingsley (1944) started to argue that the civil service needed to be representative in order to be responsive, he basically introduced a new concept of representation that was previously a domain in the study of political systems. Ever since his conception of "representative bureaucracy," a plethora of scholars and practitioners has argued the need for a diverse bureaucratic workforce that reflects the population it serves. According to these scholars, representative bureaucracy enhances its legitimacy in a democratic political system. A shift in philosophy from avoidance to acceptance of the reality that bureaucracy would continue to generate power in the policy-making process fostered the demand for a more representative bureaucracy. Rourke (1978) contends that although a powerful bureaucracy threatens the "traditional freedoms of democratic society, the bureaucratic power can be used to protect and extend those freedoms."

The idea of representative bureaucracy was further highlighted by Marini (1971), who points out that "we were reminded of relevance, social problems, personal morality, innovation, clients, the evils of hierarchy and bureaucracy." In other words, bureaucracy has power and thus needs to be included in the scheme of representation and social justice.

Representative bureaucracy has now become essential in a democratic political system. Riggs (1970) asserts that representation in all forms of government is critical to the stability of that government. He points to the rise of public rebellion in various countries as a consequence of the failure to have an equitable representation in the political dimensions of government and its administration. He maintains that there is a "need for diverse elements in a population to be adequately represented in order for a government to command their loyalty as a legitimate expression of common welfare" (1970: 570).

The concept of affirmative action in the bureaucracy is essentially an attempt to broaden the social composition of the bureaucracy to reflect that of the whole population, especially from certain under-represented groups such as women and African Americans (Kernaghan and Siegel 1989). The idea that a diverse workforce will better enhance customers' demands is also gaining momentum in the private sector. Kiel (1994) believes that an organization that is reflective of its population will have a better understanding of its clients' needs. Similarly, Dresang (1974) agrees that an organization that mirrors society allows it to serve as "an index of openness and access." Furthermore, a large number of private organizations have considered employment diversity to be a good business strategy. Howes argues that affirmative action has now become a prerequisite for future success or even survival for any organization.

Building upon this foundation, I intend to explore this issue in greater detail, especially as it pertains to Malaysian bureaucracy. The first part of this article explores the theory of representative bureaucracy, highlighting previous empirical studies that explore the transition from descriptive representation to substantive representation in government agencies. The second part explores the concept of administrative discretion and highlights how individuals' perceptions of the discretion influence the formation of a representative role. The final section explores the hypothesis that individual administrators who perceive themselves as advocators of certain groups prefer policy outcomes that are more responsive to the interests of women and minorities than those of their colleagues.

THEORY OF REPRESENTATIVE BUREAUCRACY

A general consensus maintains that the mere existence of various institutions of public accountability is not enough; they have to be effective in protecting the interests of the public. This is because the quality of governance is determined not by the objective perceptions of a few experts but by the net impact of government policies on the well-being of its citizens (Shah 1996; Huther and Shah 1998).

The quality of governance is thus enhanced by closely matching government services with citizen preferences, as well as by moving government closer to the people it is supposed to serve, something that ensures greater accountability of the public service. In recent years concern has proliferated about the consequences of governance and misgovernance (Kaufman, Kraay, and Zoido-Lobaton 1999). For example, a few empirical studies have demonstrated the link between accountability and performance.

Wade (1994) finds that when irrigation officials in India and Korea face more local pressure, they tend to perform better than traditional arrangements that insulate them from political pressure. In addition, Isham, Narayan, and Pritchett (1995) reveal that aid-financed rural water supply projects performed much better with greater participation from their beneficiaries. A wealth of crosscountry indicators of various aspects of governance now strongly suggests that good governance improves government accountability to citizens and enhances the quality of public services.

These concerns have certainly renewed interest in protecting democratic values as they pertain to control of government agencies. The growth of public agencies has forced theorists and practitioners to revisit bureaucratic paradigms such as fairness, representation, participation, accountability, responsiveness, political neutrality, efficiency, rationality, and expertise. Yet, the very nature of public administration poses problems to accommodating these values. For example, bureaucracy consists of appointed public officials and has a tendency to rely on expertise and knowledge over accountability, participation, and democratic control. In addition, bureaucrats' lack of accountability at the ballot box, as well as various civil service regulations that insulate them from political pressure, further compound the fear that bureaucratic power comes at the expense of public interest.

Hence, the essence of traditional public administration that tends to be rigid, rule-bound, centralized, insular, self-protective, and profoundly antidemocratic has often collided with the contemporary paradigm of bureaucracy that "allows qualified voters an efficient instrument through which the will of the people may be expressed; makes officers both responsive and responsible;" and ensures the common welfare (Lynn 2001). Thus, a critical question in the field of public administration is whether or not these bureaucratic characteristics are legitimate in terms of democratic principles. In this regard, David Rosenbloom (1993) opines that the legitimacy of bureaucracy occurs when bureaucratic policy making is subject to direct popular control. If bureaucracy is isolated from public accountability, then bureaucracy can in no way be responsive to public interests and desires. As a result, we are faced with the persistent problem of how best to ensure bureaucratic responsiveness and accountability to the public. Representative theory initially emerged during the Greek civilization.

Aristotle first mentioned the importance of representation of different classes of society in government (Vietri 1981). Book III of the Politics is always regarded as the foundation of political science in the West. The polis, the supreme form of community for Aristotle, is the best community, because it enables rational men to participate in the political process. However, Aristotle also believes that class conflict between the rich and the poor is inevitable in all societies. This conflict always poses a threat of instability, violence, and revolution. Hence, blending the class interests in government by supporting political equality avoids conflicts and at the same time increases legitimate sovereign authority. The writings of Karl Marx and Max Weber also contribute to the development of representative bureaucracy. The elimination of class-biased bureaucracy and the emergence of classless administrative systems came about because of Marx's fear of the danger of dominant bureaucracy. Likewise, Weber's rational-legal approach allowed unrepresented groups to seek access to government. For example, the procedures of merit-based appointment increased the democratic potential of all groups to join the civil service.

However, the contemporary intellectual roots of the idea of representative bureaucracy can be traced to J. Donald Kingsley. Kingsley's comprehensive analysis of the British civil service revealed a pattern of administrative arrangements that reflected the character of the social structure of the nation.

In his view, because the middle class dominated British society, it was inevitable that the composition of the bureaucracy was largely middle class. Since Kingsley's discovery of the term, the concept of representative bureaucracy has been widely interpreted and debated. David Levithan (1946) was the first to propose that representative bureaucracy be integrated into the American civil service. He contended that representative bureaucracy could act as an internal control on the behaviours of administrators and hence could promote democratic values. Following Levithan, Long (1952: 813) espoused a more extreme form of representative bureaucracy. He suggested that Given the seemingly inevitable growth in the power of the bureaucracy through administrative discretion and administrative law, it is of critical importance that the bureaucracy be both representative and democratic in composition and ethos.

In essence, Long believed that a representative bureaucracy enhanced the democratization of the American civil service by promoting the interests and demands of the people it represented. Building upon this theory, Van Riper (1958) argued that an "open public service" was necessary so that the American public service consisted of a reasonable cross-section of the population by occupation, class, and geography. To create a representative bureaucracy, he argued, government should accelerate the upward mobility of women and minority administrators through an equal opportunity system. He was basically the first American scholar to emphasize social characteristics as part of the representative concept. Meanwhile, Subramaniam (1967) suggested that representative bureaucracy is an organization "in which every economic class, caste, region, or religion in a country is represented in exact proportion to its number in the population." Krislov (1967, 1974) also argued that American bureaucracy should be representative in its social composition. He posited several advantages of having a diverse workforce:

The most obvious is the simple representational notion that all social groups have a right to political participation and to influence. The second one can be labelled the functional aspect; the wider the range of talents, types, and regional and family contacts found in a bureaucracy, the more likely it is to be able to fulfil its functions, with respect to both internal efficiency and social setting.

Bureaucracies also symbolize values and power realities and are thus representational in both a political and an analytic sense. Therefore, finally social conduct and future behaviour in a society may be channelled and encouraged through the mere constitution of the bureaucracy (1974: 64). However, even after 2 decades during which representative bureaucracy became a concept of considerable importance as an explanatory tool in the discussions of the American civil service, its concepts, meanings, and applicability remained ambiguous and underdeveloped. As a result of this confusion, Mosher (1968: 14-15) attempted to clarify the concept of representativeness by introducing the passive and active form of representation.

Mosher advocated the form of passive representation because the passive (or descriptive) meaning of representativeness concerns the origins of individuals and the degree to which, collectively, they mirror the whole society.

It may be statistically measured in terms of locality or origin... and its nature (rural, urban, suburban), previous occupations, father's occupation, education, family income, family social class, sex, race, religion. A public service... which is broadly representative of all categories of the population in these respects, may be thought of as satisfying Lincoln's prescription of government "by the people" in a limited sense.

Mosher believed that passive representation was important because it signified democratic values such as open service, equal opportunity, social mobility, and participatory management. Kranz (1976) further expanded the concept of representation by emphasizing the idea of proportional representation. For example, he pointed out that a bureaucracy is representative if the ratio of a particular group in an agency equals that of the group's percentage in the population. He argued that a representative bureaucracy was desirable for economic, social, and political justifications in such a way that bureaucracy was not only providing essential services but also was becoming a source of jobs, as well as "a potential form of significant group representation" (Kranz 1976: 135). He reiterated that the public sector was the preferred avenue for women and minority grievances, since it offered them greater employment opportunities.

Thompson (1976) illustrated three different forms of bureaucratic representation that could increase bureaucratic responsiveness to particular groups and advocate their interests in the policy outputs. First, he underlined the importance of demographic representation in the civil service, which would reflect certain characteristics of the population. Secondly, he emphasized the attitudinal representation in which citizens' values and beliefs must be proportionately represented among public administrators. Finally, he argued for substantive representation, such that the actual behaviour of bureaucrats should benefit intended social groups. In addition, Krislov and Rosenbloom (1981) were interested in integrating bureaucratic power into democratic government. In a similar manner to Thompson's, they also proposed three types of representation: representation by personnel (diverse workforce), representation by agencies (agencies promote specific groups' interests), and representation through citizen participation (citizens have greater access to decision-making processes). These representation models have indeed been part of administrative reforms aimed at increasing greater accountability and responsiveness. In short, the different versions of representation clearly emphasize the new perspective of the role of representative bureaucracy within the context of democratic theory.

A representative bureaucracy that broadly reflects the values, interests, aspirations, and desires of the general public has a legitimate position in a democratic country. Administrators who come from various demographic backgrounds will initially be much more sensitive to the issues and interests of their own groups and thus be able to make policy decisions that reflect those interests. However, individual administrators normally go through socialization processes that influence their values, beliefs, attitudes, and behaviours. These socialization experiences in turn shape the way they perceive their work roles as well as their policy decisions. Thus, different socialization experiences will produce different perceptions of work roles and different bureaucratic decisions. This means that administrators who first come into the civil service with specific values and beliefs might not be able to hold on to those values and beliefs anymore. The organizational values and beliefs will now be more likely to shape their attitudes and behaviour.

Administrative Discretion and Representative Bureaucracy

The essential role of government bureaucracy in formulating and implementing public policies makes it a central player in a democratic nation. Bureaucratic actions basically constitute what government chooses to do or not to do. The original politics/administration dichotomy has clearly faded because of the increasing importance of civil servants in the policy-making processes. Scholars of public administration have long recognized that bureaucracy has now become the centre of political power and authority. It has a direct impact upon the population because of its role in the decision-making and implementation processes.

However, the degree of administrative discretion required to implement public policy stands in stark contrast to the democratic government requirement of popular sovereignty. As a result, the delegation of policy-making authority to government agencies raises a serious dilemma in democratic societies. On the one hand, bureaucratic discretion is essential because lawmakers cannot foresee all possible circumstances surrounding the application and execution of public laws. On the other hand, their lack of accountability to political pressure further constrains the ability of legislatures to control bureaucratic behaviour. Consequently, bureaucrats are often called upon to make judgments based on their experiences, expertise, and intuition, rather than in the interest of the public.

In addition, a serious concern arises that certain agencies of government seem to develop a special relationship with special private interests, the very interests they are supposed to regulate, again suggesting the inability of public agencies to ensure bureaucratic responsiveness and accountability to the public. Lowi (1969) argues that the exercise of discretion tends to neglect the larger public interest. As a result, he proposes a "juridical democracy" that enlists detailed legislative action designed to eliminate discretion. In addition to specific legislation and greater legislative review of administrative actions, other proposals have suggested increasing public accountability. Cooper (1982) discusses various roles, obligations, and objective responsibilities that limit the boundaries of administrative actions. Gawthrop's (1984) system theory is a mechanism used to redesign organizational structures to achieve bureaucratic responsiveness.

Ziegler and Tucker (1978) argue that efficiency and responsiveness can only be maintained when policy initiative rests with the elected representative. Furthermore, economics-based approaches have also contributed to the search for democratic accountability. The principal-agent model that is widely used in economics, management, and sociology has become a powerful new tool for assessing bureaucratic responsiveness. This model stipulates that the principals (executive and legislative) design incentives and sanctions to control administrators' behaviour so that the behaviour is always in conformity with the policy preferences of the principals.

Finer (1972) has also argued for greater legislative control and increased supervision of administrative activities as a means of controlling bureaucrats. Fearing that bureaucrats' views become the dominant view of society, he recommends that legislatures engage in detailed supervision of government agencies. Recent theoretical and empirical studies have all highlighted the utilization of mechanisms such as administrative procedures, appointments, budgets, and oversight hearings to enhance bureaucratic responsiveness in public agencies. Other empirical studies even indicate that many public administrators believe that elected officials should exercise some degree of dominance over them.

Finally, the growing influence of the democratic accountability model on administrative theories brings forth the argument for a representative bureaucracy. Proponents of representative bureaucracy argue that bureaucratic decisions reflect the general will of the population if bureaucratic composition shares similar characteristics of the population, such as geographical locations (Denhardt 1992), social classes (Kingsley 1944), and race or gender (Krislov 1974). Van Riper (1958) argues that the concept of representative bureaucracy offers a positive perspective on the theory of administrative responsibility. Others argue that the representative nature of bureaucracy makes it potentially responsive to the needs and interests of the population. A bureaucracy that consists of people from diverse backgrounds can certainly influence policy preferences to be in sync with the interests and demands of the groups they represent.

VARIABLES IN THE MODEL

Stakeholders' Role Expectations

The focus of this variable is to examine administrators' perceptions of what significant others perceive their role should be. With such a focus, the aim is to demonstrate that an administrator defines his or her role with reference to others. For example, role theorists infer that a certain behaviour will follow a particular position. Individuals' attitudes are thus a reflection of the attitudes held by the group with which he or she associates. Michael Dawson (1994) calls this attachment being "one of us." He defines this notion of linked fate as the degree to which particular groups believe that their own self-interests are linked to the interests of others. As a result, the role itself is formed by the expectations of significant others and the expectation that the administrator attaches to it.

For example, when administrators perceive that the community of minorities and women expect them to represent women's and minority interests, they are more likely to accept this role (Kahn et al. 1964). However, when an administrator perceives that other actors have different expectations of how he or she will behave in this position, the clash of incompatible expectations leads to role conflict. For instance, political leaders expect the administrator to represent their interests and take sides on policy matters. On the other hand, the administrator also feels that his supervisors expect him to be neutral and efficient in carrying out his tasks. As a result of these different expectations, a public administrator often experiences intra-role conflict. It is generally true that administrators may have to deal with outside actors in carrying out their duties. The role expectations of other actors may significantly alter administrators' own perceptions concerning work roles. Actors such as politicians, the general public, superiors, professional associations, women and minority colleagues, and women and the minority community possess different political agendas. Most likely, the role expectations of these actors often do not coincide with the administrators' perceptions of organizational goals.

As a result, administrators must find ways to reconcile these different expectations with their own goals and commitments. For example, literature on representative bureaucracy reveals that minority and women administrators will often advocate policies that cater to the interests of their groups if other actors in the policy-making process hold such expectations for them. Likewise, administrators will tend to follow traditional bureaucratic roles if they perceive that other actors expect them to adhere to bureaucratic norms and practices. Thus, administrators who perceive that other important actors in the policy environment expect them to represent women's and minority interests are more likely to assume the role of women's and minority advocates and hence have policy preferences that reflect this role.

Women and Minority Role Acceptance

The perception of role orientations is central to this study. Selden (1997: 117) defines roles as "sets of expected behaviours to be performed by a person occupying a particular position." Role expectations are demands conveyed by significant others expressed either formally or informally. However, these expectations are not as important as individuals' own perceptions of what is expected of them (Kahn et al. 1964, Turner 1956). This is because according to Kahn et al. (1964: 16), "It is the received role, however, which is the immediate influence on... behaviour and the immediate source of... motivation to role performance." As a result, despite multiple role expectations, administrators may ultimately decide which role orientations they will meet. Several scholars have examined organizational and environmental conditions that influence the role orientations of public administrators. Although the expectations vary from one significant actor to another, Selden (1997) identifies two most common expectations: representative role orientation and traditional role orientation. The emphasis on the representative functions of bureaucracy was first codified in the "new public administration" school of thought, which essentially dismisses the old Wilsonian tradition that public administration is a value-free practice.

The landmark Minnowbrook conference of public administration professionals in 1968 was the earliest indication that the voices for inclusion had started to gain prominence in the administrative arena. Frederikson (1971), one of the proponents of this school, argues that bureaucracy has to be included in the scheme of representation and social justice. Similarly, Riggs (1970: 570) points out that there is a "need for diverse elements in a population to be adequately represented in order for a government to command their loyalty as a legitimate expression of common welfare." As a result, the idea of representative bureaucracy is not only to create a civil service that is more reflective of its population, but also to strive to make policies that promote the interests of historically disadvantaged groups such as women and minorities. Mosher's (1982) prescription for passive and active representation is reflective of his position that it is simply not enough to have a diverse workforce. Instead, public administrators should also advocate public policies that advance the interests and wishes of disadvantaged groups. Thus, when administrators perceive their role as advocates of women's or minority groups, they are more likely to pursue policy preferences that benefit women's and minority interests.

Therefore, administrators who assume the role of minority and women's role advocate are likely to prefer policies that advance the interest of women and minority groups.

Traditional Role Acceptance

The traditional bureaucratic roles emphasize economy, neutrality, rationality, meritocracy, and efficiency (Ingraham and Ban 1986). Traditional role orientation is based on the principle of merit and neutral competence. To this end, Kaufman (1956: 1,060) emphatically argues that public administrators need to "do the work of the government expertly, and to do it according to explicit, objective standards rather than personal or party or other obligations and loyalties." While neutral competence is important, the ultimate objective is efficiency in administration (Denhardt and deLeon 1993). Dahl (1947: 2) concurs that, "the doctrine of efficiency runs like a half-visible thread through the fabric of public administration literature as a dominant goal."

Similarly, Frederickson (1971: 311) asserts that the classic definition of public administration has always been "the efficient, economical, and coordinated" delivery of public services. More recent observations of public administration also underline the fact that economy and efficiency continue to remain the central values among public administrators (Ingraham and Ban 1986). As a result, it is believed that administrators who accept the traditional bureaucratic role orientation will be less inclined to conceive their role orientation representing any particular group. Specifically, administrators who assume traditional roles are not likely to engage in behaviours that support the interests of women and minorities.

CONTROL VARIABLES

I also include two control variables in this model: the ethnicity and the gender of the administrator. Since organizational socialization experiences may lead administrators to accept representative role orientation, a control variable of ethnicity is included to determine whether it has any effect on policy preferences. In addition, a control variable of gender is included because scholars examining the role of women in government tend to argue that women administrators often have a "heightened awareness of feminist issues [that] often give[s] them a better feel for the problems women encounter, making them especially adept at recognizing when policy solutions fail to account for women's unique needs" (Dolan 2000: 514). Thus, it is reasonable to assume that gender may have an additional impact on administrators' policy preferences.

METHODOLOGY

The Research Setting

The focus of the empirical research conducted in this article is the federal ministries in Kuala Lumpur. Since the focal point of the research is the discretionary power of bureaucracy, it was imperative that only higher civil servants be selected. They ranged from officers in the managerial and professional group to top managerial positions such as secretary general, undersecretaries, their deputies and assistants, and directors of departments.

The selection of higher civil servants in the study also resonates with the argument by Meier and Stewart (1992) that public administrators who are the subjects of the analysis must first have a significant amount of discretion in the decision-making process. Second, the decisions must have important implications for the groups being represented, and third, the administrators can be associated directly with the decisions they make. Because these assumptions clearly fit the characteristics of higher civil servants, they are appropriately selected in this study.

DELIBERATE DEMOCRACY AND GLOBALIZATION

The secret ballot system, according to him, erodes the very idea of democracy by letting citizens vote on the basis of "interest, pleasure or caprice" (1991: 227). The problem of electoral fallacy, which is defining the degree of democratic deliberation in Gurgaon, is the enormous gap that has occurred between the representative and the represented. This is understood through an explanation of the democratic processes in any place. The first important stage of democracy is "elections"; the second is "institutional democracy," which is an official effort between the elections; and the third is the process of sustaining these efforts by strengthening deliberative bodies of citizens.

The first stage is a short and regulated system functioning within the framework of the country's law and constitution. The second is the process of putting those many norms and values of society in place through a gradual and incremental process of adaptation and implementation. The third involves a sincere effort to give a voice to every citizen. Since every citizen has a cultural, linguistic, or occupational bonding through innumerable informal groups that act as "steam release" communes, the task of sustaining democracy would mean that these groups may not be allowed to wilt. However, the first stage becomes visually very imposing, just like the hero of a blockbuster film whose gigantic publicity hides the enormous efforts of the whole studio team which led the film to this glory.

Representative democracy has placed elections on the highest pedestal of insurance against despotism, as it bridges gaps between various policies and makes them more coherent and mutually consistent. Thus representation that originated as an instrument of democracy has now become bigger than democracy itself. Groups that are politically better consolidated have a natural advantage over others and can appropriate state resources as they want. Being a "vote bank," they become the preferred choice of the elected representative. Such nexuses manufactured through the democratic process share state resources in a way that shrinks and reduces institutional spaces that provide for open deliberations on policy issues. Thus, deliberate democracy converts into a hush-hush democracy governed by the state's ability to bring about amendments to their composition, procedures, and life span. Globalizing cities have witnessed the subjection of their local bodies to many regulatory changes brought about by the demand for efficiency, economy, and speed.

Thus, although deliberation is a process of enabling citizens to make a rational choice about the political system they desire, this process is vested with institutions that reflect the core of electoral fallacies, such as the parliament, state legislatures, or local bodies in urban and rural areas.

Marginalization of deliberate democracy leads to at least one very important aspect that sustains democratic states, which is its substantive aspect. F. W. Riggs had studied this aspect in the early days when he was working in the CAG. Its important feature, which tends to be crucial to transitional societies, is reciprocity. The relevance of Riggs's ecological framework and its consistent applicability to Indian analytical studies is due to his normative understanding of community institutions and their embedded rationality, which form the core of bureaucratic institutions. He rejected the functional argument of Almond's systems approach, and he indicated those variables where inputs did not lead to predictable outputs, and thus policy slippages remained unexplained. To Riggs goes the credit of liberating public administration theory from the US federal experience and suggesting a model based upon the cultural argument and providing an explanation of community relationships and administrative diversities, despite the fact that his path-breaking effort to reach a general theory of administration was left off half way with the early and premature demise of the CAG.

Recognizing the futility of theoretical efforts to implant Western models into India, Riggs wrote, "We may expect that a model which throws light on administrative realities in one setting may simply obscure the facts in another situation". He illustrated this in an interesting discussion on the issue of land revenues, addressing whether they should be classified as "taxes" or "rents." Since this dichotomy assumes the existence of a market system (which it was not), he drew on a study by Walter C. Neale (1957) to prove the fact that it was "neither". Neale mentions that the system prevailing in the Indian village could be called "reciprocative" and "redistributive," in which every occupational group (barbers, washermen, carpenters, etc.) performed its traditional duties for other members in the village without direct compensation. The cultivator at harvest time would distribute shares from his crop to all of them as well as to the Rajah, who also reciprocated by distributing it to his officials in the court and himself. This entails a highly specialized system of activities and exchange without reliance on markets, price mechanisms, or demand-supply forces.

Globalization has once again thrown open to debate a very pertinent question about the need for marketizing such a specialized network embedded in traditional society. Riggs (1960) further suggests that marketizing might inadvertently lead to a transformation of society by replacing or eliminating the existing benign structures. This carries the theoretical argument about the prevalence of "substantive" economics, which contrasts with the formal market system and provides a way for community members to interact with their natural and social environment in such a manner that they are able to satisfy their material needs even in times of scarcity. This is an adequate explanation about India's subsistence economy, in which a large number of rural poor are capable of surviving simply due to the availability of biomass resources (like natural produce from land, wetlands, village forests) free of any cost. When developing countries like India undergo "debt servicing," these biomass resources are subsidized for industries, as a result of which poor people lose access to them.

Thus an economic system prevails without having a formal economic structure, and an administrative system prevails without in any way having the rationally justifiable administrative model. Riggs's study suggests that an administrative system may function without having a bureau just as an economic system can work without a market. "One may discover, of course, that what exists is not at all a bad thing" (Riggs 1960: 227). Reciprocity is at the core of "deliberate democracy". Deliberation ensures cooperation and reciprocity prevents the majority from overlooking or sidelining the particular systems that regulate fairness in small communities. "Reciprocity is to justice in political ethics what replication is to truth in scientific ethics". Replication in scientific research requires public demonstration and strengthens truth; similarly with reciprocity, which justifies a law through public deliberation. In doing so, some substantive principles like cultural freedom, moral values, and access to opportunities other than the formalistic and procedural ones play a dominant role. By insulating legal processes from substantive democratic systems, the deliberative element of democratic governance is affected, as a result of which it is unable to face the moral and political challenges of globalization.

Russell Hardin's "street level epistemology", or a theory of knowledge of ordinary persons, is another defense of substantive factors that provide fundamental structures to the democratic framework ("street level epistemology is the subjective account of knowledge, not a public account" [2003: 165]). This knowledge is about usefulness, trust, and free interaction of people in a social system that is not generated by outside, exogenous forces but from within the system itself and therefore prioritizes social justice and normative values in democratic governance.

Globalizing cities are a result of exogenous pulls based upon justifications of a kind that increase FDI in the region. Consequently, the political regimes adopted the mode of legitimizing this transition from the protectionist economy to a liberal economy on the basis of free and fair elections rather than deliberations on the substantive modes of governance.

This flawed conception of democracy privileges elections over other dimensions of democracy and ignores the degree to which multiparty elections (even if they are competitive and uncertain in outcome) may exclude significant portions of the population from contesting for power or advancing and defending their interests, or may leave significant arenas of decision making beyond the control of elected officials.

This has in fact increased the hold of formal properties of governance over substantial features that consolidate societies and help democratic aggregation. Communities have become more vulnerable than ever before to the dominant interests that lubricate the procedural machinery of elections. The extent of political repression of weaker communities, marginalized groups, and the rural poor are issues that the modern liberal state tries to answer through the electoral process rather than invoking issues of substantive justice in law and governance. Fung and Wright (2003: 3) argue that the apparent decline of state capacity to govern democratically has helped the "right of the political spectrum" to escalate its attack on the very idea of the affirmative state. As they further write, "deregulation, privatization, reduction of social services, and curtailments of state spending have been the watch words, rather than participation, greater responsiveness, more creative and effective forms of democratic state intervention"

A strong critique of new institutionalism in administrative practices has come from critical theorists. Habermas, in Between Facts and Norms (1992), carried a very strong emphasis on participation and what he prefers to call "discourse democracy." This democracy emerges from those critical realities of society that solidify through participation in formal and informal forums rather than in electoral politics. Cultural presuppositions about traditional communities can model a process of informal logic that would test validity claims and design a framework of democratic participation. Social actions are regarded as the reproduction and transformation of practices and structures that are relatively enduring and exist prior to the individual. Even Riggs's advancement of the theory from Prismatic Society Revisited (1973) to Applied Prismatics (1978) was an intensive search for frameworks of ethnicities and interethnic processes and problems that continue to remain relevant for Indian administration. Kothari (1991) and Dipankar Gupta (2000) are forthrightly suspicious of the homogenization process and suggest revival of civil society institutions based upon traditions of mutuality and togetherness.

The present period of advancement calls for strengthening constitutional democracy by reviving modern rational-legal intermediate institutions, such as the institutions of local governance like the municipality, panchayat, or judiciary, or the corporate structure of the economy. It is this aspect that an affirmative state, rather than a retreating one, is more empowered to take cognizance of. The support for the affirmative state has declined in the recent years of advancing globalization because the capacity to mobilize community-guided movements has also declined. This feature manifests itself in a more pronounced manner in globalizing cities, because of their ability to draw people from all regions of the world as a technical support work force or as unorganized lowwage labourers.

Thomas and Heller (2003: 77), in their case study on decentralized planning in the Indian state of Kerala, assert, "A fiercely competitive political party system grafted onto a highly unequal and fragmented social structure has privileged narrow and opportunistic interest politics over more encompassing forms of representation."

Thus, politics has been reduced to a zero-sum scramble for public resources. To use Karl Polanyi's metaphor, these regions of the country have become "satanic mills" of the poor, where all people's movements freeze. This also suggests the growth of a shadow governance system, as elaborated in Strange's The Retreat of the State (1996), in which transnational diplomacy between national mafias has found it easier to operate economic enterprises. In globalizing cities, it is the "land mafia" that is a more visible and tangible variant on the political scene, though actual data about their influence may take more time to emerge in research.

REFORMS IN LOCAL GOVERNANCE THAT SHRINK SPACES FOR DELIBERATION

The purpose of this paper is to explore whether reforms are shrinking the arena of deliberate democracy and subordinating institutions of social deliberation to demands of the new market. Reforms undertaken at the local governance level, which affect the acquisition of village resources for infrastructure development and urbanization processes, have raised serious problems. Public administration is subjected to theoretical tensions to understand it in the background of the spirit of constitutional democracy and demands of new markets. Rosenbloom (1982: 54) suggests that the trinity of values that arrive from traditional professionalism in public administration such as efficiency, effectiveness, and economy should never be allowed to displace discursiveness and deliberations about public policies in society, or prevent autonomy of communities and the idea of common good. Long (1976: 21) also argues that we must not "substitute a market with consumers for a polity with citizens." This has, however, not been the case in globalizing cities.

Indian democracy rests upon a substratum of villages composed of communities that are ethnically, linguistically, and culturally very diversified. Yet one factor that links them into a nation is the agriculture cycle of the Rabi and Kharif cropping seasons. Since life revolves round it, their community institutions also revolve round it. Sir Henry Cotton in his book New India or India in Transition (1886) states that even the British House of Commons Report of 1812, during the peak of colonial occupation of India, carried observations about the self-supportive governance system prevailing in Indian villages. Villages have been constantly pressured by state authorities to dispense with their land and forests which, being arid types, are generally treated as wastelands under centrally sponsored schemes for land regeneration such as the Drought Prone Area Programme or Desert Development Programme. The penultimate value attached to village governance in the Constitution gets derailed due to the lopsided and exotic reforms being carried toward marketization of local governance. This has prevented the growth of participatory bureaucracy and emboldened the rule of dominant caste mafias in rural areas.

Panchayats were sacrosanct to villages in India even before they were constitutionally recognized in the 73rd Constitutional Amendment Act of 1992. This amendment was a new milestone in the democratic evolution of India, since it finally recognized this innate capacity of Indian governance. It was a landmark in the direction of decentralized decision making. Panchayati Raj Institutions (PRIs), which are the rural governance structures, and municipal bodies (urban structures) ensured people's participation in planning, decision making, implementation, and delivery. This paper takes up the reforms undertaken by globalizing cities to facilitate speedy infrastructure development and FDI investments. It would also work on the logic that reforms have to reflect people's habits and value systems and for that reason they also have to originate from people, since administrative practices can not divert from established habits and norms of society.

The element of deliberation embedded in local institutions gets weakened right from the preparation of the Master Plan prepared for the city, as it is a plan for city expansion and urbanization over agricultural lands. It is mandatory for every city to prepare a development plan. This is generally called a Master Plan, which sets in motion the task of land acquisition for development purposes in accordance with the prospective problems that the city may encounter as it grows. The problem begins when the core component of development-that is, "land"-is the scarcest commodity within the municipal limits. So this land has to be acquired from the surrounding villages. Thus, agricultural fields, land under panchayats, and village community resources such as ponds, wells, village forests, and watershed areas, which are cherished as the common property of all village inhabitants, suddenly become commodities to be sold in the market.

This process of acquiring land from villages has been going on for a long time, but as administrators from three development offices in Gurgaon reveal, earlier they were being acquired for laying a railway line, a road, an electric line, or an industry that in many ways compensated villages for the loss of land through the ethical argument of capacity development. In the present times, globalization pushes multinationals into the market, as a result of which the government acquires land and passes it to the developer, who finally becomes the major beneficiary. This is evident in the statistics on foodgrain production in Gurgaon, which has declined as a percentage of the gross value of agricultural output at current prices from 71.02% in 1970-71 to 49.01% in 2001-2002.

Even the land use pattern of the state of Haryana suggests that the area under forests has been drastically reduced, from 4.62% in 1980-81 to a mere 1% in 2004. (Statistical Abstracts of Haryana 1980-81 2004) and therefore the percentage of Gurgaon's forest area to the total geographical area of the district is a pathetically low 2.56%.

These factors are seen in the process of people's contribution to the developmental process and their participation in state programs. The Community Development statistics of Haryana reveal that people's contribution to the community development programs in Haryana, which rose from Rs. 648.19 in 1967 to Rs. 763.44 in 1981, show a sharp downturn in the globalizing period to a mere Rs. 75.00 in 2002-03.

A startling revelation here is that the less globalized industrial states have more working population, for the simple reason that these small states offer more diversified and community-based options available to every class of citizen, whereas the globalizing townships are straightline trajectories to urbanized middle-class growth, marginalizing the rural poor. This is adding to the burgeoning numbers of unemployed people in Haryana. Statistics from the Haryana Director of Employment show that the number of unemployed persons has almost doubled, from 486,706 in 1985 to 802,581 in 2002. Even though the market has opened up, the state capacity for placement has decreased from 17,253 persons in 1985 to 4,764 in 2002.

In the early era of liberalization, most of the state governments did not have the money to compensate villagers for their acquired land. This anomaly was partly rectified in 1996 when Government of India's Urban Development Plans Formulation and Implementation (UDPFI) rationalized the problems of land acquisition so that the benefits of adequate compensation go straight to the owner and the predictability of development programs for the city are also assured.

UDPFI defined "transfer of development rights" as the development right to transfer the potential of a plot designated for a public purpose in a plan, expressed in terms of total permissible built space calculated on the basis of Floor Space Index or Floor Area Ratio allowable for that plot, for utilization by the owner himself or by way of transfer by him to someone else from the present location to a specified area in the plan, as additional built up space over and above the permissible limit in lieu of compensation for the surrender of the concerned plot free from all encumbrances to the planning and Development Authority.

This system recharged the real estate developers and thus the total land cost flows from the developer to the landowner. The process was accelerated when the Government stated in November 2003 that it would permit 100% FDI, on a case-to-case basis, in the development of integrated townships. This would permit FDI in housing, commercial premises, hotels, resorts, city-and regional-level urban infrastructure facilities such as roads and bridges, and mass rapid transport systems. Two Malaysian companies, Feedback Integrated Infrastructure Development Corporation and IJM Infrastructure Ltd, have already entered into agreement to develop townships at Gurgaon and in Kukatpally in Hyderabad. According to the 2004 Global Retail Development Index by A. T. Kearney, India ranks second in the world when it comes to opportunities in the organized retail business-even higher than the People's Republic of China, which is ranked third. Investment in retail real estate yields 13-16% per year. This system lies behind the rapid growth of some of the previously sleepy and slogging townships. Reforms that have reduced bureaucracy and liberalized laws have also helped the generation of private facilitators from local areas who help in land acquisitions by suppressing the local communitarian voices.

The developments mentioned above have made rural areas and their local bodies such as panchayats vulnerable to the pressures of real estate developers. The role of panchayats in protecting and generating income for the poor landless, animal-rearing tribes and dalits (groups of communities which have remained socio-economically backward for reasons of social discrimination due to caste factors) in the village by protecting most of their resources such as land, water bodies, and forests, including the common property resources, has decreased and mostly subsided. This, however, would not mean that panchayats have acted as responsible and honest guardians of village's common areas, but they score better in traditional face-to-face accountability forums within their communities than the new structures created through exogenous pulls of the new market regimes.

The Planning Commission has also noticed this lacuna of planning, in which the higher administrative bodies of the country have failed to relate people's problems to their policies. The Report of the Task Force on Panchayats, constituted in 2001 under the Chairmanship of K. B. Saxena, had pointed out certain grave factors that prevented people's access to the planning process. "It is observed that a number of Ministries of the Central Government have not taken any concrete steps to integrate PRIs in their strategy of planning and implementation of various programmes which essentially fall in their jurisdiction" (2001: 1).

This problem has also been exacerbated due to the direct access by some NGOs to relevant ministries. The shocking fact uncovered in the report is that "PRIs do not really this strategy of implementation and in fact there is not even a conceptual recognition of it. NGOs are operating in areas and on subjects which belong to the PRIs and therefore are expected to work in tandem with them (2001: 1). The report further admits that since ministries undertake internationally funded projects, they tend to implement them directly, without any involvement of PRIs. The Ministry of Rural Development has failed to bridge this gap. Its 2001 Annual Report (2001: 5) listed 232,278 panchayats at the village level, 6,022 at the intermediate level, and 535 at the district level.

These panchayats were being managed by 29.2 million elected representatives at all levels, of whom one third were women. Ironically, this huge deliberative framework has been ignored in the process of planning, and the NGO-led decentralization has brought in experts who are delinked from the anthropological history of that region.

This paper mainly looks into the process of globalization and FDI investment in Bangalore and Gurgaon. The selection of these townships is due to their physically distinct nature. Bangalore is the largest cosmopolitan area of urban India, besides being a major software producer in India. Gurgaon has taken to that status quite recently and both the cities are called the "Silicon Valley of India." Bangalore has always been an urban, literate society, whereas Gurgaon has been a rural and traditionally a caste-dominated township, despite its proximity to the capital city Delhi. It would be interesting to begin from the panchayats of the capital city "Delhi," where the panchayati raj continues to be suspended by the state government and no effective steps have been taken to revive PRIs.

Much of the illegal activity of land mafias continues over this juridically overlapping area of governance, also called the "lal dora land." The Delhi Development Authority controls most of the development of land. Bangalore had also set up the Bangalore Development Authority in 1976 as a successor to the erstwhile City Improvement Trust Board. The Bangalore Agenda Task Force is a recent creation to act as a catalyst in realizing the city's potential. Gurgaon has the Haryana Urban Development Authority, which till 1996 was acquiring land and then giving it to Haryana State Industrial development Corporation for demarcating plots for development activities. It is a paradox that in these cities no specific body has arisen to look into these irregularities of globalization-led land acquisition from rural communities. This has helped the state government acquire the benefit of centralizing city plans including financial flows. It is imperative to study the process of development and urbanization in globalizing areas and seek ways to measure the democratic deficit of such townships. The most important administrative and political strategy is that of acquiring land from adjoining villages. It involves a number of interrelated measures. First comes the most essential ingredient, a developer-friendly legal framework, which ensures that land can be easily bought and sold. Second is the administration-friendly procedures and regulations to ensure the development of land at an affordable cost. The third measure is that of a legitimacy in which the land taxation system is designed to promote equity and efficiency in land use. This process also includes an installation of a transparent and corruptionfree local administration, which may not really push reforms to improve people's access to these measures.

Gurgaon Model

To understand the shrinking deliberative power of panchayats in Gurgaon, it is important to assess their status since the beginning of global marketization in the early 1990s. In the 1991 census, Gurgaon had 688 inhabited villages, which increased to 700 in the 2001 census because of the explosive increase of 44.64% in its population; but the number of so called "uninhabited villages" mentioned in the Director of Census Operations records fell from 42 in 1991 to 26 in 2001. This is reflected in the creation of a new town in Gurgaon district: the number of towns increased from 11 to 12 during this period.

These so-called uninhabited villages were the grazing grounds of cattle-and sheep-rearing rural inhabitants, who gained little out of a global spread of business process outsourcing companies. Gurgaon being a district with a dominant rural population, the workforce largely arrived from cities outside Gurgaon. The massive housing and construction boom that followed took place on the land acquired from villages.

The District Town and Country Planner (TCP) claims that the controlled areas that fall at the rural-urban fringes are real centres of planning for further industrialization. In Gurgaon alone it comprises something like one third of the total land in the district, out of which only 9.5% of the areas are urban, thereby leaving more than 90% of the state's area free from any of the controls of Acts enforced by the Government. There has been a substantial amount of infrastructure mismanagement, since the Municipal Committee and the panchayats are not obliged to function within this area and the TCP cannot undertake work without an officially declared plan for that area. They may more reasonably be termed as the "areas of diluted governance." The land purchased within the controlled areas needs a change of land use (CLU) Certificate from the District TCP, which the land purchased outside the controlled areas does not require. Since the industrial townships have not been able to develop plots, these industries have started buying plots directly from the farmers and managing to obtain CLU certificates from the Directorate of Town and Country Planning. This process was guided by a colonial legal system defined under the Land Acquisition Act of 1894. In 1995, on 9 February, the government constituted a committee comprising the following officers as a process to decentralize the power hereby concentrated in the Divisional Commissioner's office:

- o Divisional Commissioner as the Chair,
- o Deputy Commissioner as the Member Secretary,
- o Representative of the Concerned Member Department, and
- o District Revenue Officer as the concerned Member.

This also restricted the District Commissioner's discretion to determine the market price of land, not on the basis of 5 years' sale average but only on the basis of 1 year's sale average. Section 5A of this New Land Acquisition Act of 1995 also enabled the landowner to refer to the court under Sec. 18 of the Act. At the peak of this globalizing exercise in Gurgaon, another amendment was undertaken on 8 September 2003. Into Section 22 of the Punjab Scheduled Roads and Controlled Areas Restriction of Unregulated Development Act 1963, after clause (a), an amendment (aa) clause was added to increase the "abadi deh areas" [inhabited areas around the village] and reduce the controlled areas where numerous restrictions on construction activities apply. The explanation for the amendment given in the statement of objects and reasons by the TCP Minister of Haryana was the need to exempt construction activity in abadi deh areas. Parallel to liberalizing the process of laws related to ceilings on agricultural land acquisition and disposal of surplus area has also been a systemic restraining of the decision-making autonomy of local bodies. The 73rd Panchayat (Amendment) Act 1992 had given a constitutional status to panchayats and the Haryana Panchayati Raj Act 1994 had adopted this provision for better administration of rural areas. With the globalization of the market, certain amendments were made to the state act that raise questions about the democratic imperative of these local bodies. Three provisions may be mentioned here. First, the Act of 1994 says that "If the whole of the sabha area is included in a municipality or a cantonment, the Gram Panchayat shall cease to exist and the assets and liabilities of it shall vest in the municipality or cantonment as the case may be" (Part II, 7 [4]). Taking their cue from this, the developers constructed urban areas on village lands and thus were given the benefit of not having any taxation regime like that of cities. But the price for this anomaly is extremely high, as these villages are at the verge of extermination by real estate developers in business here, such as DLF City, Unitech City, Ansal City, or Ardee City.

These areas, exempted from the restrictions imposed by the 1963 Act mentioned above, have not been included in the Municipal Council of Gurgaon for fear of losing a vote bank, since their inclusion into a municipality would mean their subjection to a taxation system on property and land transfer deeds. But besides this tax exemption, these residents of multinational corporation-led urban areas also become entitled to vote in panchayat elections without being physically residents of the villages, historically or emotionally.

This is a total turnaround to the very idea of panchayats as a system of selfgoverning institutions for village communities, as recognized by the Constitution of India (Article 243 G). The urban voters almost outnumber the rural communities living in these village areas, who have lost their land and occupations, as well as access to their community governance systems.

Second is the series of amendments to the 1994 Act that have systematically weakened the checks and balances system embedded in the Act. Part II Art 8 (2b) of the Act, which provided for six to 20 panches (representatives) from wards in a panchayat area in the manner prescribed so that the despotism of the sarpanch (headman) could be restrained, has been omitted (vide Haryana Act No. 10 of 1999). This has abolished the power of the panches to call a special meeting with notice to the sarpanch and has also led to the Haryana Act No. 14 of 2003, in which the obligation upon the panchayats for having a circle supervisor from among the existing gram sachivs (village secretaries at the local body) to supervise the work of gram vikas sahayaks (village development volunteers) was substituted.

The third concern is that such measures becoming common in India also raises questions of constitutional propriety. In a case pending in Haryana High Court against a major colonizer in this area, DLF Ltd., and a few other minor developers, it has been recognized that a clear violation of Articles 243X and 243W exists, read with Schedule 12, in which the developer was to undertake the responsibility of maintenance under agreement between DLF and the District TCP. The contesting Resident Welfare Association of urban settlers charges it as the "Biggest Land Scam in the Country." People's awakening has led to the demise of the regime of former Chief Minister of the state, Om Prakash Chautala, and his sons in the last Assembly elections of 2004, who were instrumental in importing an uncontested rule of colonizers and land mafias in the district of Gurgaon (Amar Ujala 2003).

Bangalore Model

The Bangalore Development Authority (BDA) came into existence in 1976 as a successor to the erstwhile City Improvement Trust Board. The BDA does not have a parallel in Gurgaon. Even rural panchayats have undergone a systematic trimming through gradual amendments, but the presence of an alert and educated citizenry in Bangalore as a buffer has prevented the state government from colonizing citizens' lives through big corporate builders.

The gram sabhas (village bodies) were constituted in the 1983 Act and the first elections to panchayats were held in 1987. But in 1992, these local bodies were superceded and administrators were appointed. In 1993, following the Constitution 73rd Amendment Act, the Karnataka Panchayat Raj Act was passed, but still these local bodies could not emerge as deliberative institutions.

They have been fund-starved since their inception, and the newly created post of the Chief Executive Officer (CEO), who retains most of the powers, is not under the control of local panchayats. This Act has since been amended six times. The Nayak Committee, which was appointed in 1997, tried to debureaucratize these bodies by transferring many functions back to the panchayats. Inbanathan's (2000) study on these local bodies in Karnataka records an observation that, although panchayats are provided the opportunity for the widest section of rural society to participate in local governance, social conditions ensure that only a section of the village people actually acquire and wield power.

The rise of development authorities has also been a serious threat to flourishing local economies. The Master Plan for Bangalore was drawn to promote "urban renewal" under the Mega Cities program, similar to the cyber city program of Gurgaon. Though this brought megamalls and multistoried apartments, yet the local economies got blocked. The BDA has also demolished small enterprise-centred commercial areas to recover land that was finally allocated to higher-income groups. Procedures such as "land reconveyance," which aids in the development of land for poorer classes, is subsequently weakened. In the 2001 panchayat elections, reports revealed that an auction of seats took place (Vyasulu 2001).

Most of the intermediate local bodies are elected under development partner pressure. Government departments are given targets to set up self-help groups and other people's organizations for better people's participation. Allegations have been made about the government by the Bellandur gram panchayat and surrounding villages, which were selected for the proposed information and technology corridor project in the City. In September 2004, Janata Dal (Secular) Secretary-General C. Narayanswamy demanded a high-level inquiry into land grabbing by private land developers and influential persons (Deccan Herald 2004).

It has been reported that despite preliminary notification for land acquisition by the BDA and the Karnataka Industrial Area Development Board, influential persons, middlemen, and private land developers have cheated the farmers by paying them less than the market value for their lands and then selling the acquired lands at prevailing market rates to information technology companies like Intel.

The India Urban Indicators Programme developed by the Society for Development Studies was well received at the United Nations Habitat II Conference held at Istanbul in June 1996, and won the "Best Practice" award for excellence from among 110 participating countries. Bangalore was among the 11 Indian cities included in the program and Karnataka accounted for five of them. Thus in Bangalore also, a loose regulatory environment for land use is oriented toward mixed land use, as a result of which developers hold sway over its development and retail sale.

The Bangalore model serves governance parameters better than the Gurgaon Model and this is for one single reason. They have better civil society activism and two important measures of downward accountability: first, the gram sabhas as deliberative bodies and, second, the system of jamabandhi (social audit). When gram sabhas started deteriorating, efforts such as citizens' charters, Report Cards on Public Utilities, and right to information became important. Similarly, citizens' groups in Bangalore such as Public Affairs Survey and Swabhimaan collected a set of crucial data from candidates contesting elections and then disseminated the data to help voters make a better choice. Their survey of the industrial environment in Karnataka State has also spurred reforms in the Karnataka industries (Simplification of Procedures and Documentation Act/Rule 2001).

EPISTEMIC BONDS IN LOCAL GOVERNANCE

The last part of this paper brings out a model of governance based upon quantum physics that explains why local governance weakens when exogenous trends start dominating the processes of globalization and transnational investments. This model also explains that the weakening of local governance is the main impetus behind the rise of electoral fallacies in modern democracies.

Quantum mechanics offers a method to understand the structures of society and about the ecological bonds that may be referred to as epistemic bonds [EB], which bring people together and sustain them in a common mode of beliefs, values, and culture, or more appropriately, in an ecosystem.

Thus, EB is a "strong attractive force" composed of a set of relationships between the resources and the resource-dependent community. These bonds also provide stability and security of habitation and of the availability of needed resources from the ecosystem. All this is assured due to internal governance systems nurtured and sustained over a long period of history within the framework of ecological relationships, which an exogenous mode of development fails to visualize. The two figures given below explain the pressures of production strategies that do not adapt themselves to the community's carrying capacities within the local constraints of resources. The result is the reduced and shrinking community spaces leading toward retrogressive development or an unsustainable development. As this trend continues, the cost of governance increases and visible negative effects of growth such as inequities, lawlessness, violence, spread of diseases, and loss of environmental resources block the achievement of good governance within any society.

CONCLUSIONS

Globalization has changed the context as well as the epistemology of development policies in Indian cities. The core defense that the study makes is that of deliberate democracy, which entails consideration for reciprocative and substantial democratic principles. Institutions that have grown and evolved over a period of time in a cultural domain cherish certain ideals and values, which form the axis of sustainable governance.

Since globalization brings new transnational actors and the lure of big money-for which the development and infrastructure arrangements by state authorities are not enough-governments have been subsidizing the core value systems of substantive democracy by weakening their hold over their resources of empowerment. Panchayats have become an anathema for an ambitious Master Plan of a globalizing city. Thus the political party ruling the state undertakes measures to weaken them and even bypass the norms of constitutional propriety. This is made possible by aggressive and maneuverable measures for using the electoral machinery. Thus electoralism is treated as the condition for democracy in the state.

Two models of such globalizing experiments have been taken for analysis; Gurgaon and Bangalore. While this paper foresees a grim future for democratic standards and deliberative democracy in Gurgaon, it certainly perceives a slow but a definite return to deliberative democratic norms in Bangalore. The reason is the existence of a few committed people's organizations, which keep a check upon the records of transparency of governance and accountability of the government. Thus, deliberative democracy, which is dependent upon fearless mutuality and interaction in the functioning of institutions, is also the best information disseminator, preventing degeneration of democracy into electoralism, or electoral fallacies.

3

Administrative and Institutional Issues

Poverty means the inability of an individual to secure a normative minimum level of living. In the narrow sense, it represents the basic material condition of households or individuals in low production, consumption, and income. While economic development is central to success in poverty reduction, it is important to recognize that poverty is the outcome of economic, social, and political processes that interact with and reinforce one another. Recognition of this multidimensional view of poverty creates complexities in poverty reduction strategies, because social and cultural factors have to be taken into account. Poverty alleviation remains one of the most elusive goals confronting development specialists and policy makers at the outset of the new century. The sheer numbers of people who become poor each year, combined with the depth of their deprivation, adds urgency to the search for more effective solutions to poverty (Estes 1999).

POVERTY IN INDIA

The World Development Report 2005 says that during the period 1999- 2000, 34.7% of the population of India was living in extreme poverty (World Bank 2004). "Extreme poverty" is measured in terms of lack of money or income to meet the basic needs of life. The question of quality of living does not arise. The latest statistics gathered through the National Sample Survey indicate that 27.1% of all Indians live below the poverty line. Whatever the exact figure, the fact remains that a large portion of our population is smarting under poverty (Dutta 2002). The poor are a heterogeneous group: they are deprived not only in material terms, but also suffer from low human development and live in an uncertain and sometimes threatening environment.

Lower-caste individuals and women in particular face difficulties. Poverty is caused by low levels of assets (private goods, public goods and services, and social capital) coupled with low and uncertain returns. In addition to low incomes and inadequate consumption, poverty encompasses low human capabilities, including inadequate skills, lack of education, poor health, and malnutrition. In any country, a variety of economic and non-economic factors must be taken into consideration to obtain an accurate and comprehensive picture of poverty. India, with its rich mosaic of cultural practices and wide variety of social settings and natural environments, presents a special challenge to those wishing to measure and monitor poverty. Poverty is also associated with forms of deprivation situated in specific local contexts, such as insecurity and violence, vulnerability, and social and political exclusion, as well as lack of dignity and basic rights.

The state faces three major challenges in redressing poverty: first, to expand economic opportunities; second, to ensure that the poor are empowered to take advantage of new opportunities in a rapidly changing world; and third, to ensure that an effective safety net is in place to reduce vulnerability and protect the very poor and destitute.

POVERTY ALLEVIATION STRATEGIES

The transition of the poverty alleviation strategy from one of promoting the overall growth of the economy (and subsequently the growth of the sectors and regions where the poor are concentrated) to that of directly targeting the poor for growth is an interesting innovation of the Indian planning process. The target group approach to poverty alleviation, which originated in the 1970s, sought to provide income and employment-generating opportunities directly to poor households to enable them to cross the poverty line. With such a change in strategy, though remarkable achievements have been reported, the delivery systems evolved by the bureaucracy have not always conformed to the principles of efficiency and cost-effectiveness. It is in this context that decentralized governance and planning were seen as a new institutional strategy for managing poverty alleviation programs in an efficient and cost-effective manner.

The Study: It is a general perception that the benefits of various poverty alleviation programs are not reaching the rural poor in full measure. Against this background, a micro-study was carried out to assess the overall impact of antipoverty measures in bringing the rural poor above the poverty line, by creating supplementary income, providing employment opportunities, creating socioeconomic infrastructure in the villages, and thereby contributing to the development of the village economy. The study also examined the issues of transparency, accountability, and effectiveness of the process of administration and implementation, flow of funds, the involvement and participation of the rural poor through village-level democratic institutions (the panchayat and gram sabha) and the impact of various measures/ programs on income, productivity, capacity building, asset creation, and the quality of life of the rural poor.

FINDINGS-ISSUES AND RECOMMENDATIONS

The study revealed that, although the poverty alleviation programs under study have been targeted at weaker groups like members of the Scheduled Castes and Scheduled Tribes and at women; although some assets have been created and some employment and income generated; although a few beneficiaries have consequently crossed the poverty line and have experienced some upward occupational mobility, the overall impacts of antipoverty programs on the rural poor have been less than desirable. Only 31.6% (as against 100%) of the targeted beneficiaries could cross the poverty line within the specified period. This could be attributed to factors such as apathy and domination by the bureaucracy; lack of accountability and transparency in administration; delays in the release of funds at the district and lower levels; lack of flexibility and autonomy of key functionaries, especially at the lower levels; misidentification and wrong selection of real beneficiaries; lack of active involvement and effective participation by the rural poor, particularly women, due to lack of awareness and lack of resources; weak and ineffective villagelevel institutions; village-level politics; lack of access to information about various programs; lack of participation by the non-government organizations (NGOs); and lack of proper coordination among various implementing agencies.

Inordinate delays in the release of funds from the central Government as well as from the states have been the main cause for underutilization of allocated funds (20-30%) and an anxiety to achieve the physical targets (more than 90%) in the last quarter of the year is the main reason for poor quality performance.

Monitoring of programs is not done properly and regularly on a standard format, so timely corrective measures and follow-up are not done. Lack of a formal mechanism to receive feedback and the grievances of the beneficiaries also affects program implementation. The implementing officers should visit the field regularly to ensure that the programs are implemented properly. Periodic evaluation of the programs by an independent agency should be conducted and remedial action should be taken to improve performance.

It was observed that reliable data on physical and financial coverage for various schemes were not systematically organized and maintained at the village, block, and district levels. Proper recording systems should be installed at all levels.

The organizational structure of the District Rural Development Agency (DRDA) should be revamped and strengthened with the induction of professionals and experts and motivated and knowledgeable functionaries. The staff should be given sufficient exposure and sensitization to the complexities of poverty eradication, human resource development, and gender and related issues. DRDA should not be satisfied with achievement of physical targets only but should also ensure the quality of programs and realization of intended benefits for the targeted poor beneficiaries. Though antipoverty programs have enhanced the employment level (as well as self-employment) and consequently have increased the income level of a small number of beneficiary households as they have shifted from below the poverty line to above it, they have by and large failed in enabling a large number of poor households to cross the poverty line. Thus, these programs have had a limited impact on poverty reduction.

It must be recognized that income growth by itself is not enough to improve the quality of life of the poor. Unless they have access to certain basic minimum services such as schooling; basic health care; safe drinking water; and nutritional security, shelter, and connectivity, their living condition cannot be improved. Swarajayanti Gram Swaraj Yojana (SGSY) has been successful in providing incremental income to poor families, but in most cases the incremental income has not been adequate to enable the beneficiaries to cross the poverty line on a sustained basis, mainly because the investment per family is too low. Even the assets (e.g., animals for husbandry) provided under SGSY (individual) were neither permanent nor productive, as they have either been sold or have ceased to generate income.

It is necessary to encourage investment into high value-addition sectors and non-traditional activities that have a market potential. Financial institutions should play a more significant, proactive, and dynamic role by enhancing the credit flows through a continuous line of credit. A package approach should be employed, where the beneficiary would have access to training as required, upgrades of technology, delivery of essential inputs, and marketing and other infrastructure and services and employment opportunities in an integral and holistic manner.

Subsidies should be phased out. SGSY should be conceived as a Micro-finance program to be run by banks and other financial institutions with no subsidy. The focus should be on capacity building, credit mobilization, and infrastructure development.

Development programs are expected to promote occupational mobility among households, from less productive to more productive occupations. It was found that poor households were traditionally engaged in low-productivity occupations like wage labour and agricultural and allied activities. To the extent possible, the endeavour should be to move them to more productive non-agricultural activities like trade, business, and industry, where returns are higher and job opportunities are more sustainable. Keeping in view the district potential, rural industries should be promoted, by encouraging new and strengthening existing small-

and medium-scale industries, building capabilities, and training rural youth to become rural industrialists. The gram sabha (GS), the village assembly consisting of all eligible voters, is statutorily recognized as a vital institution of participatory democracy to ensure people's participation, (especially women, the poor, and other marginalized sections of the village community) in the process of rural development. Thus, while GS consists of people themselves, the gram panchayat (GP, the third tier of the Panchayati Raj Institutions [PRIs] of local self-government) consists of elected representatives.

The GS is required to meet at least twice in a year to discuss and approve the village level microplans based on local needs and priorities and to identify and approve the list of appropriate beneficiaries. It is empowered to monitor and audit the progress /performance of the GP in the execution of microplans and to ensure their transparency and accountability to the people. The GS is thus expected to play the role of a planner, a decision maker, and an auditor. However, the sheer size of the GS, the general lack of interest on the part of the rural poor except when some perceptible gain is in sight, the emasculated condition of the village panchayat, the paucity of resources, the high opportunity costs of attending the GS for poor villagers, and the lack of specific roles for the ordinary members of the panchayat in GS stand in the way of development of GS as a truly democratic institution. The GS, by and large, is unable to perform its statutory functions relating to granting approvals to village-level development plans and selecting appropriate beneficiaries. It can become effective if it is empowered through capacity building, political education of the masses, larger participation in development programs, more effective control over panchayat leadership, better responsiveness of the administration, better mobilization of resources, and better care of community/ village assets. Thus, GS needs to be strengthened by handing over real power.

The GPs are still dominated by the bureaucracy. Bureaucrats need to change their mindset. The middle-level bureaucrats are afraid and lack the will to transfer powers to poor and illiterate villagers. It is also important to strengthen the internal resource mobilization capabilities of PRIs for functional autonomy. They should also be given control over the natural resources such as land, water, minor forest produce, and minerals. All village-level users' groups formed under different development programs such as watershed committees, water users' groups, forest protection committees, and self-help groups, should be linked to the panchayat and brought under its control. Apart from a package of devolved powers, the PRIs need qualified trained technical staff to help them with day-to-day transactions at various levels and to advise the GP on the formulation of action plans and their technical feasibility.

The technical staff posted at block level could be assigned to work in the GP for this purpose. Orientation/training and occasional guidance should be provided to GS/village panchayats with respect to their day-to-day conduct of financial and administrative matters. The majority of the rural poor are ignorant about various government-sponsored poverty alleviation programs. This is a serious problem, especially when the majority of programs are demand-driven and users are illiterate and marginalized. Poor awareness accounts for the lack of interest and lack of involvement and participation on the part of potential beneficiaries. Consequently, the block officials, elected representatives of panchayats, and other influential persons in the village can manipulate the process of identification and selection of beneficiaries.

Personnel at the block level were found to be ill-informed, insensitive, and inefficient. Moreover, a number of posts were lying vacant. This hampers efficient implementation and proper monitoring of the programs. It is suggested that all field-level vacancies should be filled at the earliest possible time and the personnel, especially those at the block and village level, should be motivated and sensitized and their managerial skills upgraded through suitable training and field exposure. In order to improve delivery systems, in terms of both time and quality, effective cooperation, trust, and coordination among various agencies should be ensured at district and block levels. More effective liaison and interface between the state government, DRDA, PRIs, NGOs, and the rural communities is required at the local level. Each block officer is a mesostructure that links macrostructure such as state and central government with microstructures such as PRIs.

The block development officer needs to possess certain critical skills such as those in development, planning, training, and rural engineering, apart from administrative skills. In addition, such officers need to be sensitive and proactive in their approach. Staff at the village level should be better informed about various programs and properly trained and made sensitive to local issues. Efforts should be made to bring all of the country's DRDAs into an on-line network for a smooth flow of information between districts and from districts to the state to the central Government. Sensitization and training of DRDA and field-level functionaries as well as bank officials should be organized regularly.

Decentralization, which attempts to ensure local people's participation in planning and governance, is generally considered an efficient instrument for conveying benefits to the poor at least cost. Accountability and transparency, the cornerstones of decentralized governance, are expected to ensure minimization of beneficiary misidentification, better enforcement of asset acquisition, its retention and maintenance, loan repayment, capital plowback, etc. Besides, since local wisdom and local resources are readily available under decentralized governance, local human, animal, and physical resources can be effectively utilized, resulting in the creation of employment opportunities and the production of goods and services that help meet the needs of the poorer sections of society (Aziz, Meenakshisundaram, and Gayathri Devi 2000). Village development projects are expected to be executed by officials under the supervision of people and their representatives. But owing to the inadequacy of qualified officials, such works were informally assigned to contractors.

Many a time, the panchayat members themselves worked as contractors. The collusion between official members and panchayat members often resulted in leakage of funds and low-quality work. Hence, it is recommended that better conduct of GS is a must for identification of works and beneficiaries and for ensuring transparency and accountability. The panchayats should have better control over funds. This can be ensured through timely release of funds by the higher-level governments and reduction in the proportion of tied grants, so that the panchayat bodies have enough time to plan and implement poverty alleviation programs and freedom to take up works in response to local imperatives. The practice of giving special grants to members of Parliament and legislatures for local area development should be stopped. Instead, such funds should be allotted to the panchayats, which are in fact designated as governments responsible for local development. The latter, in turn, should use such funds for strengthening local development and poverty alleviation schemes

Official claims of the number of beneficiaries, works carried out, additions to productive assets, and employment generated are unreliable and exaggerated. Poor targeting is reflected in the high proportion of non-poor and other non-eligible persons among the beneficiaries. Leakages due to inappropriate works, inefficient implementation, and corruption are high. Quality of assets provided/created under these programs is poor and their impact on the income level of beneficiaries dubious. Assets and schemes are frequently not appropriate to the needs and potentials of particular regions or groups. Little consultation takes place with local communities generally, and target groups in particular, in deciding and implementing schemes. The efficacy of poverty alleviation programs can be improved by better targeting, reducing waste and corruption, making the programs more meaningful and relevant to local needs and priorities, and creating institutional conditions for greater accountability. The focus should be on rationalizing the approach, organization, and priorities of the poverty alleviation programs.

Non-government and voluntary organizations have a particularly important role in obtaining and disseminating information on the workings of government (including local government), making people aware of their entitlements and obligations, and enabling them to vent their grievances and seek redress. Besides interceding with the concerned authorities to secure benefits for the eligible and minimize leakages, they have a role in motivating and organizing local communities to take an active interest in the working of specific programs and persuading bureaucracy to work with the community to improve their effectiveness. Over time they can help promote a process of more broadly based changes in institutional mechanisms for funding/ managing local development activities to meet specific local conditions. Actively encouraging NGOs and giving them ample public space is, therefore, highly desirable for healthy evolution of local government.

CONCLUSION

All this implies a basic change in the relations between state and local governments, the role of the bureaucracy, and the attitudes of local governments. No standard blueprints are available for accomplishing the change. A great deal of experiment and learning from experience is inevitable. The upsetting of existing power balances between the various groups involved creates an opportunity for engineering desirable changes through a combination of sustained pressures on the system as a whole via the general political process along with grassroots efforts to initiate and sustain a discussion of the problem of restructuring among the concerned groups- the local-and state-level politicians, the bureaucracy, and the NGOs. Officially, the poverty line is dipping, but in the village, poverty remains more acute than ever. The poverty line came down from 55% in 1973-74 to 36% in 1993-94 and 26% in 1999-2000. However, the number of poor people remained stable: around 320 million over a long period (1973-93) and now stands at 260 million. The Food Insecurity Atlas of Rural India, published by the M. S. Swaminathan Foundation, says that 13 states are environmentally unsustainable, while five states are sustainable based on key natural resources like forest, land, and water. The environmentally unsustainable states like Madhya Pradesh and Bihar are not only the poorest but are also resource rich (MSSRF and UNDP 2003).

A typical Indian village economy is built around gross nature product. The entire ecology shares an intricate relationship between private and common resources. For example, private agricultural lands get manure from common grazing lands, which are a part of a government-owned pool of resources called the common property resources (CPRs). People depend on CPRs for survival. But these crucial commons are being rapidly depleted as the focus of poverty alleviation remains on private assets.

DATA AND METHODOLOGY

This study is based on secondary data. The data have been compiled from various sources such as publications of the Planning Commission of India (1993, 2001, 2002), Census of India, Central Statistical Organisation of India, Reserve Bank of India (1999), and Government of India (2000, 2003, and 2004). After a careful review of the literature on rural poverty, it is hypothesized in this study that alleviation of rural poverty depends upon both public policy and socioeconomic factors. The public policy factors include direct poverty alleviation programs, rural housing for the poor, public distribution systems, and loans by regional rural banks. The economic and social variables that influence rural poverty are rural non-farm employment and rural literacy. With a view to capturing:

- The overall contribution of all the policy variables and also
- That of other variables relating to the alleviation of rural
- Poverty, multiple regression analysis has been used in this study.

For regression analysis, state-level data covering 14 major states have been used. Regression analysis has been carried out at 2 levels. At level 1, only policy variables are included in the model. The regression results of this level should help to identify the impact of public programs on rural poverty alleviation. At level 2, variables other than policy variables are also included. The results of this model should help to identify the collective role of both policy and non-policy variables in rural poverty alleviation. In addition to regression analysis, statistical techniques such as percentage, means, standard deviation, coefficient of variation (CV), and correlation have also been used to analyse the data.

PUBLIC PROGRAMS FOR RURAL POVERTY ALLEVIATION

The prominent direct rural poverty alleviation programs in India can be grouped into four categories:

(i) wage employment programs,

(ii) self-employment programs,

(iii) rural housing, and

(iv) public distribution systems.

Wage Employment Programs

The federal Government has launched various wage employment programs from time to time. The important wage employment programs include Jawahar Rozgar Yojana (JRY), Employment Assurance Scheme (EAS), Jawahar Gram Samridhi Yojana (JGSY) and Sampoorna Grameen Rozgar Yojana (SGRY). With a view to improving the effectiveness of these programs, from time to time the government has merged programs, restructured them, and also redesignated a couple of them. At present the SGRY is the only major wage employment generation program. It was launched in September 2001, by restructuring the erstwhile Jawahar Gram Samridhi Yojana (JGSY) and Employment Assurance Scheme (EAS). It has two streams, namely, EAS/ SGRY-I and JRY/JGSY/SGRY-II. The objective of SGRY is to provide additional wage employment in rural areas as well as maintain food security and create durable community, social, and economic infrastructure. The rural poor who are in need of wage employment and desire to do manual and unskilled work in and around the village/habitat are eligible to get benefits from the SGRY. The scheme aims to generate 100 crore (1 billion) man-days of employment in a year. Central and state governments share the cost of each component in the ratio of 75:25 (Government of India 2003, 2004). With a view to promoting participatory democracy and decentralization, the activities under SGRY are implemented by the Gram Panchayat (village level democratically elected government). The District Rural Development Agencies (DRDAs)/ Zila Parishad (ZPs) (democratically elected bodies at the district level) release funds directly to the Gram Panchayat. On the basis of the expressed needs of the area/people, the Gram Panchayat formulate the Annual Action Plan and implement activities with the approval of the Gram Sabha, the village assembly consisting of all eligible voters. Overall guidance, coordination, supervision, and periodical reporting are the responsibility of the DRDAs/ ZPs.

SELF-EMPLOYMENT PROGRAMS

The wage employment generation program mainly supplements the earnings of agricultural labour during lean seasons. However, the extent and nature of unemployment and underemployment in rural India necessitates having programs that aim to create assets for generating self-employment on a sustained basis. With this in view, the Government has introduced a number of programs like the Integrated Rural Development Programme, Training of Rural Youth for Self-Employment, Development of Women and Children in Rural Areas, the Ganga Kalyan Yojana, the Million Wells Scheme, and Supply of Improved Toolkits. Empirical evidence suggested that each program, instead of strengthening other programs through intended linkages, gradually started operating as a separate and independent program and as a consequence, the substantive issue of sustainable income generation was lost in the process.

Recognizing this inadequacy of self-employment generation programs, the Government decided on 1 April 1999 to launch a new self-employment program, Swarn Jayanti Gram Swarozgar Yojana (SGSY), by merging earlier programs. The major objective of SGSY was to bring every assisted family or group (self-help group) of rural poor above the poverty line within 3 years through the promotion of self-employment generation opportunities on a sustainable basis. Under this program, preference was given to those activities that generate self-employment in the vulnerable groups among the rural poor like the Scheduled Castes/Scheduled Tribes and women. The SGSY envisaged providing sustainable income through micro-enterprise development, both land-based and other. For this purpose, effective linkages were established between capacity building of the poor, credit, technology, marketing, and infrastructure.

The SGSY preferred activities to be undertaken through a group approach, with a stipulation that 40% of all self-help groups should be composed exclusively of women. The SGSY also preferred activity clusters. Under the activity cluster approach, the Block SGSY Committee identified four to five activities appropriate to the resource base for each block (cluster of villages). This committee for the identification of cluster activities also made use of potential link plans prepared by National Bank for Agriculture and Rural Development, annual credit plans of commercial banks, and surveys carried out by technical organizations. The expertise of officials on local Khadi (a coarse homespun cotton cloth made in India) production and Village Industries and District Industry Centres was also available to the Block SGSY Committee. The DRDA implemented the SGSY in association with the Panchayati Raj Institutions, particularly the Panchayat Samiti (the second tier of rural democratically elected bodies having headquarters at the block level), the banks, the line departments, and the non-government organizations. Under SGSY, the central and state governments shared the funds in the ratio of 75:25.

Rural Housing

The 1991 Census data revealed that around 3.1 million households were without shelter and another 10.31 million households resided in unserviceable kutcha (mud) houses (Government of India 2003). In view of the magnitude and severity of the problem, the central Government in 1998 announced a National Housing and Habitat Policy aiming to provide "Housing for All" and also facilitate construction of 2 million additional housing units annually, with an emphasis on extending benefits to the poor and the deprived (Government of India 2003). The major rural housing programs under the Action Plan for Rural Housing are Indira Awaas Yojana (IAY), Credit-Cum-Subsidy Scheme for Rural Housing, Innovative Stream for Rural Housing and Habitat Development, Rural Building Centres, Samgara Awaas Yojana, enhancement of equity contributions by the Ministry of Rural Development to the Housing and Urban Development Corporation, and the National Mission for Rural Housing and Habitat. IAY is the most important component of the Action Plan. It was launched in 1985-86 aiming to provide dwelling units free of cost to below-povertyline (BPL) families, subject to the condition that non-Scheduled Caste/ Scheduled Tribe families do not receive more than 40% of program allocations (Government of India 2003; Government of India 2004). Beneficiaries under IAY are selected by the Gram Sabha.

Public Distribution Schemes

The major objective of the Public Distribution System (PDS) is to provide food security to the poor by supplying food grains to them at subsidized prices. PDS, started during World War II, is one of the oldest and largest systems of its type in the world and has a network of around 500,000 fair price shops. These shops annually distribute food grains worth Rs. 300 billion. About 160 million BPL households are the beneficiaries of PDS both in urban and rural India. With a view to plugging the leakages in the PDS and specially targeting the poor, the PDS was revamped under the Target PDS (TPDS) in June 1997. In the new scheme, each poor household is entitled to 25 kgs of food grain per month at prices that are less than half the economic cost. For the poorest of the poor families (i.e., the most vulnerable sector of society), the price charged is less than one fourth the economic cost (Planning Commission 2001). In rural India, the beneficiaries of TPDS include landless agricultural labourers, marginal farmers, and rural artisans/craftsmen such as potters, weavers, blacksmiths, and carpenters.

Rural Poverty Across States

The proportion of the BPL rural population at the national level has declined consistently over time. In 1973-74, more than half of the rural population (56.44%) was BPL.

This percentage has declined to one fourth (27.10%) during 1999-2000. The absolute numbers of the BPL rural population have also declined, from 261.3 million in 1973-74 to 193.2 million in 2000-2001.

A close look at interstate variations in estimates of rural poverty shows that in 1973-74, four states, namely Bihar, Madhya Pradesh, Orissa, and West Bengal, had a high (above 60%) percentage of BPL rural people. States such as Kerala, Maharashtra, Tamil Nadu, Uttar Pradesh, Karnataka, Andhra Pradesh, Gujarat, and Haryana belonged to the medium level of rural poverty (i.e., 30-60% BPL). Punjab, with 28.21% was the only low rural poverty (below 30%) state.

After a gap of about 25 years (i.e., in the years 1999-2000), the states of Orissa, Bihar, Madhya Pradesh, and West Bengal remained in the high rural BPL category, i.e., above 30%. Uttar Pradesh was the new entry in this category. Maharashtra, Karnataka, and Tamil Nadu were in the medium category (between 15-30%) of poverty states. The low level of poverty (below 15%) was a feature of Rajasthan, Gujarat, Andhra Pradesh, Kerala, Haryana and Punjab. Interestingly Punjab again had the lowest (6.4%) rural population below poverty line. The foregoing analysis shows that rural poverty has declined in all the states, but at different rates. This trend has resulted in the perpetuation of interstate disparities in rural poverty. This is confirmed by the notable increase in the value of CV of rural poverty from 22.97% in 1973-1974 to 60.84% in 1999-2000.

Assessment of Public Programs for Rural Poverty Alleviation

Rural poverty alleviation is affected by a variety of factors. In the study, as mentioned in the methodology section, the factors affecting the reduction of rural poverty have been classified into two categories. The first set of factors is from the public policy domain. It includes wage employment and self-employment programs, rural housing, credit advanced by regional rural banks (RRBs), and the PDS. The second set of variables has its roots in socioeconomic development and includes the variables of rural non-farm employment and rural literacy.

In order to investigate the combined role of these variables and also the role of each independent variable in explaining variations in rural poverty for the year 1999-2000, correlation and regression analyses have been carried out by using state-level data. The variables included in the model are given as the percentage of rural people below the poverty line; X1 per capita expenditure on wage employment and self-employment programs for the rural poor (in rupees); X2 per capita expenditure on rural housing programs for the rural poor (in rupees); X3 per capita monthly supply of rice and wheat for rural BPL people under the PDS (in kilograms [kg]); X4 per capita advances by RRBs to the rural poor (in rupees); X5 rural non-farm employment (%); X6 rural literacy (%).

The correlation coefficients between rural poverty and other variables. All the variables have negative correlation with rural poverty. However, three variables-per capita expenditure on wage employment and self-employment programs, per capita monthly PDS supply of rice and wheat, and per capita advances by RRBs-have very high and significant (1% level) negative correlation with rural poverty. Of the remaining three variables, two-rural non-farm employment and rural literacy- have low negative correlation with rural poverty, which is significant at the 5% level.

The third variable-per capita expenditure on rural housing programs-has a very low negative correlation with rural poverty, which is significant at the 10% level. Regression analysis has been used to identify the extent of cause and effect relationships between rural poverty (dependent variable) and independent variables. As mentioned in the methodology, regression analysis has been carried out at two levels.

Conclusions and Policy Recommendations

In India, the proportion of rural BPL people has declined over time. The same trend is noticeable in all the selected states. The pace of decline, however, has varied considerably across states. Kerala has experienced maximum decline (49.79%), whereas Bihar has witnessed minimum decline (18.69%) between the study periods. Though the declining trend is noticeable in most of the states over time, interstate disparities have widened.

Factors such as per capita public expenditure on wage employment and self-employment programs for the rural poor; per capita monthly PDS supply of rice and wheat for rural BPL people, per capita advances by RRBs to the rural poor, and rural non-farm employment have helped in reducing the percentage of rural poor in the country.

In contrast, rural housing schemes and rural literacy programs have adversely affected rural poverty. From the policy perspective, the study recommends allocation of more public funds for wage employment and self-employment programs and for the PDS. Non-farm activities should be promoted in the villages to provide employment to the rural poor.

The number of rural regional banks should also be increased; this would play an important role in reducing the numbers of the rural poor. The leakages and corruption in housing programs for the rural poor need to be reduced or stopped, with a view to improving their delivery. Introduction of a focused literacy program for the rural poor could also help in mitigating rural poverty in India.

WELFARE STATE

In his paper, Dr. Djonet Santoso examines the role of the Social Safety Net (SSN) program in Indonesia in poverty reduction. It is a general understanding that government should work to boost economic growth, reduce poverty, and develop the human resources through expanding public health spending and schooling. In this regard, the Indonesian Government created the SSN program in 1998. Though the effectiveness of the program varies across regions, the study reveals that on many occasions the program has missed the target groups.

The SSN program has four sub-programs: food security, employment creation, education, and health care. To further improve the effectiveness of the SSN program, the author recommends that the Government implement several strategies: consult with non-government organizations; take new approaches; improve the transparency of information dissemination to the public; bring about effective and efficient public consultation; monitor the progress of programs or projects; encourage citizen participation; and look for accurate demographic data.

Public Programs

In their paper "Rural Poverty Alleviation In India: An Assessment of Public Programs," B. S. Ghuman and Gurpinder Chima use secondary data and identify the impact of public programs on rural poverty alleviation as well as highlighting the collective role of both policy and non-policy variables in rural poverty alleviation.

The authors use regression analysis to find out that four variables-per capita (rural poor) expenditure on wage employment generation and selfemployment programs for the rural poor, per capita monthly supply of rice and wheat by the Public Distribution System (PDS) for below-poverty-line rural people, per capita funds advanced by regional rural banks for the rural poor, and rural Non-farm employment-help in reducing the percentage of India's rural poor. Thus, from the public policy perspective, the authors recommend allocation of more public funds for wage employment and self-employment programs, and for the PDS. Moreover, the number of rural regional banks should also be increased, which would be effective in reducing the number of rural poor. Our panelists cover a number of issues that manifest the value orientation of conventional public administration, such as efficiency, effectiveness, social equity, democratic participation, and public accountability. While traditional values are emphasized, the more contemporary ideas of New Public Administration are also highlighted, such as entrepreneurship, market orientation, and result and outcome orientation.

Poverty is a historical phenomenon; only if economic development reaches an advanced level can poverty ultimately be eliminated. Nevertheless, even in rich countries like the USA, fighting poverty is still a significant issue. Therefore, public administration shoulders the responsibility of redistributing social wealth through a number of means, such as tax policy, diverse welfare programs, and other regulatory policies. Public administration has a large role to play in facilitating economic growth as well as ensuring social equity. Although our panelists and other participants have greatly contributed to our understanding of the state of the arts of poverty alleviation in so many countries and areas of Asia-Pacific region, they do not exhaust the issue. New problems and questions will surely emerge from time to time. In this regard, we look forward to the next NAPSIPAG conference for the new means and new ideas about governance from and for Asia-Pacific areas.

Improving Governance and Services: Can E-government Help?

Introduction: Since the late 1990s, the prospect of using information and communication technologies (ICTs) to improve effectiveness, fairness, and accountability in government has attracted widespread enthusiasm. However, early hopes that e-initiatives would bypass intractable questions of government organization and transform citizen experience of the delivery of public services have given way to more modest claims.

At the same time, thinking about how to use ICTs most effectively in government has generated widening questions about what governments should try to do and how they should do it. As Fountain (2001) has argued, einitiatives reconfigure bureaucracy and disturb settled understandings about politics and the nature of the state. ICTs open up diverse patterns of personal and group interaction. But managing ICT infrastructure and applications to provide better government demands coordination. Within government, e-government initiatives pose sharp questions about the roles and capabilities of the executive. They challenge the executive to organize itself for integrated policy making and management, respond to what citizens actually need, and manage multilayered and reciprocal interactions between government organizations and technology.

These challenges are linked, but linking them in a "whole-government" agenda creates large tests of executive capability.

A recent study by the Organisation for Economic Cooperation and Development (OECD) sets out key dimensions of the challenge in these terms:. "Key questions include: How to collaborate more effectively across agencies to address complex, shared problems; how to enhance customer focus; and how to build relationships with private sector partners" (OECD 2003: Such questions lead directly to a familiar dilemma "How to capture the benefits of coordinated action and shared approaches while maintaining individual agency responsibility and accountability for operations and results" (OECD 2003: 15). Many governments have gone to great lengths to craft pluralist or decentralized strategies for improvement. In such models, connections between diverse initiatives depend on consultation and negotiation. Many large and complex businesses have followed similar paths.

However, the opportunity costs of e-initiatives are high. Such initiatives need to provide value. For governments, e-initiatives need to provide policy, management, and service outcomes that citizens value. The concept of public value provides a useful framework for making such assessments (Moore 1995; Kelly and Muers 2002; Stoker 2003; UN 2003; Smith 2004). For businesses, e-initiatives need to grow the business, build shareholder value, or maximize dividends. This has led to steadily more assertive rethinking of the role of coordinating and framework-setting bodies for the use of ICT in both business and government.

Themes of decentralization, devolution, and differentiation associated with New Public Management, neoliberal, or Washington Consensus agendas, which had a pervasive influence in the 1990s, are critically reconsidered. The OECD e-government project team (OECD 2003: 99) sets out a long list of benefits of central coordination. For the private sector, Nicholas Carr argues controversially that similar considerations apply:

Hierarchies... may outperform markets when it comes to integrating complex information systems, leading to a re-emergence of the vertically integrated company (Carr 2004: 12).

In a major study of information technology (IT) governance, Peter Weill and Jeanne Ross (2004) go further; they concentrate on the private sector but include significant public sector cases. They set out a concept of IT governance in which decision rights about IT are carefully allocated to ensure that business strategies drive IT investments. They propose that as dependence on IT spreads throughout organizations, IT governance increases in importance. In words that mirror the phrasing of the OECD team, Weill and Ross argue that the task of good governance is to handle effectively a longtime management paradox-encouraging and leveraging the ingenuity of all the enterprise's people while ensuring compliance with the overall vision and principles (Weill and Ross 2004: 236).

Governments introducing e-initiatives thus face contradictory pressures. Making e-government initiatives work demands significant resources. E-initiatives are hungry for political, organizational, human, and financial capital. Investments and potential gains are large.

But to date, actual gains, however measured, are modest. Further, the price of even modest gains is to open up controversial agendas of governance. Central coordination is back. And it is joined by demands for more responsive and participative government. The propositions outlined above provide a framework for exploring these issues. Examples will be drawn from international surveys of e-government (OECD 2003; UN 2003; Yong 2003) and from the state of Victoria and the federal government in Australia. This paper argues that

- o e-government can help improve governance and service delivery by refocusing consideration of the purposes and tools of government;

- o e-government initiatives pose challenging questions of management, especially about coordination in government and the design of services for citizens; and
- o progress toward implementing e-government raises critical questions about preferred styles of governance and about how governments relate to citizens.

Refocusing the Purposes and Tools of Government

E-government initiatives focus attention on the long-term impacts of the interaction of technology and organizations. E-government is not just about using ICTs throughout the institutions and operations of government. It is also about how organizations in government perceive and apply technology. The reciprocal relations between technology and organizations drive longterm change (Fountain 2001, Bellamy 2002). Ambitions for e-initiatives in government are large. A recent UN survey argued that E-government is about opportunity. Opportunity for the public sector to reform to achieve greater efficiency and efficacy. Opportunity to reduce costs and increase services to the society. Opportunity to include all in public service delivery. And opportunity to empower the citizens for participatory democracy. But the greatest promise of e-government is the historic opportunity for the developing countries to "leap frog" the traditionally longer development stages and catch up in providing a higher standard of living for their populations (UN 2003: 182).

Similarly, in Australia the state government of Victoria stresses the need for positive social impacts. Recently, it reframed its e-government strategy around people-centred government. Its aim is [t]hat Victorians [be] assisted to meet their everyday needs through timely, convenient and relevant support from government, made possible by harnessing the capabilities of information networks and communications technologies as they evolve. Further, E-government should be about people, not technology... Putting People at the Centre... is our vision for creating a new era of richer interaction between the government and citizens.

E-government is thus about the potential for a transformation of government and governance. Many early discussions of e-government outlined stages in the development of e-government in which the final stage was "transformation," "integration," "seamless service delivery," or some similarly ambitious state. However, the path to transformation is tricky. Early, discrete, and bottom-up e-government initiatives tended to meet barriers. Such barriers included costs of ICT infrastructure, lack of interoperability, and problems of coordination. It proved easier to initiate specific projects than to bring together integrated packages. It also proved easier to use the Internet to provide information than to facilitate transactions.

Thinking about the path to transformation raises large questions. Three deserve particular attention. First, is how is change in the application of technology is to be managed?. Whether the focus is on determining requirements for IT infrastructure, finding funds to invest and accounting for those invested, outsourcing responsibility for technology supply, redesigning office procedures, or redefining requirements for skills and knowledge possessed by public employees, governments are expected to assume substantial responsibilities for the management of change.

In a study that combines technical and organizational perspectives, Lionel Pearce uses the evolution of selected stages models to set out the extent of the change agenda. He argues that the specialists in information systems management who originated stages models found themselves drawn progressively more deeply into issues of organization and management. He advocates an organization development model in which each step forward is checked against progress in four dimensions: financial, business process improvement, organizational learning, and customer satisfaction (Pearce 2004:147).

The second question is how to determine the focus of desired transformations. Much discussion focuses on citizens as customers. Government is treated as a retail business and initiatives focus on individual transactions, for example, paying taxes, receiving benefits, renewing licenses, or finding information. E-government in Singapore is notable for the number of transactions now available electronically. Victoria On-line provides users with access to Victorian agencies through a single entry point. It also provides access to federal and local levels of government. At the federal level Australia Goverment and provides access to a series of portals with entry points to federal government services and to state governments.

However, citizens expect more from governments than to be treated as customers (Mintzberg 1994). Pressures emerge for holistic initiatives that benefit citizens as a group. Such initiatives may include institution building, policy development, or the management of information on which both the internal operations of government and the delivery of services depend. The statements quoted above from the UN and the government of Victoria make this explicit. However, progress on such initiatives is at a very early stage. The third question is how to measure progress and learn lessons. Initiatives need to provide value to citizens and to be integrated. The country recognized consistently as an outstanding leader in e-government, Canada, makes a point of using citizen surveys, focus groups, benchmarking tools, and advisory groups. Canada also explicitly links the achievement of efficiency gains with improving and integrating services.

The federal Government in Australia follows a similar course. In a recent study, it found that e-initiatives returned favourable cost-benefit ratios and that, if anything, agencies underestimated "the financial benefits to people of government on-line initiatives." It also found a demand from citizens for more participation:

> Focus group participants indicated a strong desire for more information, greater interaction with government agencies and active participation in development of future community-focused e-government initiatives.

For the two largest countries in Asia, the People's Republic of China and India, a whole government perspective is also emerging as critical. James S. L. Yong and Janice L. K. Leong provide an example of the management difficulties facing e-initiatives in the Beijing Government: We still lack a clear uniform standard in constructing e-Government, since different departments have different standards. Also, it's very difficult to redefine the work responsibilities of those departments (Yong and Leong 2003: 86).

Unless such problems are addressed, Yong and Leong foresee that "islands of automation" will emerge in different government agencies, and the overall e-government interface will remain disjointed (2003: 93). Yong and Sachdeva identify similar issues in India, stating that ...the road to an integrated e-Government system in India is still a long one. The projects are emerging disparately without much replication and interoperability... There is a great need for a comprehensive national e-Governance Plan.

If such issues assume high priority in countries that are making conspicuous efforts, they assume even more significance in countries that are still starting out. In Indonesia, for example, Ayuning Budiati (2004) found that e-government initiatives needed stronger leadership from the President and central agencies. Progress was further inhibited by the strong tendency for agencies and levels of government to work alone.

E-government thus refocuses the purposes and tools of government by contributing to agendas that place a high priority on coordination, integration, and providing citizens with value.

Rethinking Coordination and Design of Services

Ensuring that ICT infrastructure supports e-government strategies requires explicit strategies for the governance of ICT. Once information and transactions are available on-line, attention refocuses on integrated services. In turn, this leads to proposals for service redesign. Both governance of ICT and service integration have consequent impacts on the distribution of agency responsibilities and relations with users.

Governance of IT

The approach to IT governance proposed by Weill and Ross is designed to manage change. They argue that the need for IT governance increases as change accelerates (2004: 184). In brief, their case is that good IT governance pays off: IT is expensive, IT is pervasive, new ITs bombard enterprises with new business opportunities, IT governance is critical to organizational learning about IT value, IT value depends on more than good technology, senior management has limited attention spans, and leading enterprises govern IT differently (2004: 14-18). Through an extensive survey of IT management practices in leading corporations and several public sector agencies, including the

Metropolitan Police Service in London and UNICEF, they aim to identify effective governance strategies.

For governments, their argument about organizational learning is especially important. Weill and Ross state that [e]nterprises have struggled to understand the value of their IT-related initiatives because value cannot always be readily demonstrated through a traditional discounted cash flow analysis.

Value results not only from incremental process improvements but also from the ability to respond to competitive pressures... Effective governance creates mechanisms through which enterprises can debate potential value and formalize their learning (2004: 16-17).

The examples cited above reflect the difficulties many governments have in managing contending e-initiatives. Governments need to learn how to manage them better and convince citizens that they are getting value for money. Further, governments need to learn how to learn about managing e-government. Weill and Ross's analysis is based on an IT governance arrangements matrix related to different governance archetypes for different kinds of decisions. They identify five interrelated IT decisions:

- o IT principles-clarifying the business role of IT;
- o IT architecture-defining integration and standardization requirements;
- o IT infrastructure-determining shared and enabling services;
- o business application needs-specifying the business needs for purchased or internally developed IT applications; and
- o IT investment and prioritization-choosing which initiatives to fund and how much to spend. (2004: 10-11).

They identify six archetypes for the kinds of people involved in making IT decisions:

- o business monarchy-top managers;
- o IT monarchy-IT specialists;
- o feudal-each business unit makes independent decisions;
- o federal-combination of the corporate centre and the business units with or without IT people involved;

o IT duopoly-IT group and one other group (e.g., top management or business unit leaders); and

o anarchy-isolated individual or small group decision making (2004: 12).

They use the matrix to plot the distribution of arrangements used by the organizations in their study, relate arrangements for the overall making and monitoring of strategic business decisions, and identify effective patterns of governance.

Weill and Ross find that any decision archetypes can be associated with effective business strategies (2004: 158-175). However, patterns fall into three main groups. Companies that focus on operational excellence use highly centralized IT governance to facilitate high-volume, low-cost transaction processing. Companies that focus on customer intimacy face more complex needs and try to combine decentralized organizational structures with strong business and IT monarchies to "define and enforce shared technology, business processes, and data definitions" (2004: 168). Companies that focus on product leadership need to encourage creativity while sharing results and building synergies. They can use duopolies and IT monarchies. They can even use feudal arrangements for identifying IT application needs.

Generally, Weill and Ross argue that IT governance in corporations is moving from "more autonomous to more synergistic organizational designs. As firms evolve toward more synergistic designs, they adopt more complex IT governance" (2004: 175).

The distinguishing features of most government organizations are greater organizational complexity and difficulties in performance measurement. Weill and Ross recommend

o using joint business and IT decision making for setting IT principles,

o considering IT infrastructure principles to be strategic business decisions,

o not using a feudal model for business application needs, and

o using joint decision making for IT investments. (2004: 203-205).

They suggest that high-performing public sector bodies regularly use the following mechanisms:

- o executive committees focusing on all key assets including IT,
- o IT council comprising business and IT executives,
- o IT leadership committee comprising IT executives,
- o architecture committee,
- o tracking of IT projects and resources consumed, and
- o business/IT relationship managers (2004: 205-206).

The most conspicuous result of improved IT governance is improved management of information. For example, they attribute the transformation of business processes in the United Nation Economic and Social Council to construction of an effective intranet.

Weill and Ross conclude that, compared with corporations, government and not-for-profit organizations need to govern IT in subtly different ways: Successful IT governance in not for profits relies even more on partnerships and joint decisions between business leaders as well as heavier use of formal mechanisms such as committees. More and more not for profits will include representatives from outside the organization on their IT governance mechanisms to reflect their broader definition of value (2004: 214).

The strength of Weill and Ross's analysis is that it is based on case studies of large government or not-for-profit organizations and reinforced by considerable familiarity with government operations. However, it does not examine arrangements for whole governments. The following brief examination of governance arrangements in the federal Government in Australia and the state government of Victoria makes a start at filling the gap. This examination reinforces Weill's and Ross's conclusions about business complexity and improved governance by evolution. However, as Canadian observers have noted, a government is an "enterprise of enterprises." For this reason, federal models are highly attractive. The problem is that, as Australian experience shows, "whole-of-government" models are very difficult to sustain. Making business-IT duopolies work at agency level does not necessarily create support for a cohesive, whole-of-government federal system. Federal models provide thin restraints on feudal temptations, and the culture of agencies and departments operating in isolation is well entrenched.

Federal Government in Australia: In the federal Government, the history of IT governance and of e-government initiatives is of successive attempts to improve coordination, which decay, and a profusion of single-agency or single-transaction initiatives, which succeed but do not always connect. Whole-of-government approaches to IT governance began in the early 1990s with a review commissioned by the Minister of Finance. The Finance portfolio had, and still has, a leading role in management reform across the federal public sector. While the review recommended improved coordination between agencies, it also recommended contestability and outsourcing for IT solutions. A new Government in 1996 attempted to drive outsourcing from the Department of Finance. Although it was forced to abandon this strategy, because of it a substantial legacy of mistrust of central direction of IT remains.

In 1997, the Government set up the National Office of the Information Economy (NOIE) as a separate office within the portfolio of Communications, Information and the Arts. The office had a dual role: it encouraged internal coordination of e-initiatives; it also had responsibility for developing the regulatory and physical infrastructure for e-commerce. NOIE absorbed responsibilities from other departments, including the Office of the Government On-line, but it did not have overall responsibility for e-government. Meanwhile, in 2002, the government set up an Information Management Strategy Committee (IMSC), supported by a Chief Information Officer Committee.

The IMSC included heads of significant service delivery agencies and the Department of the Prime Minister and Cabinet. The head of Communications, Information Technology and the Arts chaired the committee. The Department of Finance was not represented. The committee encouraged a "big picture" approach to ICT issues, but agencies continued to be responsible for their own arrangements. As Teicher and Dow have commented, these arrangements reflected ...the fragmented nature of public management and the difficulty of achieving a whole-of-government perspective in the wake of two decades of managerialist reforms which have been partially successful in developing an organization specific culture (Teicher and Dow 2003: 243).

However, the Management Advisory Committee, a meeting of departmental and significant agency heads, began to take a larger interest in the use of ICTs. The e-government benefits study, referred to above, also developed a substantial whole-of-government agenda:

- o consistent methods for demand assessment and a demand assessment approach that will respond to the whole-of-government perspective;
- o consistent mechanisms for tracking all government service delivery options so adoption of e-government can be placed in perspective;
- o consistent methods for assessing value and determining which projects have an acceptable benefit/cost ratio and should proceed;
- o a whole-of-government e-service architecture that focuses on the user and the interface to the user that will honour the intention of citizencentric and cross-agency expectation;
- o a mechanism for cross-agency cooperation that allows agencies to take the lead as well as deliver services on each other's behalf; and
- o a funding mechanism that responds to the social value being created and supports e-government initiatives that reflect cross-agency cooperation and citizen-centric development (AGIMO 2003).

In 2004, the Management Advisory Committee followed up with a forthright report on coordination entitled Connecting Australia: Whole of Government Responses to Australia's Priority Challenges (MAC 2004). Also in 2004, the Government split NOIE, absorbed it into the Department of Communications, Information Technology and the Arts and created the Australian Government Information Office (AGIMO). AGIMO inherited NOIE's internal coordination tasks. Further, as part of a post-election reshuffle, the Government created in the Finance portfolio a new Department of Human Services, charged with improving service delivery, and transferred AGIMO to Finance. The impact of these changes is yet to be seen. After several years and by a zigzag path, the federal Government has put together arrangements that may be able to fulfil Weill and Ross's governance tasks. It has moved from a stance of differentiation and outsourcing to one of collective leadership by department and agency heads.

Setting up the Department of Human Services suggests that it may also be willing to tackle the task of integrating services by redesigning their organizational architecture, and in the process reconfiguring the bundles of government services. Putting AGIMO and Human Services together in the Finance portfolio provides a platform for serious reform. Under NOIE the federal model tended to become confederal. Under the new arrangements it has gained a potential centre.

Victoria

In Victoria, the history of e-government is of initial enthusiastic political leadership, substantial redirection following a change of government, and recent steps to institutionalize political and bureaucratic leadership in the interests of further ambitious initiatives.

In the early 1990s, a neoliberal government created Multimedia Victoria as a new agency to encourage e-commerce and e-government. In 1999, a new government, as noted above, introduced themes of "people-centred government." It recognized also the need for a holistic approach, including:

- o effective governance-the mandate or authority to act in a given situation, a framework for reporting and accountability, a recognized budget process and reward system;
- o business systems-the operating business and decision-making processes that support cross-government activities; and
- o physical infrastructure-the ICT and other systems needed to combine agency services for presentation to the community in an integrated way.

It developed Victoria On-line as a joint venture between Multimedia Victoria and the Department of Premier and Cabinet, in conjunction with a range of external stakeholders. The project relied on extensive social research. Victoria's approach is a counterpoint to its initial centralized, politically led initiatives, with a strategy to link citizens, technology, and community development. However, this strategy was easier to articulate than to implement. More recently, Victoria has opted for a radical reorganization of decision making. Central to the new arrangements is a new position of system-wide Chief Information Officer (CIO) "to improve efficiency, promote innovative and integrated service and cut waste" (Moran 2003). A new position of Chief Technical Officer (CTO) was also created.

The initiative was supported by a report by the Boston Consulting Group (Government of Victoria 2003). The consultants made extensive studies of private sector CIO models and of government ICT management roles that the consultants thought to be overly decentralized. The office of the CIO is located in the Department of Premier and Cabinet, which, with the Department of Treasury and Finance, provides advice across the full range of government responsibilities. The office of the CTO is located in the Department of Infrastructure. As with NOIE at the federal level, Multimedia Victoria has been divided. The CIO supports an ICT Strategy Project Board at head-of-department level and an ICT Strategy Sub Committee of the Expenditure Review Committee at Cabinet level. Similar central consolidation of roles, consistent with Weill and Ross's recommendations discussed above, is envisaged for each department and agency.

The Boston Consulting Group consultants made extensive studies of private sector CIO models and of government ICT management roles which the consultants thought to be overly decentralized. The approach is designed to build a continuing conversation among stakeholders about governance principles and a thorough examination of all existing plans and investments. It includes significant foundation projects, such as a single data centre servicing all agencies, a government-wide document management system, and a shared application hosting environment (Office of the Chief Information Officer 2004;

Woodhead 2004). The foundation CIO received praise for his diplomatic approach to securing the support of secretaries of departments: "he accepted they held unambiguous accountability for the outcomes of their departments. He adopted mechanisms to make allies rather than trying to wrest power from them" (King 2005).

In the words of the foundation CIO, He argued that the approach provides strong reasons for people to work together (Woodhead 2004): What we've established are mechanisms for ensuring that agencies have discretion in regard to the evolution of decisions that their operations depend on, but in exercising that delegation we reversed the onus of proof.

We essentially said that secretaries are to have regard to plan developments and to demonstrate why non-compliance would be beneficial (Woodhead 2004). In terms of Weill's and Ross's archetypes, the approach places strong emphasis on joint decision making based on shared understandings of complex patterns of interdependence. It aspires to a federal model in which business and IT infrastructure needs are bound tightly together.

In the short run, the results of the Victoria initiatives are ambiguous. Two other states have followed Victoria's appointment of a CIO with overall responsibility for ICT.

However, in Victoria itself, the foundation CIO resigned unexpectedly after less than a year. While the government promptly appointed a respected replacement, speculation has continued about the viability of the role. Such speculation is fuelled by the high turnover of CIOs in both business and government in Australia (King 2004, 2005).

However, how to make CIO positions a part of stable top management teams remains vigorously contested. In different ways, the federal government in Australia and the government of Victoria have raised the priority of IT governance in plans for e-government.

They have accepted that it is essential to align IT infrastructure with business needs. Like Weill and Ross, they have tried to solve the puzzle of how to encourage creativity by allowing discretion while ensuring effectiveness by providing leadership.

RECONNECTING CITIZENS AND GOVERNMENTS?

The cumulative impact of e-government initiatives holds out the prospect of creating substantial public value. Recent initiatives in Australia recognize the need to provide citizens not only with improved services but also with improved opportunities for participation.

Strengthening links between the current internal focus on IT governance and the benefits made available to citizens will become urgent. E-initiatives will promote new agendas of relationship management and institution building. Five examples make this clear.

First, initiatives in single electronic transactions, including procurement and licensing, improve transparency, accountability, and timeliness in decision making. Some citizens will be satisfied with quick, fair decisions. Others will want to develop wider agendas of transparency and accountability. Second, looking at government services as retail operations has led to initiatives in service integration. Such integration has proved harder than it looked because service redesign leads to agency redesign. In turn, agency redesign changes relationships with users. Third, sharing information within the public sector raises questions about accuracy, security, and privacy. Within government, sharing information poses challenges of technology and management. Information once gathered can be shared and analysed. Aggregating information can itself create new information. In turn, this may lead to new policy and management options.

However, within the community, such activity raises questions of accuracy, security, and privacy. High value is placed on ensuring that information shared is accurate, that it is not shared between organizations serving conflicting interests, and that personal information is not shared without safeguards. How to determine citizen preferences about what can be shared and what must be kept private is emerging as a task of strategic importance.

Fourth, experiments with e-consultation and e-democracy join e-government agendas with wider agendas about new forms of national governance. As Canada has shown, citizen surveys can help shape effective einitiatives.

Weill and Ross and recent Australian initiatives acknowledge the need for stakeholder involvement. So far, experiments with e-democracy are modest. However, together with other e-initiatives, especially about the management of information, they have the potential to raise new agendas. These include demands to renegotiate relations between executives, legislatures, and the citizens on whom both executives and legislatures depend.

Fifth, e-initiatives have the potential to transcend national boundaries. So far the strongest impacts on organizational boundaries have concerned agencies in government. Initiatives to integrate services have already led to questions about the realignment of responsibilities within federal systems. In Australia, relations between federal and state levels of government have swung between competition and collaboration. Current relationships are strongly competitive. Building integrated e-government initiatives will depend on negotiating a new agenda for collaboration. This suggests that similar attempts to collaborate between national governments are likely to open up substantial new agendas.

Many discussions of e-government have kept it quite separate from agendas in e-governance. This discussion suggests that these agendas are already merging.

CONCLUSION

This discussion has examined the challenges for governments of making effective connections between technology and business strategy against the background of early, ambitious claims for e-government. It suggests that internal agendas about IT governance connect with wider issues of national and international governance.

It concludes that, at present, interactions between citizens, the institutions of government, and ICT raise more agendas than governments can handle. However, trying to find ways through these agendas is to confront questions of wide interest to citizens. At the very least, e-government thus helps improve governance and services by asking questions.

This discussion also makes clear that the most successful structures for managing e-government are likely to be based on carefully balanced federal models. Agency-specific approaches with weak coordination lend themselves to a transactional approach to service delivery and to e-government more generally. Such approaches understate the potential of both e-government and good governance.

A CASE STUDY OF KERALA

The World Development Report 2001 argues that major reductions in all dimensions of poverty are indeed possible when the interaction of markets, state institutions, and civil societies can harness the forces of economic integration and technological changes to serve the interest of poor people and increase their share of society's prosperity.

Actions are needed in three complementary areas: promoting economic opportunities for poor people through equitable growth and better access to markets and expanded assets; facilitating empowerment and removing social barriers that exclude women, ethnic and racial groups, and the socially disadvantaged; and enhancing security by preventing and managing economy-wide shocks and providing mechanisms to reduce the sources of vulnerability that the poor face (World Bank 2001).

Poverty reduction strategies vary depending on a country's macroeconomic, structural, and social policies and programs to promote growth and reduce poverty. Nevertheless, all strategies should reflect the country's characteristics and should be participatory, with proper diagnostics, appropriate targets, and indicators and systems for monitoring and evaluating progress. The widely acclaimed strategy of promoting self-help groups (SHGs) of the poor has proved ideal in many countries for alleviating poverty and fostering rural development. By the early 1970s, welfare and charitable organizations concentrated on working with neighbourhood or village groups on self-help initiatives and grassroots economic projects.

Now SHGs worldwide foster a process of ongoing change in favour of the rural poor in a way that allows them to sustain this process through building and managing appropriate and innovative locallevel institutions rooted in values of justice, equity, and mutual support.

The Concept of the Self-Help Group

The concept of SHGs gained special significance after 1976, when Professor Muhammad Yunus of Bangladesh began experimenting with microcredit and women's SHGs. The strategy made a quiet revolution in Bangladesh in poverty eradication "by empowering the poor women." SHGs are small informal associations created for the purpose of enabling members to reap economic benefit out of mutual help, solidarity, and joint responsibility. The benefits include mobilization of savings and credit facilities and pursuit of group enterprise activities.

The group-based approach not only enables the poor to accumulate capital by way of small savings, but also helps them gain access to formal credit facilities (Shylendra 1998). By way of joint liability, these groups enable the poor to overcome the problem of collateral security, thus freeing them from the clutches of moneylenders (Stiglitz 1993). Moreover, some of the basic characteristics of SHGs like small membership size and homogeneity of composition bring about cohesiveness and effective participation of members in the functioning of the group (Fernandez 1994).

In general, the SHGs created on these criteria have been able to effectively reach the poor, especially the women, help them obtain easy access to facilities like savings and credit, and, in the long run, alleviate poverty by empowering them (NABARD 1995)

Poverty in Kerala

Among developing countries, India has a relatively good record in addressing the issue of poverty. Kerala, when compared with other states of the country, has performed well in tackling this problem, both from the "entitlements" point of view and the "capabilities" point of view (Economic Review 2001). The 1999-2000 data show that Kerala's poverty level is only 12.72%, against the all-India 26.30%. However, the problem of poverty remains persistent, particularly due to unemployment and underemployment, limited land availability, and social disadvantages (Economic Review 2001). Poverty reduction strategies in Kerala moved in tandem with the national policy of direct attack on poverty till the early 1990s. However, a breakthrough in participatory poverty reduction was made through the introduction of SHGs and the Community Development Societies (CDS) in Alappuzha district in 1993 as part of the implementation of the centrally sponsored Urban Based Service for the Poor and the UNICEF-assisted Community Based Nutrition Program. Women from poor families were identified through a transparent process using the nine-point noneconomic criteria and organized into Neighbourhood Groups (NHG) of 15 to 40 families. The NHGs, organized at the grassroots level, are federated democratically into Area Development Societies (ADS) at the ward/panchayat level and these are further federated into CDS, which would be a registered body at the Municipality/District level.

The entire three-tier structure is envisaged as an extension of the Panchayati Raj System, providing a support system as well as a delivery mechanism for the converged implementation of all poverty eradication programs. The success of the Alappuzha CDS and its smooth replication in another district, Nakappuram, inspired the Kerala Government to expand CDS throughout the state (Kudumbasree 1999). The urban Poverty Eradication Mission ("Kudumbasree") is the outcome of this and it envisages eradicating poverty from Kerala over a period of 10 years. This will be done by organizing women of the poor community into groups.

Kudumbasree-the Poverty Eradication Mission

Kudumbam in local language means "family" and sree refers to prosperity. Started on 1 April 1991, Kudumbasree is a partnership between four major actors (the central Government, state government, local Bodies, and National Bank for Agriculture and Rural Development [NABARD]). The objective of the project is to eliminate absolute poverty from the state of Kerala within a decade. It is exclusively focused on women, women in family and women in community. It is an organization of women from below the poverty line. The core activity is women's empowerment through micro-finance, micro-enterprise, and convergent community action. Kudumbasree-the unique effort of the Kerala government-stands for organizing the poor into a community-based organization.

Study Objectives and Limitations

This paper seeks to examine the performance of selected SHGs in the state of Kerala and identify the factors contributing to the successful functioning and sustainability of groups. It also attempts to examine the impact of SHGs on poverty by their empowerment of women. However, being a case study, though the findings could not be generalized, some of them may reflect on the implications of this strategy and suggest areas of concern. It has attempted to find how the SHG intervention has changed savings habits, attitudes, incomeearning capacity, and asset expansion, thereby leading to empowerment.

Methodology

The above objectives were examined through an explanatory study of the functioning of selected SHGs in Kerala. Malappuram, which is considered to be the most backward district in the state, with the lowest per capita income, highest population, educational backwardness, etc., was purposely selected. Chungathara Panchayat, which is considered to be the pioneer in promoting the SHG concept, was chosen and promoted by three voluntary agencies or non-government organizations (NGOs)-Shreyas, Boothan Vikas Mandal (BVM), and the Community Development Society. Five groups each from CDS, BVM, and Shreyas were selected for an in-depth study. A detailed socioeconomic survey of the members was conducted and the members' perception of factors contributing to the groups' sustainability and their attitudes, skill, and knowledge after joining the groups were collected using a structured interview schedule. For this, 10% of the members from the selected groups of the three voluntary agencies were randomly selected. The field data collected were supplemented with focus group interactions and short interviews with the office-bearers and coordinators of the three voluntary agencies.

Sustainability of SHGs

Several studies reveal that certain elements / factors are crucial for the successful functioning of an SHG. They may be categorized as external and internal. The external factors usually include an agency (e.g., a Mahila Samajam-voluntary, small formal women's association formed at the local level, Gram Panchayat-a democratic structure functioning at the village level, a banker, or even a government organization) that promotes and motivates the members.

The Bangladesh and Myrada experiences show that in the initial years, the role of the external promoting agency is vital for motivating, nurturing, and equipping the group to reach the stage of self-reliance. Deliberate external intervention of the promoting agency (in the initial stage) helped in laying a strong foundation in the Myrada group. However, whether it is the government or the voluntary agency, the role of these promoting agencies is significant, because it is not confined to mere mobilization of rural women. The agency is also expected to inculcate in them a spirit of self-help, mutual help, and creating a better understanding about the mission and goals of the SHG concept.

Groups cannot be built overnight. Group formation is a slow, time-consuming process. Once the members get the crux of the concept and realize the benefits, they will be loyal throughout and will never leave the group. When the group becomes stabilized in its functioning, internal factors like good leadership, unity, and mutual understanding among the members determine the pace of growth and development. The internal factors contributing to group success include:

(i) the presence of an educated, sincere, and dynamic leader;
(ii) stability in leadership;
(iii) homogeneity in membership (members belonging to same income or social strata, etc.);
(iv) democracy and transparency; and
(v) cooperation, unity, and mutual understanding.

Based on these criteria, we have identified a few internal and external factors that have influenced the functioning of the selected groups under the three agencies. The role of the promoting agency and the coordinator were the most important external factors contributing to the groups' success: 46% of the members interviewed felt that the promoting agency and the coordinators had a crucial role in the initial years, till the groups reached the stage of self-sufficiency.

However, in BVM, the role of the bank and the promoting agency was highlighted by 54% of the members. In CDS, 25% gave multiple responses, and 23% did not respond or were neutral. In the consideration of the internal factors contributing to groups' success, group-wide variations were not observed. Sixty-nine percent of the members, irrespective of the group, remarked that good leadership, cooperation among the members, transparency in decision-making, etc., were essential for the groups' smooth functioning and sustainability.

However, members felt that the role of the group leader was one of the foremost factors responsible for the groups' success/ failure. In some of the defunct groups, the absence of a strong secretary to inculcate in the members the real spirit of group dynamics had led to its failure.

Micro-credit and the Extent of Women Empowerment and Poverty Alleviation

Micro-finance programs for women are promoted as a strategy for poverty alleviation and women's empowerment as well (Mayoux and Johnson 1996). In the past decade, empowerment has become a key objective of development. In our present context, empowerment may be defined ideally as "the continuous process where the powerless people become conscious of their situation and organize to improve it and access opportunities": an outcome where women take control over their lives, set their own agenda, gain skills, solve problems, and develop "self-reliance" (Mayoux and Johnson 1996).

It is the expansion of assets and capabilities of poor people to participate in, negotiate with, influence, control, and hold accountable institutions that affect their lives. Within the SHG approach, empowerment is embedded at many levels. In the present study, to examine the impact of SHGs and micro-credit on empowering women and thereby reducing poverty, the framework developed by various micro-finance institutions, aid providers, and international agencies was adopted and modified to suit the context, the area of study, and the culture of the people. The following indicators were used to assess the extent of empowerment and poverty reduction.

Economic and Financial Empowerment

The status of women is intimately connected with their economic position, which in turn depends on opportunities for women to participate in economic activities. Women's ability to save and access credit would give them an economic role, not only within the household but also perhaps outside it as well. Investment in the economic activities of women would improve their employment opportunities and thus have a "trickle down and out" effect. Here the specific issues examined are the income-generating activities (IGAs) taken up by the members of the three groups and the monthly returns from them, their contribution to the monthly family incomes, their level of savings, repayment behaviour, and changes in their physical assets and amenities after joining the group.

Income-Generating Activities and Increase in Income

In the Micro Credit Summit Preparatory Meeting (1995), Hillary Clinton said: "It is called micro, but its impact on people is macro. We have seen that it takes just a few dollars, as little as $10, to help a woman gain self-employment to keep her family out of poverty. It is not a hand-out, it is a helping hand" (Proceedings of Micro Credit Summit 2001) It is widely accepted that the returns from the economic activity are used for the welfare of the family and the community at large.

An examination of various IGAs taken up by the members of the groups under the three NGOs shows that irrespective of the voluntary agency, the majority of the members had gone in for poultry, cow, and goat-rearing. Of the total, 27% belonged to this category. As in other rural areas, animal raising has proved to be a low-risk, low-cost economic activity for supplementing family income without much effort. In Chungathara panchayat, goat-keeping is an ideal activity, as grazing is possible in the nearby forest. Moreover, their high prolificity combined with their ability to breed throughout the year have rendered goat-rearing a highly remunerative activity; it has therefore induced a large number of the poor to take it up.

In spite of the tendency among beneficiaries to under-report income, most of them generated a stated monthly income ranging from Rs. 50 to Rs. 3,000 (Rs. 3,000 on sale of kids). Most of them also had availed themselves of repeat loans. In CDS and Shreyas, some of the members who were labourers said that they could not afford to forego their work and wages to take up cattle rearing. Hence, such members had sold off cattle, while all the unemployed members found this activity highly remunerative.

Agriculture-vegetable cultivation, including cultivation of banana and tapioca-proved a viable venture. The group cultivation of vegetables undertaken by BVM groups was found to be highly remunerative. We found that the area in which the BVM groups function is highly fertile, surrounded by three rivers.

In CDS, four members had taken loans for tailoring and purchase of sewing machines. The innovative group activity taken up by some members of direct marketing of Sabari tea and Supplyco's other products on a commission basis was also very remunerative, yielding an average of Rs. 1,500 per month per member. The soda-making unit, which had been a viable one earlier, now faces tough competition from branded soft-drink products. In BVM, the Chippy Umbrella group has availed itself of a loan from NABARD and two other voluntary agencies. The average gross monthly income from this enterprise ranged from Rs. 700 to Rs. 1,500. Though the market is assured, this activity is seasonal and during the rest of the year, they remain unemployed or engaged in some small activities. They are planning to start a paper plate-making venture, for which they were looking forward to getting training.

It is remarkable to note that in Shreyas some of the members had undertaken some innovative economic activities. Sericulture done as a group activity seems to have generated an average of Rs. 2,000 per month. The seed nursery set up by a group with support from Krishi Bhavan is a welcome step. The loan amount accessed by the members of Shreyas ranged from Rs. 500 to Rs. 40,000, amounts of micro-credit notably higher than those of other groups.

Also, the number of members who took loans for consumption was comparatively high. It is observed that a significant number of members (not from the sample) in Shreyas had taken loans to repay old debt.

Contribution of IGAs to the Family Income

The basic assumption underlying the provision of micro-credit is that the investment made with the credit will generate income, adequate to contribute significantly to family earnings. In Chungathara Panchayat, unemployment is an acute problem and the poor families are the worst hit.

The women in these families are unable to contribute toward their families' income, as they do not have the skills or the opportunities for employment. Joining a SHG, though the returns from IGAs taken up under it remain irregular and in many cases unstable, would make a lot of difference to the lives of the poor. The increased incomes have helped reduce poverty to a great extent in several families. Some members take up more than one activity (goat rearing and tailoring, for example) to make up the loss during off-seasons. It could be inferred that in the case of 80% of the members with economic activities, their incomes from micro-enterprises contributed considerably to the family incomes directly or indirectly.

In BVM, 55% of the selected members were reported to have taken up IGAs, while in Shreyas and CDS the corresponding figures were 33% and 42%. In order to examine the impact of the program, the income generated from the economic activity (resulting from micro-credit) was collated with the total monthly family income.

The contribution of micro-enterprise to total family income is found to be significant, indicating the positive impact of the strategy. The contribution was the highest in BVM (35%) and the lowest in CDS (24%). It is noted that in Shreyas, monthly income from the economic activity formed 27% of total family income, which was higher than in CDS.

Relationship between Income and Micro-credit

The preceding analysis suggests that the provision of micro-credit to poor women has created a positive impact, since the enterprises they began were able to produce substantial returns. All the increase in their incomes might not have come from these enterprises, however. The coefficient of correlation shows that the correlation between these two, though positive, is not statistically significant (the figures are 0.2554 and 0.3896 in BVM and Shreyas, respectively). A fairly high correlation is seen in the CDS groups. Thus, it is obvious that factors other than the investment made with micro-credit must have influenced to a significant extent the increase in income of the members of groups in BVM and Shreyas.

On the other hand, it was seen that the CDS members were comparatively poor and had invested only the micro-credit amounts in their enterprises and that most of the activities were new ones. The returns from these were meager and irregular. However, in BVM and Shreyas, members either took up highly remunerative ventures or used the micro-credit for diversification of, or addition to, ventures already under way. Thus, they could generate substantial income out of the activity using the micro-credit. For instance, in CDS, some of the members who started making pappad (spicy snacks/wafers made from ground rice), curry powder, etc., had to stop the venture due to low demand for the product. However, in Shreyas one of the members could carry on the activity of pappad-making successfully, as he was a traditional pappad-maker and had regular clients. It is thus evident that those who had some previous business experience were able to make use of micro-credit more effectively.

Political and Legal Empowerment

The empowerment of women extends beyond economic and social aspects. It includes increased respect from the community, participation in social activities and decision-making forums, acquisition of entrepreneurial skills, and legal and political visibility. The study shows that about 20% of the members were able to acquire livestock and poultry. However, the majority of the respondents (73%) reported that the impact on creation of physical assets was almost nil.

Regarding awareness and capacity building, SHGs have been very effective in improving the levels of knowledge and skill of rural people through informal education and training programs. Social interaction is reported to be much better among the members after joining the groups. Fifty-four percent are well informed about health care and family welfare programs. The occasional classes arranged by the voluntary agencies on health and hygiene proved to be extremely beneficial. The most striking advantage of SHGs is that 91% learned about the banking system after joining the group and were confident about going to the bank to transact business. Over 86% of the respondents reported that they have not undergone any vocational or skills development training.

However, the awareness level about local planning and legal rights is an area that is almost neglected. Some groups have introduced participatory learning approaches, which is an exercise in awareness building and articulation of needs through social mapping.

Regarding participation in the political process, 75% of the members remarked that their participation was nil. Though 91% of the members attended the gram sabhas (a local-level meeting convened by the panchayat president to discuss and decide on all development issues pertaining to the local area), some of them saw no use in attending, as the major share of panchayat funds went to politically affiliated persons. The respondents remarked that they merely sat as spectators. However, the president of an SHG remarked, "We take efforts to see that members participate in gram sabhas and raise the voice of their needs."

However, it is seen that participation has not led to involvement of the members in local planning, decision making, or implementation of development programs in the area. In rare instances, "group needs" like requests for streetlights and ferry service across the lake, or a bus permit for transit in remote areas, etc., could be addressed.

Experience in Alappuzha shows that the leadership in SHGs may serve as a gateway to more active political participation and empowerment. In many panchayats, it was found that in the recent election, the group leaders were considered candidates by political parties because of their proximity to and close contact with the local people and their awareness of each and every problem of the area. In the words of Ms. Usha, "If I participate in local elections and opt to become a party candidate, I am afraid that I would not be able to discharge the present duties of CDS president effectively. My functional freedom will be curtailed by political interference. When a decision is taken, people would then consider it politically biased. I turned down the offer"

Performance Evaluation and General Findings

This part discusses the performance of the selected groups using secondary information and through observation and short interviews with members and group leaders. The groups promoted by the three agencies were performing well and each had its own positive and negative features. It was evident during the field survey that the most powerful attributes that SHGs have helped to foster are the awareness of one's rights and the ability to transform their lives. The success of the movement in Malappuram has been mainly due to the sincere services of the group coordinators and community organizers. Also, the more backward an area, the greater is the intervention required.

Group formation was rushed through in many cases, with inadequate preparation of the participants and clarity about the goals of the SHG. This is evident from the fact that in inactive groups, members were found to have left the group after availing themselves of a loan. The enthusiasm seen in the newly formed groups was lost, at least by some members, in about 2 or 3 years of functioning.

None of the voluntary agencies was found to be making efforts to develop a second line of leadership or groom members to take up the leadership role. It was observed that a few women were dominating the show. A trend seemed to have emerged of the educated and the "better off " leaders dominating the groups and getting re-elected again and again due to the following factors:

(i) illiteracy, absence of numerical skills, and educational backwardness of the members; The Role of Public Administration in Alleviating Poverty and Improving Governance

(ii) lack of enthusiasm among the members to partake in the group activity, and complacency in continuing with the traditional role of housewife;

(iii) interest shown by leaders for continuing in their leadership positions;

(iv) resistance from family members or the community, mainly in the case of Muslims, about attending meetings outside the ward or the locality; and

(v) unwillingness on the part of members to take up responsibilities for fear of the additional workload.

Overdependence on leaders is found among members in all the successful groups. The members seem to depend on them for each and every decision. This system of spoon-feeding cannot be considered a positive result; a strategy of gradual and slow withdrawal of the helping hand of the leader, as has been shown by some NGOs in other places, seems to be the ideal mechanism for making the groups self-reliant.

One major impact on the women members of SHGs promoted by the Grameen Bank has been the creation of awareness about newer economic opportunities available to women and the abilities needed to tap them. It is seen that despite 3 to 4 years of functioning, some members remain unemployed but are willing to take up an economic activity provided sufficient guidance and credit is made available. None of the groups in Malappuram is seen to be making efforts to help the members to identify suitable IGAs based on their skills and aptitudes. Wide scope exists for accessing micro-credit from various agencies.

More members of the poor households have to be brought into the credit network, together with necessary guidance and technical support. All the groups have taken up individual economic activities, but group activities are very few.

The leaders were apprehensive about the success of group enterprises, because cases in which the group activity failed had led to financial imbalances and difficulty in loan repayments for all the members of the groups. The situation was not so complex in the case of failure of individual units. It was felt that individual activity was better, especially in the first 2 years, until the group attained sufficient maturity and confidence to take up group enterprises.

In general, the lessons of the training and the awareness courses imparted to community organizers and other leaders do not seem to be effectively passed on to the members. Dissemination of information to the grassroots level is inadequate. Unless the training given to the community organizers is disseminated to the members, empowerment of the members may not take place.

We found that even after 5 to 6 years, only the group leaders were fully aware of various government schemes and programs and other opportunities, while the members remained passive. A tendency has emerged among members to leave one group and join other groups, when the latter are found more attractive. In some cases, the secretary of the CDS group was also the president of BVM, or vice versa. Instead of promoting healthy competition among the various agencies, the coordinators and leaders consider other NGOs as their rivals. A coordinated effort of all voluntary agencies at the gram panchayat level would pave the way for overall development, solve problems of infrastructure development and marketing, and put an end to social evils such as early child marriage and dowry.

Summing Up

Elimination of poverty requires both macro and micro strategies. At the macro level, a conscious choice has to be made to achieve pro-poor growth. This means that attention should be on developing agriculture and encouraging labour-absorbing industries, particularly small and village industries. Also, a massive capacity-building exercise needs to be taken up to enhance the capabilities of the poor. At the micro level, a convergence of programs, resources, and services is called for. This can be achieved only through a demand-led process, which means that the poor have to be organized and empowered to participate in the development process. In concrete terms, it means setting up micro-enterprises, providing wage employment while creating rural infrastructure, targeting basic services, and providing direct social security measures to the most vulnerable. Only such a concerted approach can tackle the multiple dimensions of poverty and their ratchet effect on the poor.

It has been proven beyond doubt that interventions through SHGs can make a big change in living standards, through regular savings, improved levels of family earnings, expanded assets, and better sociopolitical access, thereby reducing vulnerability and poverty and contributing to a wide range of development goals. SHGs have not only produced tangible assets and improved living conditions for their members, but have also helped in changing much of their social outlook and attitudes.

The group dynamics have reasonably helped many members to overcome the feeling of low self-esteem and lack of confidence and empowered them. Considering the time span of SHG functioning and the backwardness of the area, we feel that the "takeoff stage" has been successful. The general backwardness of the area, i.e., poor educational background, ignorance, adherence to traditional values, etc., has hindered the pace of development. The foremost thrust of all the voluntary agencies should be on informal education, building awareness, and organizing skills upgrade programs at the grassroots level.

Considering the presence of a large number of active groups and the drive created by the movement, the strategy can help alleviate poverty, provided the movement is sustained. However, the overdose of politics and the entry of communal organizations have threatened the very concept of SHGs and the collective spirit for which these informal setups were formed.

Political parties, becoming aware of the vast potential of these SHGs in mobilizing people, have set their eye on "intruding." Even the religious organizations have been encouraging their members to penetrate into SHGs with a parochial agenda, thereby creating a dangerous trend. This may have serious repercussions in the long run, and the desired role of SHGs in poverty alleviation and women's empowerment may come to a standstill unless adequate policy measures are taken.

4

Citizen Participation in Local Governance

Local government is the frontier of governance, and the quality of local government is related to the welfare and benefits of the citizens. Local governance plays a very important role in modern public administration. Public administration stresses the views of New Public Management (NPM) at the end of the 20th century, and it emphasizes the importance of customer orientation to enhance the effectiveness of and competition within local government.

However, it is not apparent that a scenario where NPM principles dominate the administrative functions of a local government is compatible with an increasing demand for citizen participation. Recently, research into local governance has become a popular subject. Scholars of public administration, however, do not define the core values and concepts of local governance clearly. Besides, there is no doubt that at this time local governance has some institutional problems of its own.

It is most important to note that if we use the term without the concept of citizen participation, local governance will in fact become a source of troubles. In this paper, several points will be discussed. First, we will review the formation of local governance using the approach of NPM, and will review the related problems. Second, we will discuss institutional problems and solutions from the viewpoint of institutional design and reform when local government adopts the measures of local governance. Third, we will discuss measures related to how local governance connects with citizen participation; and finally, we will analyse the case of local governance in Taipei, China.

FORMATION OF LOCAL GOVERNANCE WITH A NEW PUBLIC MANAGEMENT

Starting in the early 1980s, some countries were under financial pressure, and a wave of reorganizing the structures of government began to occur. New ideas emerged. Some scholars stressed the importance of effective management and of redefining government functions. What emerged was a new paradigm, known almost universally as NPM. Its main idea is to re-establish democratic principles in governments by reducing the ambiguities of delegation. Its main features:

- o devolving authority and added flexibility;
- o ensuring performance, control, and accountability;
- o developing competition and choice;
- o providing responsive service;
- o improving the management of human resources;
- o optimizing information technology;
- o improving the quality of regulation; and
- o strengthening steering functions at the centre (Jan 1999: 75).

From these features, we may infer that NPM is about achieving higher levels of performance by governments. Some countries have adopted NPM style government reforms to improve governmental and managerial performance.

The general mission of NPM thinking is achieving better governmental performance in democratic regimes. A key concept of NPM is managerialism. Managerialism stresses the following: hands-on professional management, explicit standards and measures of performance; managing by results; value for money; and, more recently, closeness to the customer (Rhodes 1997: 48). This transformation of the government involves less government but more governance (Osborne and Gaebler 1992: 34). Some organization experts had introduced the NPM-inspired government model and a set of government roles during the final decade of the 20th century. Around the same time, in Taipei, China, some consultants or scholars, such as C. Jan (1999) and T. Lee (1999), had also introduced the NPM-inspired governance models and roles. Above all, local government transforms the main governance issue into an interagency working group or partnerships among organizations.

NPM advocates less input control and more emphasis on evaluation and performance, with the criteria used in the evaluation largely driven by the private sector rather than by bureaucratic theories. It accords a lesser role to the state and more to market forces. So the government's reform emphasis on the boundaries among organizations has become very blurred. The Organisation for Economic Cooperation and Development (OECD) notes that for the public sector to remain responsive to the needs of those it serves, governments must be willing and able to learn about client needs and adjust the provision of services accordingly (OECD 1995). Decentralized management would provide feedback from clients and ultimately enhance consumer choice. Incrementally, some scholars and proponents have taken off from NPM techniques and philosophies to improve upon the public sector's performance.

In recent years, some public administration scholars have questioned and even criticized the NPM approach. Although NPM ideas and reforms help provide multiple opportunities to local government, they blot out the role of local government and decrease the connection between local government and citizens. So, many scholars have also suggested strengthening local governance to offset the disadvantages of NPM. Governance can be defined as "the tradition, institutions, and processes that determine how power is exercised, how citizens are given voice, and how decisions are made on the issues of public concern" (Denhardt 2002: 4). Bovaird and Löffler (2002: 16) define local governance as "the set of formal and informal rules, structures and processes defining the measures with which individuals and organizations can exercise power over the decisions by other stakeholders capable of affecting their welfare at the local levels." According to the definition, perfect local governance involves six groups of stakeholders: citizens, third sector (such as non-profit organizations, non-government organizations, etc.), business, media, higher-level government, and local authorities. This means that governance includes cooperation, competition, and conflict management. The main issue for governance is whether it constitutes a new paradigm of how to solve common problems and create win-win situations for all stakeholders. However, just as NPM is not a panacea for all conditions, governance also does not provide a complete answer to all current challenges to the public sector.

Institutional Perspective of Local Governance

From an institutional perspective, governance involves creating capable political actors who understand how political institutions work and are able to deal effectively with them. Institutional governance involves building and supporting cultures of rights and rules that make possible the agreements represented in coalition understandings. It involves building and supporting identities, preferences, and resources that can make a polity possible. It is related to many institutions that are not suitable when the idea of governance is propagated. So we have to consider the institutional issue of local governance.

Local governance will influence the existing framework of local government. When the idea of governance is propagated, some mechanisms have to be adjusted. Such institutional reforms have to stress the relationship among local governments in a political system: on the one hand, it is a subordinated level expected to effectively implement the objectives of the higher levels of government; on the other hand, local government has to offer space for democratic choice for local actors in accordance with local preferences. These reflections point to institutional reforms in local government as one approach to solve government failures in participation, transparency, and effectiveness.

One way to guarantee efficiency is to monitor performance through continuous policy evaluation. Parts of these budget-oriented reforms are changes in the organizational structure, especially changes that seek to strike a new balance between the public and private sectors: in other words, the introduction of market-type mechanisms to public tasks. This has become a key part of management reform strategies: government positioning in a competitive environment. Among the various reforms mentioned, there are several that stand out. In Taipei, China, for example, we can see some cases; these include the "build-operate-transfer" model (such as the Taiwan High Speed Railroad Company) and the public-private partnership (such as contracting out). In addition, models are still being developed. These models will help take the evaluation of local governance further. For example, the Commonwealth Association for Public Administration and Management (CAPAM) has, as of this year, initiated an award for innovations in governance. There are nine criteria in the CAPAM evaluation process:

- o Partnering,
- o Accountability,
- o Communication and information revolutions,
- o Demands for citizen engagement,
- o Integration of horizontal and vertical management,
- o Maintenance of policy coherence in a fragmented policy community,
- o Political or parliamentary structures,
- o Evolution in required human resource competencies, and
- o Values and ethics.

Promoting local governance, therefore, means local government accepting the influence from outside and amending the existing laws. Then, local government has to combine the ideas of governance with laws to create new mechanisms. Citizens would disapprove and resist if local government promoted new mechanisms that would negatively affect their benefits. So there is a focus of tasks at the local level as well as of the expectations of citizens toward local government.Hood (1995: 15) observes that "unintended effects of policy and management measures are a recurring theme in social science." Local government reforms also tend to emphasize legitimacy. A traditional reform path has stressed the accountability of officeholders. Local governance focuses on the efficiency of local politics and administration, while "alternative modernizers" have stressed the element of direct citizen participation. As Blair (1998: 13) notes: "Local government will still deliver some services but their distinctive leadership role will be to weave and knit together the contribution of the various local stakeholders." One of the important stakeholders is the citizens; we will therefore discuss the ties between local governance and citizen participation in the next section.

LOCAL GOVERNANCE AND CITIZEN PARTICIPATION

New governance institutions are being developed at the local level that require local authorities to consult with, and directly involve, the general public on an ongoing basis. It is important to recognize a number of practical issues that concern participatory mechanisms. Among those questions that have been raised in debates about participation and local participative structures in a number of countries are the following:

- o The need for continuity, and for processes to be institutionalized;
- o The frequently very high financial costs of consultation and participation;
- o Whether the complexity of some issues for decision is compatible with participation;
- o Whether to involve in decisions a large group of people, which might result in relatively superficial opinions, or a small group, to obtain more developed opinions;
- o The prospect of creating new elites, and processes being captured by minority groups or the well mobilized; and
- o Opposition from the professional bureaucracy to increased participation.

Local government is the frontier of governance, and the quality of local government is related to the welfare and benefits of the citizen. Local government is experimenting with "finding new forms of legitimacy for decisions made in loose networks of relationships. This strategy requires trials and errors and constantly searching for solutions that work in both the functional and democratic senses" (John 2001: 166).

But because unlimited citizen participation will become populism, public administration scholars have aimed at "deliberative democracy."

The philosophy of deliberative democracy is social justice. It means that everyone should have equal opportunity to participate in public affairs. In the context of deliberative democracy, local governance would play a very important role in affording citizens an opportunity to participate and in establishing some norms. Lindblom (1965) noted that effective governance is actually generated by participation. So "participation is the most valuable element of representative democracy. In that context, accountable representatives have the authority to evaluate needs, balance demands, arrange priorities, and monitor the outcomes of the political system" (Lowndes 1995: 169).

Clay researched the process of public institution building and pointed out the meanings of citizen participation in local governance (1996: 109-110):

- o serving as an important means of meaningful negotiation, both within the public institution and with its policy subsystem;
- o building relationships within the public institution and among institutions;
- o resting on a degree of trust among the participants;
- o requiring both explicit and implicit rules and norms to guide performance and behaviour;
- o becoming institutionalized through the infusion of institutional values; and
- o requiring continuous interaction to be maintained but with some degree of institutional memory.

Some scholars agree that citizen participations has two advantages. One is that participation is in the first place important in defining the expected outcomes of political interventions, together with the policy; the other is that participation is effective in the realization of policy objectives because it can help solve problems associated with making and implementing policy (Haus and Heinelt 2004).

Citizen participation can certainly contribute to good governance, if it is targeted at enhancing the deliberative quality of policy making and at activating the endogenous potential of local communities. If local communities could contribute to citizen participation by making the public sector closer to the citizens at the local government level, neighbourhood and grassroots organizations are important for more responsive governance. Therefore, citizen participation could act as a real source of strength for a public sphere well informed of its responsibility to safeguard its interest in establishing a system of accountable and transparent governance (Salih 2003).

Hence, the connection between decision making and deliberative democracy is very important. Local government has to prepare and build well-designed institutional and managerial mechanisms. One of OECD's projects picks up on this renewed recognition of citizen agency.

The project is entitled "Strengthening Government-Citizen Connections." It recapitulates that the conditions of local governance have made the policy-making process highly complex and virtually unfathomable to the ordinary citizen. At the same time, some scholars are noting, "Many citizens are faced with such complexity and the perception of a loss of influence over national and local policy decisions, and they are complaining of a democratic deficit" (PUMA 1999).

However, even though citizen participation could assure effective governance and increase legitimacy, it has some disadvantages as well.

First, governance and legitimacy depend on their forms, in that they are selective of the citizens involved, but citizen participation seldom covers all levels of citizens, and instead groups only those who would be affected.

Thus, the principle of political equality, requiring equal opportunities to participate in the decision-making process, is not fulfilled (Dahl 1989).

Second, while in most cases at least some of the outcomes must be transformed into binding decisions by representative bodies, the crucial difference between i) a traditional process of government, and ii) a process resting on interactive governance as well as some component of formalized government is that in the latter case the particular outcomes would not have been possible without the participation of societal actors (Haus 2003). Third, there is always the danger that those who are not well mobilized to represent their views may become even more marginalized by the process.

The most marginalized citizens in society are not heard through participatory mechanisms. On the other hand, those who shout the loudest and whose voice is heard may not always be the most representative. One potential solution to overcoming this distance might be to put in place arrangements by which representative democracy is complemented by increased mechanisms for public participation and increased contacts between government and civil society (Boyle and Humphreys 2001: 80).

Some scholars have suggested that local government should propose some mechanisms to encourage citizen participation. One of the mechanisms is a measure to build up the local citizen participation network through information and communication technology (ICT). Such a mechanism is called "digital democracy." The measure of digital democracy includes the following (Clift 2002):

- o e-mail notice,
- o in-person public hearing recordings and materials,
- o online public hearings and consultations,
- o wired politicians who reach out and serve,
- o local civic deliberations and global networking, and
- o e-voting.

One of the bases for the reform process is the introduction of ICT for all employees in government, especially in local government. The organizationwide use of ICT not only makes service delivery more efficient; it also breaks down communication barriers between professional groups within the local authority. Nevertheless, the local councils are only interested in the ICT project to the extent that it helps to reduce the budget deficit.

In particular, they have not been able to use ICT as an instrument to improve the information basis for political decision making. Furthermore, ICT has not been used as a means to improve communication with citizens. Even though some basic information about local services is provided to the citizens on the Internet, the local authority has taken no steps to open up real dialogues with citizens through ICT (Bovaird, Löffler, and Parrado-Diez 2001: 8).

In particular, e-voting in public elections seems to be an extension of digital democracy. We view it as tinkering around the edges of digital democracy, having the technical capacity to make voting more convenient for citizens. With the proliferation of e-voting methods, we should put more emphasis on the participation of citizens.

Furthermore, we should focus more on such groups as the youth, who tend to be less involved in political activities. The participation by voters that is essential to a healthy democracy could be increased with the use of Internet technology. The digital divide between those who do and do not have computers and access to the Internet decreases every day as Internet technology becomes more affordable. Internet voting could also create gains in efficiency and effectiveness for voting technology, democracy, and the voting process. Internet voter registration could efficiently and effectively accomplish this and could also increase overall voter registration, especially among young people, who have always had the lowest levels of voter registration.

Thus, e-channels could create a more efficient and effective voting process. The efficiency and effectiveness of e-channels could also result in increased voter participation. Clearly, e-voting could increase voter participation rates among those who have never voted or have voted infrequently. However, while the Internet could yield many potential benefits to the democratic process, some shortcomings may need to be overcome first.

CONCLUSION AND RECOMMENDATIONS

The issues of local governance are structure, process, and analysis framework (Rhodes 1997). The study and planning of local governance should focus on institutional design, and local governance should play the most important role of integrating and aggregating citizens.

Local governance is related to the interaction of citizens and promotes the structure and process of citizen participation. So we have to connect different citizens, aggregate more social capital, and allow for sufficient government information.

There is little doubt that the integrating function of the local governance process is the ability to transfer resources. If we want to enhance that ability, the central Government should offer more incentive mechanisms and encourage citizens to participate in local government activities.

When we discuss the issues of local governance, one topic focuses on enhancing citizen participation, and this is what we mean when we talk about "increasing the degree of direct democracy." In Taipei, China, we have been promoting citizen participation and e-democracy programs. But the most important thing is that we believe these are "oxymorons," mechanisms are not general ideas, and principles are generally not detailed.

5

Gender Responsive Governance

In a country with a history spanning more than 5,000 years; a multiplicity of languages, customs and cultural practices; hierarchies based on caste and class; and varieties of religions and sects, layers of discrimination are almost inevitable. Gender discrimination is one such layer that is firmly embedded but, very ironically, is often not perceived as discrimination. Once India became independent, the next step was to initiate the policies and programs for realizing the ideals of the welfare state. The postcolonial state was to be an instrument of social transformation, formulating policies to achieve the goals of justice-social, economic and political-enshrined in the constitution.

These goals included melioration of disadvantaged groups, emphatically including women. Jawaharlal Nehru, India's first prime minister, highlighted the need for a special policy toward women. He wrote, We talk about a welfare state and direct our energies towards its realization. That welfare must be the common property of everyone in India, and not the monopoly of the privileged groups, as it is today.

If I may be allowed to lay greater stress on some, they would be the welfare of children, the status of women, and the welfare of the tribal and hill people in our country. Women in India have a background of history and tradition behind them, which is inspiring. It is true, however, that they have suffered much from various kinds of suppression and all these have to go so that they can play their full part in the life of the nation (Nehru 1955).

On the whole, however, it seemed in 1950 that India had ushered in a new era of liberty and equality, where women were equal to men.

Through the institution of the adult franchise and Article 15, which prohibits discrimination inter alia on grounds of sex, the Indian Constitution mandates political equality. This recognition of political equality of women was a radical departure not only from the sociocultural norms prevailing in traditional India, but also in the context of the political evolution of even most advanced countries of that date. With the exception of the socialist countries, no other state in the world had accepted women's equality as a matter of course.

The United States and the United Kingdom granted the franchise to women only after World War I, after decades of struggle by their women. Most other countries, Eastern or Western, conceded it only after World War II. Japan granted the franchise to women in 1946, the People's Republic of China in 1949. The exceptions were Thailand and the Philippines, which granted a limited franchise, similar to the Indian case, in 1932 and 1933, respectively. Among the West European countries, France granted the franchise to women in 1945, Switzerland in 1971.

In the case of India, the two major forces that acted as a catalyst in the achievement of political equality of women were the national movement and the leadership of Gandhi, who declared himself to be "uncompromising in the matter of women's rights." He wrote, "Women must have votes and an equal legal status. But the problem does not end there; it only commences at the point where women begin to affect the political deliberations of the nation" (Gandhi 1929).

CONSTITUTIONAL PROVISIONS FOR GENDER EQUALITY

Improvement in the status of women was a pledge made by the constitution makers, which found embodiment in the form of Fundamental Rights and Freedoms. They include freedom of speech, protection of life, and personal liberty, which may be termed as positive rights; as well as negative rights, which emphasize prohibition of discrimination or denial of equal protection (Basu 1985: 69).

Article 14 promises equality before the law and equal protection by the laws. Article 15 prohibits discrimination on grounds of religion, race, caste, sex, or place of birth, and also provides that the state may make "any special provision for women and children, even in violation of the fundamental obligation of non-discrimination among citizens, inter alia of sex." Article 16 guarantees equality of opportunity in public employment or in appointment to any office under the state, and Article 17 (2) forbids discrimination "in respect of any employment of office under the State" on the grounds only of "religion, race, caste, sex, descent, place of birth, residence or any one of them."

The obligation not to discriminate in matters relating to employment or appointment to any office under the state at least normatively ensures a significant position and status to Indian women. Article 23 prohibits traffic in human beings as well as forced labour.

Apart from the important provisions in the Fundamental Rights, some guidelines are given in the Directive Principles of State Policy enunciated in Part IV of the Constitution. They concretize, together with the chapter on Fundamental Rights, the constitutional vision of a new Indian sociopolitical order. The Directive Principles are declared nonjusticiable, but "nevertheless fundamental in the governance of the country," and the state is charged with "a duty... to apply these principles in making laws" (Article 37). Some of them concern women indirectly or by necessary implication. A few are "women specific."

The first category includes the omnibus provision of Article 38, which in brief directs the state to secure a just social, political, and economic order, geared to promote the welfare of the people; Article 39 (b), (c), and (f) stipulates distribution of ownership and control of material resources of the community for the common good, prevention of concentration of wealth and means of production to the common detriment, and protection of childhood and youth against exploitation and moral and material abandonment; Article 40, on the organization of village panchayats (councils) to promote self-government; Article 41, on the right to work, education, and public assistance in cases of unemployment, old age, sickness, disablement and other types of undeserved wants; Article 43, on the provision of work, a living wage, conditions of work ensuring a decent standard of life and full enjoyment of leisure and social and cultural opportunities, and the promotion of cottage industries; Article 44, on the Uniform Civil Code; Article 45, on free and compulsory education for all children up to the age of 14; and Article 47, on raising the level of nutrition and the standard of living of the people and improvement of public health.

Directive principles that concern women directly and have a special bearing on their status include Article 39 (a), on the right to an adequate means of livelihood for men and women equally; Article 39 (d), on equal pay for equal work for both men and women; Article 39(e), on protection of the health and strength of workers-men, women and children-from abuse and entry into avocations unsuited to their age and strength; and Article 42, on just and humane conditions of work and maternity relief. Article 51, inserted in 1976 by the 42nd Constitutional Amendment, imposes a fundamental duty on every citizen to renounce practices derogatory to the dignity of women. The Constitution has accepted the principle of affirmative action favouring women and children. This principle has activated the state to make provisions for reservation for women in elected bodies of local government and other selected bodies.

The special attention given to the needs and problems of women, to enable them to enjoy and exercise their constitutional equality of status, along with other specific provisions relating to the hitherto oppressed sections of society, have led many scholars to describe the Indian Constitution as a "social" document embodying the objectives of a social revolution.

The Constitution contemplates attainment of an entirely new social order by making deliberate departures in norms and institutions of democratic governance from the inherited social, political, and economic systems. In doing so, the Constitution assigns primacy to law as an instrument directed toward social change. It thus demands of the legislature, the executive, and the judiciary continuous vigilance and responsiveness to the relationship between law and social transformation in contemporary India.

MILESTONES IN WOMEN'S DEVELOPMENT

The first 2 decades after assertion of the principle of "We the People" were full of optimism over the achievement of goals. Planning was high on the agenda of independent India. It was geared to improve the quality of life of the people, and it therefore contained the welfare perspective to protect the deprived and the neglected sections of society. The Planning Commission of India defined three major areas in which special attention was paid to women's development: education, social welfare, and health care. The First Five Year Plan (1951- 1956) was concerned mainly with the challenges of reconstruction after the war and partition. Its approach to women's issues was welfare oriented. It focused on the services that had to be promoted for the welfare of women: family planning, maternity and child care centres, schools, feeding schemes for children, and expansion of facilities for women's education. The voluntary agencies were expected to share the major burden in the field.

The Central Social Welfare Board (CSWB) was established in 1953 to promote welfare and development services for women, children, and underprivileged groups. Social Welfare Boards also came to be appointed at state levels. The CSWB remains an important national body involved in women's development at three levels: policy, programs, and implementation.

The Board frames policies at the central level through links with women's voluntary organizations, charts its own development programs for women on the basis of funds given by the Government, and implements programs through its welfare extension projects, which reach out to remote areas of the nation.

The second Five Year Plan (1956-61) envisaged the welfare of women and children under CSWB schemes and encompassed a comprehensive social welfare program; family planning featured prominently in health plans. The Third, Fourth and other Interim Plans (1961-1974) emphasized women's education; steps were taken also to improve maternal and child health services and supplementary feeding for children, and for nursing and expectant mothers. Women continued to be seen as beneficiaries of programs of social welfare, mainly through voluntary organizations, with the help of the CSWB. The period from the 1970s onwards witnessed new awareness and sensitivities toward women's issues. In 1971, the Government of India appointed the Committee on the Status of Women in India to undertake a comprehensive examination of all the questions relating to the rights and status of women in the context of changing social and economic conditions in the country and new problems related to the advancement of women, and also to suggest further measures that would enable women to play their full and proper role in the building of the nation.

The committee submitted its historic report entitled "Towards Equality," which proved to be an eye-opener for the Government and concerned citizens.

After having thoroughly examined the four Five Year Plans and the draft of the Fifth Five Year Plan, the Report of the Committee on the Status of Women in India noted:

> An examination of the Five Year Plans reveals that in spite of the policy emphasis on welfare or investment in human resources, the share of investment in the social services in terms of the actual allocation has been steadily declining in successive plans. The objectives emphasized in the various plans, as well as the share of allocations, indicate that among programmes specifically designed for women's development, the order of priorities up to the Fourth Plan has been education, then health, and lastly other aspects of welfare because it was generally assumed that all other programmes will benefit women indirectly if not directly.

This Report pointed out that the dynamics of social change and development had adversely affected the majority of women and had created new imbalances and disparities. The Report stressed that disabilities and inequalities imposed on women had to be seen in the total context of the society, where large sections of the population-male and female, adults and children-suffer under the oppression of an exploitative system. Any policy or movement for the emancipation and development of women has to form part of a total movement for removal of inequalities and oppressive social institutions if the benefits and privileges won by such action are to be shared by all women and not to be monopolized by a small minority.

After a debate on the Report, Parliament adopted a unanimous resolution to initiate a comprehensive program of legislative and administrative measures aiming at removing the economic and social injustices, disabilities, and discriminations to which women in India were being subjected. After the mandate from Parliament, the Government of India framed a National Plan of Action for Women based on the suggestions recommended in the Report. The recommendations of the U.N.'s World Plan of Action of the 1975 Mexico World Conference on Women were also incorporated.

A Women's Welfare and Development Bureau was established in the Ministry of Social Welfare to act as the nodal point within the Government, to coordinate policies and programs, and to initiate measures for women's development. It was backed by an interministerial study committee; special cells for women were also established in the Ministries of Labour and Employment and Rural Development.

POLICY SHIFT

Gradually a policy shift occurred: from viewing women as targets of welfare policies they began to be seen as critical groups for development. The scope of social welfare was enlarged in the Fifth Plan (1974-1978) to cope with several problems of the family and the role of women. The Sixth Five Year Plan (1980-1985) included for the first time a chapter on women's development, due to the continuous efforts of the women's movement and the international visibility that women's issues gained because of the International Women's Decade. It emphasized women's economic independence, educational advancement, and access to health care and family planning, and adopted a multidisciplinary approach with a three-pronged thrust on health, education, and employment.

As preparations began for the Sixth Five Year Plan, the Planning Commission appointed a working group on employment of women and encouraged the Ministry of Agriculture and Rural Development to review the programs and policies. The Ministry of Education, already involved in the promotion of the National Adult Education Programme, appointed a special committee to advise the Adult Education Programme for Women. The Ministry of Industrial Development also appointed a working group on self-employment for women. Researchers and representatives of organizations also started deliberating with the government representatives. With the beginning of the 1980s, special attention to women's issues was initiated at the centre.

The document "Forward-Looking Strategies for the Advancement of Women," which emerged at the end of the International Decade for Women, gave new importance to women's issues. An important response of the Government to this document was to revitalize the machinery at the national level by setting up a separate Department of Women and Child Development under the newly created Ministry of Human Resource Development. The Women's Welfare and Development Bureau under the erstwhile Ministry of Social and Women's Welfare became part of the new Department and now functions as the nodal agency for the advancement of women. This shift in approach is therefore no longer aimed at the hitherto "developmental goal" but in fact the thrust is on "empowerment" of women. The manifestation of this shift is evident in the following trends:

(i) The need to educate women is being emphasized in order to achieve the goal of empowerment.

(ii) "Economic self-reliance" of women and not merely provision of "economic aid" is informing the orientation of programs and policies.

(iii) Political process is being redefined: the concept of women as a distinct "class" has gained recognition and is being addressed in the sociopolitical realm.

The realization that, although women have a stake in politics as large as that of men, they do not have their share of political power prompted the initiation of the 73rd and 74th Constitutional Amendments. These provided for 33% reserved seats for women in Panchayati Raj Institutions (rural units of local governance and urban societies of local government). The former "voters" have gained ascendancy and are being geared to become "cosharers" of political power. Reservation of 33% of seats at the grassroots level in institutions of government and the ongoing debate for similar reservation in the state and national-level institutions are ample evidence of this new phenomenon.

A review of the state welfare policy on women during the past decades of the Indian Republic brings the reality to the surface. The picture that emerges is both positive and negative. It is a truism that in the early decades women were looked at as components of social welfare programs, not of development. Women's subordination was due not only to male domination, but also to the basic economic and political structure of society, which was reinforced by the same male domination. Initially, planners and policy makers were reluctant to question these, though they were contrary to the constitutional guarantee of social, economic, and political justice.

The National Perspective Plan for Women (1988) was drawn up to facilitate mainstreaming of women's issues in major policies and programs. It contains recommendations aimed at the development of women by focusing on the sectors of rural development, health care, legislation, political participation, education, employment, support services, communication, and voluntary action.

An important milestone of this period was the historic report "Shramshakti" prepared in 1998 by the National Commission for Self-Employed Women and Women in the Informal Sector appointed by the Government under the Chairmanship of Ela Bhatt (National Commission for Self-Employed Women and Women in the Informal Sector 1988). It highlighted the contribution of the marginalized women in the rural and urban areas to the national economy. It made some important recommendations such as recognizing women's work as homemakers and producers, setting up an exclusive credit body for poor and self-employed women, and linking training programs to employment.

Some of these recommendations have been implemented. The National Credit Fund for Women called the "Rashtriya Mahila Kosh" was set up in 1993 to give poor women credit at reasonable rates of interest through non-government organizations working in rural areas. Another major initiative to raise the economic status of women was the "Mahila Samridhi Yojna." It gives rural women greater control over their household resources and enables them to save and improve their financial assets. A high-level statutory body, the National Commission for Women, was also set up to monitor matters relating to the constitutional and legal rights of women. Since 1986-1987, Women's Development Corporations have been set up in the states to play an important role in strengthening the economic activities of women, and Mahila Samakhya schemes have been initiated to empower women.

The Eighth Five Year Plan (1992-1997) made an attempt to shift the approach from "development" to empowerment of women. It stressed that the benefits of development from different sectors should not bypass women. Special programs for women were framed to complement the general development programs. The Ninth Plan continued along the same lines. It is noteworthy that the Plan outlays have increased to meet the needs of women and children. The outlay of Rs. 40 million in the First Plan (1951-1956) has gone up to Rs. 20 billion in the Eighth Five Year Plan (1992-1997) and has been further increased in the Ninth and Tenth Plans respectively.

Following are some of the other significant steps taken by the Government regarding women's issues:

(i) A chapter on Education for Equality within the National Policy on Education (1986);

(ii) The Report of the National Expert Committee on Women Prisoners (1986);

(iii) 27 women-specific beneficiary-oriented schemes monitored by the Prime Minister's Office;

(iv) The National Plan of Action for the Girl Child (1991-2000);

(v) Provisions of reserved seats for women in elected bodies at local level by 73rd and 74th Constitutional Amendments (1993);

(vi) Poverty eradication programs and self-help groups under the National Bank of Agriculture and Development;

(vii) Support to training and employment programs for upgrading the skills of poor women and for providing them employment under the Integrated Rural Development Programme (IRDP);

(viii) The Training of Rural Youth in Self Employment; Jawahar Rozgar Yojana; Indira Awas Yojana; Development of Women and Children in Rural Areas;

(ix) A network of support services for women and children belonging to the weaker sections, programs for training women in nontraditional areas, gender sensitization, awareness generation, literacy and legal literacy programs and extension of support services such as hostels and creches.

An overview of the government initiatives on women's issues shows that in the last 4 decades, development planning for women has straddled principles spanning welfare, development, equity, efficiency, and empowerment.

Development planning was the pride of the new nation, which involved massive investment of financial and physical resources. The main goal of the State was achievement of economic growth, with a hope of realizing self-sufficiency in food; creating a strong industrial base in the public sector; and generating employment opportunities. The planning process further included welfare orientation, so that the interests of the deprived sections of society were protected. The independent state was far more concerned with higher growth, modernization, and industrialization; social welfare activities were identified as appropriate interventions to deal with the problems of certain target groups, including women. It was mentioned in the National Plan of Action that women are "handicapped" by social customs and social values, therefore social welfare services should specially endeavour to rehabilitate them.

The growing erosion of optimism regarding the "Nehruvian model," the ideal of wiping the last tear from the eye of the poorest man and creating a socialistic society, coupled with the impact of market forces unleashed by liberalization and globalization, led to structural adjustments. The important role of women that was previously invisible-in social and economic development-began to be focused and highlighted. The United Nations Declaration of the Decade for Women (1976-1989) played a crucial part in it.

This led to considerable shifts in approaches by academic researchers and policy makers. The earlier preoccupation of researchers with the role of women within the family and their reproductive responsibilities was replaced by attempts to understand the complexities of women's employment and their productive activities. Research on both waged workers and those in the informal sector, in urban areas and rural areas, helped in identifying the range of low income women's income-generating activities in the national economy.

Policy makers also began to shift focus from a universal concern with welfare-oriented, family-centred programs that assumed motherhood as the most important role for women in the development process to a diversity of approaches emphasizing the productive role of women.

Thus the women in development (WID) approach gained ascendancy, the underlying rationale of which was that women are an untapped resource that can provide an economic contribution to development.

The WID approach, despite its change in focus from one of equity to one of efficiency, is based on the underlying rationale that development processes would proceed much better if women were fully incorporated into them instead of being left to use their time unproductively. It focuses mainly on women in isolation, promoting measures such as access to credit and employment as the means by which women can be better integrated into the development process.

However, the introduction of the New Economic Policy after the mid-1980s, led to structural adjustments that were even more pronounced in the 1990s, targeting production for global markets, opening up the economy to other nations, and making market forces the sole determinant of economic and other activities. This affected all spheres of life and led to the emergence of new issues that affected Indian women substantially.

New market forces, with their emphasis on technology and management, began determining the contours of national development, including women's issues. The political, administrative, and ideological changes also raised pertinent issues regarding the deprived sections, viz., women.

Approaches to issues of women in developing countries therefore took a further shift, principally in academic research. The limitations of focusing on women in isolation are being recognized, and attention is being drawn to the need instead to look at "gender and development" (GAD). This focus on "gender" rather than "women" is influenced by the manner in which the problems of women were perceived in terms of their "sex," that is, their biological differences from men, rather than in terms of their gender, that is, the social relationship between men and women in which women have been systematically subordinated.

The focus on gender rather than on women makes it critical to look not only at the category "women"-since that is only half the story-but at women in relation to men, and the way in which relations between these categories are socially constructed.

Men and women play different roles in society, with their gender differences shaped by ideological, historical, religious, ethnic, economic, and cultural determinants.

These roles show similarities and differences between other social categories such as class, race, ethnicity, and so on. Since the way they are socially constructed is always temporally and spatially specific, gender divisions cannot be read off on checklists. Social categories therefore differentiate the experience of inequality and subordination within societies. A brief reference to some issues in the Indian context might aid comprehension of the ground reality.

After the mid-1980s, communal issues escalated, especially with such events as the Shah Bano case for maintenance in 1985,[2] the Roop Kanwar incident of Sati in Rajasthan 1987,[3] and the Adyodhya dispute in 1992.

All these events gave a communal colour to various policies, and drew attention to the plurality and diversity of people and issues. The trend of articulating demands through the community perspective gave rise to identity politics; the perception of Indian women as a homogenous entity was shattered, giving rise to different voices articulating varied concerns.

Though the diversity of women's status had been recognized earlier, and, to an extent so had issues of region, community, caste, and class, it was nonetheless felt that at least a few problems were common to all women as victims of patriarchy. The major shift came when difference meant that one group could not speak on behalf of another. Thus, one of the major challenges today is the articulation of women's issues not as a unified agenda but as demands based on different identities.

The acceptance of globalization and the entry of multinationals and market forces as dictated by the World Bank and the International Monitory Fund changed the thrust of the economy, and the polity, education, and culture underwent a perceptible change. The visibility of women as agents during communal and caste conflicts brought about significant change in the thrust of research. The studies shifted from considering women as victims to considering women as agents with power to influence the politicocultural system, positively and negatively. The phenomenon of docile, illiterate, subordinated women becoming articulate and assertive leaders in the new panchayats has also gained the attention of researchers.

In pre-independence India, while provisions of health care and education services had been increasingly demanded from the state, social welfare programs were administered mainly by voluntary agencies. No comprehensive nationwide program provided welfare services. After the attainment of independence, it was felt that the social and economic uplifting of the masses required government assistance to strengthen the services rendered by voluntary agencies.

The administrative structure inherited from the colonial government was clearly not equipped for this task. In 1953, the central Government therefore created a new agency, the CSWB, to promote welfare and development services for women, children, and other underprivileged groups by providing assistance to voluntary agencies, improving and developing welfare programs, and sponsoring them in areas where they did not exist. Following the creation of the CSWB, the state governments set up, at the request of the CSWB, state social welfare (advisory) boards, for the same purpose. This was necessary, as welfare is a state subject.

THE RAJASTHAN EXPERIENCE

The concept of social welfare included in its ambit the underprivileged sections of society in totality. The categories requiring the attention of the responsible department were so variegated that the gender issue did not acquire the requisite visibility and attention.

Therefore, in 1984 the government of Rajasthan established an altogether new department, the Women and Child Department. Implementation of comprehensive programs aimed at women's development and empowerment was the specific purpose of this newly created department.

Programs and policies initiated by both the central and state governments were to be implemented through this department. Various programs and schemes related to women's development have seen the light of day due to this department. Considerable overall improvement of the women in the state has been noted. A gradual increase in female literacy, access to credit and employment, etc. took place.

Besides the Women and Child Department, on the pattern of the National Commission for Women, a State Commission for Women was also set up in Rajasthan through an act of the state legislature in May 1999, to monitor matters relating to the constitutional and legal rights of women and also to eliminate gender discrimination.

The wide range of the functions of the commission includes hearing and investigation of complaints regarding misbehaviour against women. The commission has been empowered to conduct criminal proceedings in relevant matters and also recommend measures for the redress of grievances.

With the acceptance of New Economic Policy, liberalization, the information explosion, the market economy, etc., the role of women in society has undergone tremendous change. As stated earlier, the WID approach to development proved inadequate and the GAD approach appears more suited to the ideal of empowerment of women. The adoption of the Women Policy in the State of Rajasthan in 2000 is a vivid reflection of this GAD approach.

The policy was the manifestation of the intention to improve the status of women in the state. It was also aimed at evolving mechanisms for the eradication of discriminatory and exploitative practices toward women. Creation of a congenial environment for overall development and empowerment of women has been emphasized.

The following measures have been identified as leading to the attainment of this policy's objectives:

(i) Implement schemes and programs that would enhance the capacity of women in the enjoyment of their constituted and legal rights, and also ensure gender equality and justice.

(ii) Recognize the productive role of women in family and society.

(iii) Prioritize fulfillment of girl children's and women's needs in acute conditions of poverty and adverse conditions.

(iv) Eliminate malnutrition, ill health, and early-age pregnancy and initiate health care facilities catering to all stages of life.

(v) Provide compulsory education for girls, at least at the primary level, and provide opportunities for basic and continuing education to illiterate women. Provide opportunities to women for acquiring the highest possible levels of education.

(vi) Create a congenial atmosphere and appropriate mechanisms to generate gender sensitivity in the personnel of all departments, opinion makers, media, and politicians.

(vii) Enhance the participation of women in the political process and also ensure their involvement in decision making for development.

The Women and Child Development Department established in 1984 has been made the nodal agency to implement the above policy, and also to coordinate and supervise the activities of different agencies and departments engaged in the implementation of various government policies and programs designed for the development of women. This nodal agency has been assigned the responsibility of ensuring coordination between relevant government departments, public institutions, banks and other financial institutions, and women's groups and organizations. It has also been assigned the specific responsibility of procuring progress reports from the concerned departments and agencies that are to be submitted to the State Commission for Women. This Commission has been expected to make recommendations in this context to the state government, and the latter would ensure the compliance with the same.

To ensure enforcement of the recommendations, a committee under the chairmanship of the Chief Minister was contemplated. This has been supplanted by a committee under the chairmanship of the Chief Secretary of the State to monitor and review biannually the implementation of policies and programs for women's development.

CONCLUDING OBSERVATIONS

A review of the implementation of the above policy and various programs in the state reveals that women's empowerment, as it has been articulated, has been mostly rhetoric. Gender has been co-opted in the language of various policies but the fact remains that mere rhestoric cannot solve problems.

The burgeoning of conflicts and caste and community identities in recent years has yet to elicit an adequate response from the administrative system. In the pursuit of liberalization, the state is gradually withdrawing from vital areas of education, health care, environment, and social services, thus deepening the suffering of the deprived sectors. Undoubtedly the role of civil society in democratic governance is crucial, but the state cannot be absolved of its accountability.

The 73rd and 74th Amendments have proved to be milestones in the process of enhancing political participation in Rajasthan. Women are being absorbed into formal politics at the local level and are gradually shattering the myths regarding their inefficiency, inability to govern, rule by proxy, etc. Evidently the success stories of these elected representatives at the local level (e.g., Panchayati Raj Institutions) have sent signals of the determined efforts of women for change, creating anxiety in male-dominated power structures and scaring them about the extension of power assertion if reservation is extended to state and parliamentary elections. Thus, relevant opposition to the Bill proposed for reservation for women in Lok Sabha (Central Legislature) and Vidhan Sabhas (State Legislatures) is strong.

An attempt at stocktaking of the "gender responsiveness" of the state government reveals that the proliferation of policies and plans of action for women still too frequently fail to be translated into practice. Unfortunately, in India the term "culture" has been frequently used as a blanket explanation for constraints responsible for the "gender blindness" in policy formulation. The use of this term in such a pejorative manner as a casual explanation of failure raises the issue of whether planning is really a neutral activity and likewise, the planning and implementation processes.

A review of governance in the state of Rajasthan (India) with specific reference to "gender-responsiveness" in the last decade reveals that the issue of "gender" is an "add-on" rather than an integrative approach to the mainstream policy and planning exercise.

Pertinent issues such as policy shifts in approach toward hitherto "invisible" gender issues by successive governments in the states are yet to be translated successfully into practice. In conventional analysis, political participation means activities related to electoral politics like voting, campaigning, holding party office, and contesting elections.

But now such views are being challenged and conceptualized in a broader context. The concept now encompasses all voluntary actions intended to influence the making of public policies, the administration of public affairs, and the choice of political leaders at all levels of government. Political participation is no longer concerned only with the organization of the state and government and the dialectics of the exercise of power; it also seeks to reorganize the lives of the members of society.

Implementation of gender policy is also confronting technical as well as political constraints. The traditional view of planning methodology as a neutral activity needs to be overhauled. The separation of planning from the concrete reality of its context has proved to be "empirically vacuous." The "manning" of departments responsible for the implementation of gender-oriented policies themselves need to be gender balanced in structure and organization. In other words, organizations need to adopt a more "gendered" approach.

This could be accomplished by undertaking extensive training programs aimed at changing the working practices of colleagues within organizations. Formulating policies without the backing of a sound institutional framework is proving meaningless.

The majority of the policies, programs, and projects have not yielded the expected results due to lack of coordination among the relevant departments and agencies entrusted with the onerous tasks. The majority of the programs, projects, and policies lack an integrated approach responding to their multiple socioeconomic roles. A sensitive understanding about women's different roles has still not emerged in the development planning schemes, and efforts for the betterment of women still remain piecemeal.

6

Public Policy and Administration

Ever since Plato's Republic, the question of how to groom future public leaders for their future roles has been laden with philosophical, even moral, significance. Answers touch on core beliefs: What makes good public policy? What skills and dispositions would, if possessed by public managers, both inform and lend authority to their decision making?

The authors in this section engage in three interconnected debates that in a generic form were probably as relevant to the Republic as they remain today. Briefly, they concern the content, methods, and ultimately the consequences of policy education.

WHAT SHOULD BE TAUGHT?

To begin with the obvious, the fields of public policy and administration have a bountiful and diverse inheritance. Dan Durning's chapter traces the rise of public policy programs since the 1960s and the more recent advent of public management programs modelled to some extent after schools of business administration. Leaving aside the question of what separates such programs from public administration-an added layer of complexity-multiple disciplinary identities and influences have led to perennial debates over what belongs to the "core" of a policy or administration curriculum.

What knowledge of economics, political science, and management is vital for public administrators or policy analysts to possess, and with what skills of integration? Durning makes an interesting observation that mainstream policy analysis in quest of technical sophistication has moved away from the problem-solving orientation that inspired scholars to launch public policy as a separate discipline. An anecdote may help to illustrate the diversity of views within public policy circles alone. Our colleagues at the newly established Lee Kuan Yew School of Public Policy recently conducted a review of the core curricula of major policy schools worldwide.

It revealed a wide range of configurations of such programs. Most included some form of economics, statistics, and political analysis in the core, but the relative emphasis varied from one to several courses in each of those fields. Other programs incorporated management or leadership courses as well. Clearly a range of visions of what an appropriate policy program should look like are available among the leading purveyors of such education. Not least because faculty members in these departments are as likely to identify themselves with component disciplines (such as economics or political science) as with the less well delineated "policy science," it is likely these debates will be with us for some time.

The same review turned up a mandatory course entitled "Democratic Governance" at a prominent policy school. The course title itself might fit uneasily in the core curriculum of some countries otherwise keen to promote policy education, even though the content is probably not vastly different from less colorfully entitled courses in "political and organizational analysis" at other institutions. This raises a second area of tension regarding the content of policy education. To what extent, and how, is it necessary to localize the content of policy education to fit non-Western contexts? Or to put it more radically, are entirely new models of, and modalities of teaching, policy and administration necessary for such settings?

The question takes on a particular edge in the attempt to transplant core curricula-and the content underneath course titles-from countries with long-established "democratic" traditions to authoritarian one-party governance settings. And it takes the form of a visceral frustration for many educators of policy and administration programs in non-US settings in particular; because so many of the basic texts-let alone the textbooks-of public policy and administration are built around that country's rather unique set of institutions. Several of the authors in this section address such issues. Ngok Kinglun outlines the development of teaching of public administration and policy in the People's Republic of China (PRC). Developing a relevant curriculum has been especially important due to the PRC's shift from a planned to a market economy requiring new institutions and mindsets in the public sector.

Baulderstone and O'Toole highlight the interesting case of international students studying public administration in Australia, for whom the existing curriculum and mode of delivery may not be entirely appropriate and require modification. It is far from easy to introduce modifications to key courses in these fields that maintain coherence while catering to a diverse student body. Robert Laking gives a detailed account of how this challenge was addressed in training Vietnamese participants in public management in New Zealand.

How Can Public Administration and Policy be Most Effectively Taught?

The question of what teaching methods would best serve adult learners has long been debated in universities and in the specialist literature on pedagogy. One form this challenge takes for teachers of policy and administration is how to prepare students for the complexities of a public sector environment, in which ethical dilemmas, conflicting notions of the "public interest," and multiple accountability pressures are all common.

The generic answer in many professional schools has been to promote problem-based learning in various forms. It arises from a long-standing critique-much in vogue in university centres devoted to teaching methods, and given a new interpretation in Steven Aufrecht and Xie Ming's chapter- of hierarchical, lecture-based methods. These methods take various forms. Faculties of medicine perhaps have the most plausible application: rigorous, closely supervised clinical education to accompany theoretical learning. Yet the subjects of policy analysis and administration are rather unlike the controlled environment of hospital examination rooms. Business schools have developed a more applicable model, emphasizing group work, internships, and applied case analysis. An important point to note is that none of these methods is free of controversy or practical challenge.

Take the use of case studies. They are widely employed in both business and public administration classrooms, and are widely thought to provide the opportunity to integrate political, economic, and organizational analysis for "real-life" problem-solving and to stimulate the development of managerial "wisdom." Yet typical public policy cases have also been criticized as portraying the policy world in terms of "high-level, lone protagonists beset by hostile political forces," and of de-emphasizing the institutional and historical contexts of policy action. If the critique rings true for American policy contexts, it may have even greater traction when case studies "cooked" in Western contexts are served to current or future public managers from developing or non-Western country settings.

Several chapters look beyond case analysis for problem-based learning methods. Carole Comerton-Forde and her colleagues from the University of Sydney explore group work in public policy programs, while Richard Hayllar offers a detailed description of the use of extended role-plays "to develop policy and decision-making skills in cases where interpretations of what is in the 'best public interest' are strongly contested," as he puts it in his evocative title. While no chapter focuses on e-learning methods, there is little doubt that this new technology will be increasingly important in the years to come, and an important way to provide distance education and in-service training to public sector personnel in a wide catchment area.

Does it Matter?

This is a third type of question that can be asked of policy education. Put differently, what impact does training in public policy and administration have on the practice of governance or the quality of governmental decision-making? The question may sit uncomfortably for educators; indeed, only one of the chapters in this section-that by Mangahas on the potential impact on Millennium Development Goal attainment-addresses this type of issue. The reluctance stems largely from the general difficulty of quantifying the impact of higher education in any field-except on the subsequent wages of graduates, a measure which is decidedly unhelpful for the public sector. The question may also be uncomfortable for university administrators. After all, policy and administration schools-particularly those catering to students from developing countries-probably have among the highest percentages of students whose tuition is paid by third parties among all the professional schools. Are these generous funders, whether donors or governments, getting their money's worth?

In this regard one might recall Chambers' (1983) evocative (if simplistic) description of the cultural and attitudinal gulf separating "positive practitioners"-for whom every problem is solvable with the right mix of resources and skills-and "negative academics"-annoyingly insisting on the profound structural constraints on effective policy intervention. Professional schools of public administration and policy everywhere straddle, even embody, this divide. But it is a tension that can border on "schizophrenia" when the context is policy education in less developed settings.

We know that the productivity and "room for maneuver" for individual public managers depends heavily on how facilitative their work environments are: on the incentives, resources, information, and public authority that these managers can mobilize. If all such incentives and resources are weak to the breaking point in many developing country settings (as many "negative academics" might contend), what will a better grasp of benefitcost analysis bring our well-trained public servant? To put the question more strongly, how tenuous is the link-for it must be tenuous-between the short exposure of mid-career managers to expensive, short-duration executive education programs and the quality of policy outputs emerging from the systems in which they must operate?

There may be good answers to this question. Indeed, some aspects of developing country environments may enhance managerial discretion and, by extension, the importance of its sensitive application (Grindle and Thomas 1991). But to ask the question underlines the difficulties of moving the pedagogical discussion from one based (to use public management-speak) on the "process and outputs" to the "outcomes and impacts" of policy education.

Ultimately, educators of the "guardians" of once and future Republics can always fall back onto Oscar Wilde's famous dictum: "If you think education is expensive, try ignorance." But perhaps we can do better than this. Examining the impact of policy education in producing not just more capable, but more effective public managers is an important future arena for discussion-one the chapters point toward without directly addressing.

ENHANCING THE ROLE OF PUBLIC ADMINISTRATION EDUCATION

The Millennium Development Goals (MDGs) establish targets for reducing poverty, improving health care and education, promoting economic growth, empowering women, and creating an enabling environment for sustainable development (UNDP 2003). The magnitude of the challenge for achieving the MDGs is formidable. Unless drastic and concerted actions are undertaken at all levels-from global to local-it is unlikely that the desired results and outcomes will be significantly realized (DFID 2003). The attainment of the MDGs requires collective action and commitment of international, national, and subnational institutions involving governments, civil society, and the private sector.

Addressing the enduring problems of poverty and environment degradation is predicated on the successful implementation of governance reforms to rectify the policy and institutional frameworks that discriminate against the historically disadvantaged and marginalized sectors. The MDGs are expected to be resisted, since new concepts and paradigms must be introduced to the policy arena, together with new administrative systems that challenge strongly held views and practices. Any effort to promote citizen-centred policies and pro-poor change will understandably be opposed by well-organized and influential groups that benefit from the status quo.

Critical to the achievement of the MDGs is the promotion of institutional and organizational development, which requires the learning of new skills, strategies, approaches, and tools. Building capacity for identifying and responding to citizens' needs, particularly those of the poor, is an imperative for most developing countries. Functional skills in cooperating with others, managing stakeholders, and establishing networks and partnerships should be improved. Measuring and reporting performance to enhance efficacy and promote accountability of public officials are also necessary.

To meet the MDGs, public administration education must play a key role. Despite the global interest in and broad support for work toward realizing the MDGs, they are yet to be formally introduced in the teaching and learning processes of many schools of public administration in the Philippines. This paper seeks to suggest what such schools can and should do to support actions toward fulfillment of the MDGs. It also aims to examine how the academic curricula for teaching public administration may be strengthened to develop competencies for institutional and organizational development looking toward the MDGs.

This paper begins with a brief discussion of what will it take to achieve the MDGs. This is followed by a description of the agenda for promoting good governance and its link to reaching the MDGs. The paper then explains a framework for promoting institutional and organizational development. A discussion of perspectives in effective curriculum design follows. Next, the paper provides some general observations on academic curricula in public administration. The paper concludes with recommendations to strengthen programs of instruction and educative roles to help achieve the MDGs.

PROVIDING AN ENABLING ENVIRONMENT FOR ACHIEVING

Targeting poverty reduction, women's empowerment, and environmental sustainability require substantial changes in political, economic, and social systems (Brinkerhoff 2004). The enduring problems that the MDGs seek to address are the consequence of decades of policies and practices at international and national levels. As such, significant improvements in living conditions in developing countries will be realized through specific reform measures at the national and subnational levels, matched with focused interventions from the international community.

International and national instruments are the key to reaching the MDGs. International instruments involve effective debt reduction, trade-related policies, reform of the Bretton Woods Institutions and the World Trade Organization, and increased quantity and better quality of international aid (GFID 2002). National instruments include improving the delivery of basic services, particularly to the poor; a more equitable and transparent taxation system; and a guarantee of peace and order (GFID 2002). Public policies are too often insufficiently focused around issues related to poverty, health care, education, gender, and environment. Likewise, administrative capacities are inadequately prepared and resources are scarce for promoting change and pursuing pro-poor development. Although the attainment of the MDGs is not the sole responsibility of governments, governments actually play a critical role in making services work for the people and raising the quality of life. Governments perform thousands of functions, but in essence, they perform four major types of activities that affect almost every aspect of living:

(i) They formulate and monitor policies;

(ii) They raise revenues to implement policies;

(iii) They implement policies, some through provision of goods and services; and

(iv) They provide an enabling environment for private sector growth and social development.

The reduced or nonexistent capacity for good governance has nonetheless weighed down government performance. Good governance or sound development management is therefore a sine qua non for achieving the MDGs.

Governance is broadly defined as the sound exercise of political, economic, and administrative authority to manage a country's resources for development. It involves the institutionalization of a system through which citizens, institutions, organizations, and groups in the society articulate their interests, exercise their rights, and mediate their differences in pursuit of the collective good (ADB 1995).

It embraces not only the affairs of government, but also the proactive role of the private sector and civil society in national development. Governance is, thus, not the sole province of government. Instead, its functions are delegated to, or assumed by, other institutions and organizations in the business sector and civil society (UNDP 1997). Its concern with the sound exercise of authority underscores its ethical moorings. Thus, its basic elements are accountability, participation, predictability, and transparency, which are also the key principles of sound development management (ADB 2003). The basic elements of governance, its key dimensions, and specific areas of action. Promoting good governance poses opportunities as well as challenges as it brings together the public sector, civil society, the private sector, and communities in the tasks of evolving policies, programs, organizational and operational mechanisms, and institutional arrangements that can effectively respond to the needs of the people, ensure the judicious and transparent use of public funds, encourage growth of the private sector, promote effective delivery of public services, and uphold the rule of law.

Mainstreaming good governance not only requires capacitating individuals and institutions, but also providing the appropriate policy environment to institutionalize reforms (ADB 2005). At the individual level, capacity building for good governance focuses on the process of equipping civil servants and stakeholders with the understanding; skills; and access to information, knowledge, and training that enable them to work together and perform effectively. At the organizational level, governance reforms involve the elaboration and establishment of enabling management systems, structures, processes, and procedures, not only within organizations but also in the management of relationships between and among the different organizations and sectors. At the institutional level, capacity building includes making legal and regulatory changes to enable organizations, institutions, and agencies at all levels and in all sectors to enhance their capacity.

Sound development management identifies the roles of the state as:

- o Creating a conducive economic environment,
- o Protecting the vulnerable,
- o Improving government efficiency and responsiveness,

- o Empowering people and democratizing the political system,
- o Decentralizing the administrative system,
- o Reducing gaps between rich and poor,
- o Encouraging cultural diversity and social integration, and
- o Protecting the environment.

IMPORTANCE OF INSTITUTIONAL/ORGANIZATIONAL DEVELOPMENT

Institutions are often creations and instruments of the powerful elite, and usually discriminate against the poor (DFID 2003a). Without institutional reform, policies and programs to support the MDGs can be stymied. Poor development performance is rooted in institutional factors. Institutional causes of poverty can be:

- o *Economic*: inadequate funding for basic services, inefficient allocation and use of resources, debt burden, weak planning and budgeting links, lack of competitiveness, weak revenue generation capability, and poor access to credit;
- o *Legal*: poor regulatory framework, corrupt administration of justice and law enforcement, policy conflicts/gaps, and a closed system of policy making.
- o *Political*: political instability, a strong patronage system, a highly politicized civil service, and corrupt leaders.
- o *Social*: low labour productivity, unemployment, a poor work ethic, a high incidence of crime, insurgency (DFID 2003a).

The 2002 World Bank Development Report emphasizes the importance of institution building for poverty alleviation (World Bank 2002). The United Kingdom's Department for International Development (DFID) similarly points out the pressing need for governments to enhance their capabilities if they are to work better for poor people to achieve the MDGs (DFID 2003a). As such, building capabilities for good governance and MDGs is very much a matter of institutional development. It is in this context where teaching and research in public administration can make a difference. Promoting good governance and achieving the MDGs are likely to succeed if they pursue improvements in wider institutional capacities as well as in technical competencies.

More efficient and responsive services for the poor require technical competencies (i.e., knowledge, skills, and attitude) for doing so; but these must be matched with institutional changes to allow the technical improvements to work.

For example, Filipino civil servants need technical competence to identify and improve specific aspects of service delivery through application of benchmarking and continuous improvement techniques.

At the same time, their superiors and work structures should allow them to perform better and make the necessary improvements. According to DFID, technical interventions (e.g., training or ICT applications) that leave unsatisfactory institutions intact achieve nothing (DFID 2003b).

Institutional/organizational development must be directed at achieving a specific outcome. In the context of realizing the MDGs, the change intervention should clearly identify what is to be done and why. Once the purpose has been defined, a timeframe is set for achieving the milestones and results. The context or starting point is then situated. Participants and allies to the change process are identified and managed. Accountability measures are likewise established.

The institutional development process consists of five stages. The first phase involves analysis and diagnosis that examine the overall institutional framework. It seeks to answer questions like "What is to be achieved and why?" and "What are the main institutional strengths/ weaknesses?"

The second phase refers to the analysis and diagnosis of the concerned organization in its wider institutional context. This stage aims to identify the main organizational strengths/ weaknesses. The third phase is designing the intervention, which identifies the best way to promote change. Next is implementation or managing the change intervention. Finally, the monitoring and evaluation phase is concerned with establishing mechanisms for measuring performance.

PERSPECTIVES ON CURRICULUM DESIGN AND DEVELOPMENT

Blueprint for Teaching and Learning Processes: The academic curriculum is an essential component of any educational institution. The curriculum is the blueprint for instruction and student assessment. It sets out the learning objectives and the means for achieving them. The curriculum therefore sets out not only the content of each course but also the inter-connectedness and sequence of courses to systematically provide the learners with a rational process for acquiring and building upon their know-how and skills over a specified period of time. Being at the core of educational functions, resources must support the successful achievement of curriculum goals and objectives.

A carefully planned and well-structured curriculum provides a strong foundation for quality delivery of education, thus realizing the desired learning outcomes. Serious curriculum design involves a long and iterative process. Curriculum development stresses the importance of identifying educational opportunities that are most critical to an organization or community. The learner groups and their learning needs are properly identified. Learning objectives are subsequently determined and ordered in relation to required competencies.

The appropriate number and mix of courses or modules are likewise specified. The content outline is developed for each course. Instructional strategies and media are selected. Lesson plans are also developed for each course including the timing and duration. Logistics of the total curriculum delivery system are planned and finalized. The design may be scaled down or expanded based on the resources that will be made available. The content and objectives of the curriculum design are validated and field tested prior to adoption and full-scale implementation. Other mechanisms must be put in place to monitor and evaluate whether or not the curriculum is meeting its intended purpose. Moreover, the system of responsibilities and accountabilities for managing and implementing the curriculum must be established.

Poor curriculum designs achieve minimal educational benefits. Too often they are manifested by the lack of goal orientation and convergence in the program of instruction, unnecessary overlaps of courses, disjointed subjects, wasteful use of scarce resources, low completion rates, substandard teaching, and ineffective assessment of learning. At the end of the day, the curriculum should be able to effectively, efficiently, and economically provide the desired learning outcomes.

Curriculum development is a complex process. It requires iteration, dedication, perseverance, and, more important, the technical expertise to get it going. Pitfalls can be avoided by observing the principles and logical process of curriculum design, applying benchmarking and continuous improvement techniques, and enhancing learner participation in curriculum development. There is an increasing trend for curriculum designs to shift from the traditional subject-based, input-oriented, and teacher-centred learning to systems-integrated, competency-based, community-oriented, and student-centred programs. The continuing challenge for educational institutions is how to make their academic curricula respond to changing needs and demands, thus bringing about favourable results and outcomes.

The curriculum must be directed at providing students with the necessary competencies to make them productive members of society. The curriculum must not only respond to individual learning needs of students, but also to societal and/or organizational demands. Such needs and demands serve as the bases for developing a responsive and viable curriculum. The curriculum defines the scope and content of what students should learn and what must be taught. Teaching and learning methods are assembled around achieving curriculum goals and objectives. Formative and summary assessment techniques are likewise formulated and administered to measure/ improve the curriculum and instruction.

Curriculum design encompasses the horizontal and vertical organization. The horizontal organization is concerned with the side-by-side arrangement of curriculum components. The vertical organization, on the other hand, is concerned with the longitudinal arrangement of curriculum elements-the placement of additional skills development. Under the horizontal organization are scope and sequence. Scope is the breadth and depth of the content of a curriculum-from simple to complex principles, required common content, and elective or special content. Sequence is the order by which the curriculum content is presented. Under vertical organization are continuity and integration. Continuity refers to the vertical reiteration of major curriculum elements. Integration refers to the horizontal relationships of curriculum activities. Inasmuch as the academic curriculum is a very important element in ensuring quality delivery of educational services, it must be emphasized that learning outcomes are shaped by:

(i) university/school factors,

(ii) system/ supporting inputs,

(iii) student characteristics, and

(iv) contextual factors.

Overall, the effectiveness of a university or school is conventionally measured in terms of learning achievement, completion rate, and competitiveness of graduates in the labour market.

University/School factors consist of:

(i) university/school vision/mission,

(ii) university climate/culture,

(iii) curriculum and instruction,

(iv) leadership and quality of staff, and

(v) teaching/learning processes.

Although the vision/ mission statement predictably sets high expectations, it needs to clearly state the expected outcomes. The educational institution must have a strong commitment to excellence and the organization geared toward delivering better services and results.

The university/school must have a capable teaching force. It also requires competent leadership to manage school resources and, more important, provide effective instructional supervision. A system of responsibilities and accountabilities must also be established and operationalized.

Rewards and incentives are likewise necessary. Teaching/ Learning processes alongside assessment/testing techniques must be aligned with the curriculum. Both teachers and students must strive for academic excellence. Students have to assume learning responsibilities.

The university/school must have supporting inputs from the educational system as well as from the community and parents/ families of students. The concerned educational institution must have the legal mandate and resources to carry out its functions. Of course, the quality of students admitted into the degree programs is contributory to the success of the university/school. Institutional, political, economic, language, and cultural factors are also important in appreciating the capacity of the university/ school to produce good graduates.

What Makes a Good Curriculum?: A quality curriculum must be very clear about what is to be covered, how it is delivered, and how to measure/assess learning. Learner objectives, activities, and assessments must be closely linked to one another. An effective curriculum requires the following (MDESE 2004):

- o a rationale that relates the goals and objectives of each subject area and course to the educational mission and philosophy;
- o a general description of the content of subject areas at the undergraduate and graduate levels;
- o statement of general goals for students in each subject area;
- o specific, measurable learner objectives for each subject;
- o alignment of the measurable learner objectives for each subject to the knowledge, skills, and attitudes that students need to meet the curriculum goals and standards;
- o instructional strategies (activities) and specific assessments (including performance-based assessments for a majority of the learner objectives);
- o evidence that individual learner objectives have been articulated by subject and by course sequence; and
- o review and approval for each curriculum guide.

Another perspective of an effective curriculum identifies five critical components:

(i) meaning,

(ii) coherence,

(iii) articulation,

(iv) high standards, and

(v) alignment.

The first element, meaning, refers to setting measurable objectives that focus on fundamental knowledge and processes. It includes a clear, defensible rationale and contains explicit course descriptions. In addition, meaning should articulate scope and sequence. Furthermore, meaning should provide assessments and instructional activities to measure established objectives.

Coherence pertains to the provision of adequate opportunities at each level in the curriculum or certain points in the learning process to build on prior knowledge and learning experiences.

Articulation in the effective curriculum model focuses on the promotion of learning at different year levels that is appropriately sequenced and related. It also connects topics within year levels/ courses by unifying themes/ concepts.

High standards establish a core set of challenging benchmarks or yardsticks of performance for all students. High standards promote in-depth learning and they help address student learning styles through a variety of instructional strategies. High standards in a curriculum also utilize a variety of assessments to evaluate levels of student understanding (and achievement).

Alignment is equally important in a curriculum. The curriculum must exhibit strong connections between written, taught, and evaluated learning. The curriculum must likewise provide direction to the course content, process of delivering instruction, and methods for measuring progress of learning. Other characteristics of an effective curriculum, instructional strategies and activities, and assessment program, which reemphasizes alignment and integration of the curriculum content, pedagogical tasks and activities, and assessment.

Formation of the curriculum content begins with defining and sequencing aims, goals, and objectives of instruction. Knowledge and skills to be taught are prioritized in the curriculum in terms of being mandatory (must know), essential (need to know), and worthy (nice to know). Themes and topics are included and prioritized in the curriculum as a result of a systematic, well-informed, and highly consultative process.

The vertical and horizontal linkages and inter-connectedness of courses/ subjects are likewise decided. It is also preferable that the philosophy or tone of a curriculum be guided by specific and acceptable learning models. Instructional delivery is another important aspect that can make or break a good curriculum. Apart from the curriculum, instruction is shaped by teacher quality, pedagogical approaches, and instructional materials.

The teacher (or medium) needs not only to have mastery of the subject matter, but must also apply appropriate processes and methods. The organizational structure and mechanisms to govern curriculum implementation and improvement must likewise be put in place. Assessment relates not only to measuring if and how learning has taken place, but is also concerned with evaluating whether the goals and objectives of the delivered curricula have been obtained. Assessment methods are formulated to accurately provide information to measure learning and to improve instruction and curriculum.

Curriculum Design Prototypes: Prototypes of curriculum design are represented by three types:

(i) subjectcentered,

(ii) learner-centred, and

(iii) problem-centred.

The relative strengths and limitations of three prototypes. The subject-centred curriculum design is the oldest and most widely used. The scope and content of the curriculum are determined by the conventional range of subjects worthy of inclusion. The sequence of topics is largely a function of the logic of the subject matter.

The learner-centred curriculum design emphasizes individual development. This kind of curriculum design is more sensitive to learning needs, which makes it more effective than the traditional subject-centred design. The design is developed based on the needs, interests, and purposes of students. It is not "pre-planned" or "off-the-shelf." It evolves as teacher and students work together on content and tasks. The scope and content depend on what the learners need to learn. The sequence of topics is aligned with the absorptive capacity and even preferences of the learners. The problem-centred curriculum design is similar to the learner-centred design, as they are both rooted in individual-centred epistemological assumptions.

It is focused on building and strengthening competencies to enable the learner to function more effectively and productively in the community or society. The design aims to perform strongly in providing problem-analysis and problem-solving skills. Problem-centred design is nonetheless "pre-planned" in the sense that it is oriented to addressing pressing or common problems, which shape the scope, content, and sequence of instruction.

Approaches to Curriculum Review and Development: Academic review of high degree programs in United Kingdom is conducted using a phased approach. First, necessary preparations for the review are undertaken. Scope and preference surveys are undertaken to gather information on the following:

(i) The range of subjects offered,

(ii) Desired programs to be included under each subject heading,

(iii) The estimated number of full-time equivalent students for each program, and

(iv) The institution's preferred timing for the review and any preferences for subjects to be reviewed.

With the time schedule mapped out, initial profiles are prepared to commence a dialogue with the concerned educational institution on the overall approach to and intensity of the review. Selfevaluation documents and program specifications are prepared at this stage.

Second, the points of reference for the review are laid down. A framework of higher education qualifications is used to provide reference points to determine whether the intended outcomes for programs and actual student achievement are appropriate to the level of the qualification awarded. Subject benchmarks are likewise established, which represent the general expectations about standards for the award of qualifications at a given level in a particular subject area. Third, the review is conducted. One approach involves a peer review, where judgments are made by those who understand the subject under scrutiny and who are familiar with the teaching and learning processes. The other approach is to review against the broad aims of the concerned educational institution.

Fourth, judgments are made on academic standards and quality of learning opportunities based on the results of the review. Reports are written, disseminated, and discussed to come up with decisions on what to do with the curriculum under review. The University of British Columbia in Canada suggests a step-by-step circular procedure to design an effective curriculum:

(i) Convene faculty members,
(ii) Develop the concept,
(iii) Draft the content,
(iv) Consider the learners,
(v) Prioritize the substance,
(vi) Evaluate learning, and
(vii) organize for learning.

Convene Faculty Members

When proposing a new curriculum/course or revising an existing curriculum/course, the idea must be explored with colleagues. Questions that might be helpful in identifying who could join the dialogue include

- o Who is willing to talk about teaching?
- o Who will be involved with the course?
- o Who should be part of the discussion?

Develop the Concept

Faculty members usually have a good grasp of the courses they teach and why they are taught. What is clear to them, nonetheless, may seem vague when made public to the students and to colleagues. When preparing a course, a series of courses, or university-wide curricular objectives, it is useful first to establish a clear understanding of the course. A very helpful way to do this is to ask and answer relevant questions about the important aspects of the "what" and "why" of any course. Some guide questions may include

- o What is the critical idea, skill, or attitude that students must learn from the course?
- o How will this course improve the present program?
- o What are the specific problem(s) this course is meant to address?
- o Why should this course be included in the departmental and program offerings?

Draft the Content

Having deliberated on the concept and how it will fit, the question now becomes, exactly what:

(i) knowledge,

(ii) skills, and

(iii) attitudes or beliefs the concerned educational institution wants its students to learn.

Options may include wanting students to understand concepts or master ideas, to be able to critique established ideas and formulate something better, or to demonstrate the ability to follow a procedure. Attitudes or beliefs may focus on personal growth and the appreciation of certain ideas. Possible content may consist of all suggestions of individual faculty members, disciplinary strictures, degree program requirements, and university objectives. The end result is a pool of rich ideas from which the course will be structured.

Consider the Students

Courses/Subjects are taught to students who enroll/ take them with both homogeneous and heterogeneous levels of knowledge, skills, and attitudes. Since the aim of the curriculum is to build on what they already know, thus helping them reach new levels of competence, it is important to know what they know, which is helpful in determining course level and the necessity of prerequisites. Some useful questions to ask are

- o Who should take the course/subject?

- o What should they know, be able to do, and believe before they take the course/subject?
- o Who else may take the course/subject?
- o What will they most likely know, be able to do, and believe before they take the course/subject?

Prioritize Topics

After the possible substance has been gathered and the potential student identified, topics for inclusion in any course/subject must be prioritized. Establishing a ranking system not only helps in identifying the course/subject content, but also provides areas of enrichment for students or possibilities of further course development. Useful questions include

- o What must a student know, be able to do, or believe as a result of this course?
- o What might be nice to know, but not as essential?
- o What is redundant?
- o What is less relevant? Or irrelevant?

Evaluate Learning

The evaluation of the course, if properly designed, provides the operational definition of the course. As such, the "what", "when" and "why" of course evaluations are essential in any type of assessment.

Evaluations are the most powerful feedback to teaching and learning instruments and it is necessary to begin immediately to determine how to know what students are learning.

Evaluations should be focused and specific. If the goal is to make students learn to think, then thinking is evaluated. Similarly, if the goal is for students to learn a skill, evaluation should require demonstration of the skill. Learning goals related to changes in attitudes and beliefs are obviously more difficult to evaluate. Such evaluations are usually derived through feedback from their peers, colleagues, and co-workers.

Before structuring how a course is to be taught, it is best to decide if it is appropriate for students to compose a term paper, do a synopsis of a journal article, critique a chapter of a book or the entire book, make an oral report, answer a quiz or examination, prepare a role-play, analyse a case, solve a problem, or answer ambiguous multiple choice questions. Other useful questions:

- o How frequently should evaluation be conducted?
- o What should be the weighting of various evaluations?
- o How will fairness be monitored?

Organize for learning. Once the content of learning has been formulated, it is imperative to think about how to make this knowledge and these skills, attitudes, and beliefs accessible to students. Teaching methods should be selected on the basis of how students can learn most effectively and efficiently what the concerned educational institution wants them to learn. Some questions to ask include

- o How can the material be sequenced most effectively?
- o What will the students need to do to enable them to learn? (Will they need to talk, listen, argue, do experiments, write, compute, discuss, criticize, analyse, apply, synthesize, evaluate, or what?)
- o Which teaching methods will work best for what we want students to learn? (lecture, discussion, lab seminar, self-study, cooperative learning group, problem session, etc.)
- o What additional material will facilitate student learning? (Would a course manual, a case study, a field trip, a lab exercise, a problem set, a question sheet, or a simulation be helpful?)
- o What needs to be included in the course outline?

Strengthening Public Administration Education

In light of the agenda set by the MDGs, how can schools of public administration make themselves more relevant? What must public administration students know? What should be taught? In sum, what is the appropriate program of instruction in support of the MDGs?. Learning competencies in the study and practice of public administration need to emphasize the following:

- o Communicating the MDGs to leaders, policy makers, service providers, and citizens;

- o Generating and sustaining policy and institutional commitment;
- o Building partnerships and networks;
- o Translating the MDGs into specific actions that can be taken at the national, subnational, community, and family levels;
- o Identifying the process and implementation arrangements for achieving the MDGs;
- o Benchmarking, monitoring, evaluating, and reporting progress on the MDGs;
- o Generating and allocating resources for the MDGs; and
- o Promoting and managing institutional and organizational development.

Some fundamental issues need to be addressed to improve existing curriculum designs in public administration. First, the MDGs need to be integrated into academic curricula of public administration. A survey conducted by this author involving 102 participants in the recent national conference of the Association of Schools of Public Administration in the Philippines reveals low levels of awareness of the MDGs among the participants before attending the said conference and a desire on their part to learn tools and techniques for achieving the MDGs.

Second, curriculum development needs to be more systematic, researchbased, and oriented toward addressing student learning needs. As a matter of practice and norm, the teacher has complete flexibility and discretion in what themes or topics to include in his/her course.

The teaching methods, course references or readings list, and course requirements are likewise decided by the teacher. Previous course syllabi or the experience of having studied the same subject before serves as a guide in designing and delivering the course. There are no explicit guidelines or standards to follow in teaching the subjects. Institutional mechanisms for instructional supervision or peer review-which are key in ensuring quality and high academic standards-are scarce, if not nonexistent. In the absence of written guidelines, newcomers may find it difficult to teach.

Academic curricula commonly lack efficient organization of subjects. In addition to the vague vertical and horizontal integration of subjects, the curriculum is unclear as to relative emphasis that needs to given to an "agreed" set of topics (e.g., what topics should be discussed and how much time should be given to discussing each).

The lack of clarity and specificity of learning objectives and outcomes can create problems in delivering instruction and assessing teaching/learning. Third, most academic curricula in public administration tend to be subject-centred. The logical structure and sequence of courses and topics of academic curricula are greatly influenced by textbooks or references. Too often, curriculum designs have been oversimplified and reduced to a mere list of courses with the corresponding academic credits that must be accrued over a prescribed period of time. Even worse, such a list has been copied or drawn from other schools perceived to be leaders in the field. Written and explicit curriculum guidelines are rather uncommon.

When the curriculum is subject-centred, there is a tendency for lessons to be fragmented, to the extent that students find it difficult to appreciate the inter-connectedness of the different subjects studied. The courses also generally tend to be detached from concerns and events of the real world. A study shows that graduates and students clamour for more practical examples.

Degree programs are usually shaped by what the school wants to teach instead of what the student needs to learn or what the larger community demands. Many programs of instruction favour passive concepts of learning, which rely heavily on lectures and oral reports. Fourth, curriculum objectives should be made more specific and measurable.

Similarly, the learning objectives and outcomes should be clearly articulated. The contents and instructional strategies will therefore be organized around the desired learning objectives and outcomes. The statement of objectives and outcomes also serves as the reference points to measure learning. The desired curriculum must be properly disseminated with adequate guidelines and standards to implement it.

In a recent curriculum study, content analysis of course syllabi indicates varying interpretations of public administration courses among the faculty members (Mangahas 2004). Course requirements for the same subjects vary according to the teacher. The study also points out wide variations in the number and emphasis of course topics or sessions for a course being taught by different teachers. Teaching and learning inputs similarly vary.

Issues have therefore been raised regarding the validity and fairness of questions during the examinations. Summary and formative forms of evaluating learning, such as examinations, should be congruent with what has been taught to the students. The quality of current degree programs in public administration can be further strengthened by putting in place reasonable, consistent, and objective standards for providing teaching/learning inputs. Improving the curriculum is absolutely a step in the right direction by aiming to provide quality education in public administration and governance.

Given the challenges facing public administration education in this country, the Association of Schools of Public Administration in the Philippines should be able to provide leadership in standards setting, curriculum development, and measurement of learning outcomes.

7

Administration in Public Sector

The public sector is the part of economic and administrative life that deals with the delivery of goods and services by and for the government, whether national, regional or local/municipal. Examples of public sector activity range from delivering social security, administering urban planning and organising national defences. The organization of the public sector (public ownership) can take several forms, including:

- o Direct administration funded through taxation; the delivering organisation generally has no specific requirement to meet commercial success criteria, and production decisions are determined by government.
- o Publicly owned corporations (in some contexts, especially manufacturing, "State-owned enterprises"); which differ from direct administration in that they have greater commercial freedoms and are expected to operate according to commercial criteria, and production decisions are not generally taken by government (although goals may be set for them by government).
- o Partial outsourcing (of the scale many businesses do, e.g. for IT services), is considered a public sector model.

A borderline form is:

- o Complete outsourcing or contracting out, with a privately owned corporation delivering the entire service on behalf of government. This may be considered a mixture of private sector operations with public ownership of assets, although in some forms the private sector's control and/or risk is so great that the service may no longer be considered part of the public sector.

The decision about what are proper matters for the public sector as opposed to the private sector is probably the single most important dividing line among socialist, liberal, conservative, and libertarian political philosophy, with (broadly) socialists preferring greater state involvement, libertarians favouring minimal state involvement, and conservatives and liberals favouring state involvement in some aspects of the society but not others.

Public Services

Public services is a term usually used to mean services provided by government to its citizens, either directly (through the public sector) or by financing private provision of services. The term is associated with a social consensus (usually expressed through democratic elections) that certain services should be available to all, regardless of income. Even where public services are neither publicly provided nor publicly financed, for social and political reasons they are usually subject to regulation going beyond that applying to most economic sectors. Public services is also a course that can be studied at college and/or university. These courses can lead entry in to the: police, ambulance and fire services. It is also an alternative term for civil service.

Sectors

Public services tend to be those considered so essential to modern life that for moral reasons their universal provision should be guaranteed, and they may be associated with fundamental human rights (such as the right to water). An example of a service which is not generally considered an essential public service is hairdressing. In modern, developed countries the term public services often includes:

o education

o public transportation

o broadcasting and communications

o electricity and gas

- o fire service
- o healthcare
- o police service
- o waste management
- o water services

Characteristics

A public service may sometimes have the characteristics of a public good (being non-rivalrous and non-excludable), but most are merit goods, that is, services which may (according to prevailing social norms) be under-provided by the market. In most cases public services are services, i.e. they do not involve manufacturing of goods such as nuts and bolts. They may be provided by local or national monopolies, especially in sectors which are natural monopolies. They may involve outputs that are hard to attribute to specific individual effort and/or hard to measure in terms of key characteristics such as quality. They often require high levels of training and education. They may attract people with a public service ethos who wish to give something to the wider public or community through their work and are prepared to work harder for less pay as a result. (John Kenneth Galbraith has looked at the role of such "public virtue" in economic growth.)

History

Historically, the widespread provision of public services in developed countries usually began in the late nineteenth century, often with the municipal development of gas and water services. Later, other services such as electricity and healthcare began to be provided by governments. In most developed countries such services are still provided by local or national government, the biggest exceptions being the U.S. and the UK, where private provision is more significant. Nonetheless, such privately-provided public services are often strongly regulated, for example (in the US) by Public Utility Commissions. In developing countries public services tend to be much less well developed. Water services, for example, may only be available to the wealthy middle class. For political reasons the service is often subsidised, which reduces the finance available for expansion to poorer communities.

PUBLIC OWNERSHIP

Public ownership (also called government ownership, state ownership or state property) refers to government ownership of any asset, industry, or corporation at any level, national, regional or local (municipal); or, it may refer to common (full-community) non-state ownership. The process of bringing an asset into public ownership is called Nationalization or Municipalization. A government owned corporation (sometimes state-owned enterprise, SOE) may resemble a not-for-profit corporation as it may not be required to generate a profit; although governments may also use profitable entities they own to support the general budget. SOE's may or may not be expected to operate in a broadly commercial manner and may or may not have to face competitive tendering. The creation of a government-owned corporation (corporatization) from other forms of government ownership may be a precursor to privatization.

Arguments for and Against

For:

- o Public Services: Some services, such as defence, cannot be provided by the private sector directly-only a government system of taxation can finance them. Others (merit goods), such as education, can be under-provided by the private sector (according to social standards concerning access to them).
- o Essential Services: In the case of an essential service-particularly one on which lives may depend-Nationalization may ensure the continuation of this service regardless of commercial or environmental pressure (saving lives is not always profitable). Furthermore, there may be externalities which mean it is in the interests of all to ensure a good service is available to everyone, even beyond moral concerns.
- o Efficiency: In natural monopolies, competition is wasteful, and will tend to be eliminated by competitive forces (leading to a private monopoly or oligopoly). A public sector monopoly can be held to account via democratically-elected governments, in a way in which a private monopoly

cannot. (A private monopoly may be subject to regulation, but this may be an inefficient way of securing the public interest.)

- o Accountability: As mentioned above, while a governmental monopoly is nonetheless still a monopoly, it is answerable to the electorate rather than a small group of shareholders. (e.g. if the telephone service is nationalised, voters can bring pressure onto the government to provide better services, and parliament may have the power to sack anyone responsible for a reduction in the quality of service).
- o Consumer Interests: Public ownership can protect consumer interests in sectors where competition is low, where choices are important but made infrequently, and/ or where consumers do not have the expertise to make good decisions (such as in health care).
- o Common Good: A profitable nationalised industry contributes with its profits directly to the common wealth of the whole country, rather than to the wealth of a subset of its population.
- o Financial Security: Public sector institutions have access to finance at government interest rates, which are (almost) always lower than even the most financially secure private sector firms, because the government cannot go bankrupt, which means less risk to the lender.
- o Work Ethic: Employees may be more inclined to view their work positively if it is directed by a management appointed by a government that they have a say in electing, rather than a management representing a shareholding minority. Also, they may gain intrinsic satisfaction knowing their work is important and essential for society as a whole. There has been discussion of a public service ethos which makes public sector workers work harder than they would for a private employer.
- o Equity: Public ownership can help prevent extreme imbalances of wealth.

Against:

- o Waste: Government ownership may lead to waste (x-inefficiency) if it proves unable to motivate management and personnel through appropriate incentives, including appropriate pay and threat of redundancy.

- o Consumer Choice: Public ownership in an industry which could be competitive in private hands may stifle innovation if proper incentives are not provided by the government. Consumer choice may be reduced and there may be no alternative sources-and no catalysts for alternative sources- of goods or services that better meet consumer preferences.
- o Mis-investment/over-investment: Public ownership of profitable services may lead to "gold-plating" (over-investment in assets) if decisions are driven by engineering ideals and not efficiency concerns.
- o Unprofitable Companies Survive: Public ownership of a loss-making service or industry (such as flu vaccines) may inhibit the changes needed to ensure long-term profitability (or permit bankruptcy). This may mean subsidising unnecessary losses indefinitely.
- o Misallocations of Labour and Money: The government may be inefficient in running production, trading, or service operations, in the sense of causing misallocations of labour and capital, with consequent reductions in the standard of living and economic growth.
- o Accountability: Accountability to the market may be eliminated, and accountability through government may be an insufficient replacement, particularly if an industry or service does not have a high public profile or if the government is not democratic.
- o Influenced by Politics: Decision-making in the public sector may be prone to interference from politicians for political or populist reasons. The industry may be over-staffed in order to reduce unemployment; it may be forced to conduct transactions or actions in certain areas in order to win local votes; it may be forced to manipulate its prices in order to control inflation. Of course, some of these measures may be considered positive rather than negative, but if they are not taken properly, in the long run they are likely to be an inefficient way to meet the desired goals.

- o Source of Income Sometimes governments are accused for overcharging for products where they hold a monopoly, thus utilising them as an additional source of income, or hidden tax.

Government

A government is a body that has the authority to make and the power to enforce laws within a civil, corporate, religious, academic, or other organization or group. In its broadest sense, "to govern" means to administer or supervise, whether over a state, a set group of people, or a collection of assets. The word government is ultimately derived from the Greek (kybernan), which means "to steer" or "to control".

Typically, "the government" refers to the executive function of the state. In many countries (particularly those having parliamentary systems), the government refers to the executive branch of government or a specifically named executive, such as the Blair government (compare to the administration as in the Bush administration in U.S. usage). In countries using the Westminster system, the party in government will also usually control the legislature. Forms of Government: Governments are often classified according to the number of people who hold political power.

- o In Autocracies one individual holds all the power.
- o In Oligarchies political power is held by a small group of individuals who share interests. For example a plutocracy is composed of the wealthiest members of society.
- o Democracies are governments where the people as a whole hold political power. It may be exercised by them (direct democracy), or through representatives chosen by them (representative democracy).

The lines between some of the above forms of government can sometimes be ambiguous. For example, during the 19th century, most self-proclaimed "democracies" restricted voting rights to a minority of the population (e.g. property-owning males). This could qualify them as oligarchies rather than democracies. On the other hand, the voting minority was often quite large (20-30% of the population) and its members did not form the compact group with common interests that is the hallmark of most oligarchies. Thus, this form of government occupied a space between democracy and oligarchy as they are understood today.

Ideas about the Origin of Government

There are a wide range of theories about the reasons for establishing governments. The four major ones are briefly described below. Note that they do not always fully oppose each other-it is possible for a person to subscribe to a combination of ideas from two or more of these theories.

Force Theory

Many political philosophies that are opposed to the existence of a government (such as Anarchism, Nihilism, and to a lesser extent Marxism), as well as others, emphasize the historical roots of governments-the fact that governments, along with private property, originated from the authority of warlords and petty despots who took, by force, certain patches of land as their own (and began exercising authority over the people living on that land). Thus, it is argued that governments exist to enforce the will of the strong and oppress the weak, maintaining and protecting the privilege of a ruling class. It states that the government emerged when all the people of an area were brought under the authority of one person or group.

Order and Tradition

The various forms of conservatism, by contrast, generally see the government as a positive force that brings order out of chaos, establishes laws to end the "war of all against all", encourages moral virtue while punishing vice, and respects tradition. Sometimes, in this view, the government is seen as something ordained by a higher power, as in the divine right of kings, which human beings have a duty to obey.

Natural Rights

Natural rights are the basis for the theory of government shared by most branches of liberalism (including libertarianism). In this view, human beings are born with certain natural rights, and governments are established strictly for the purpose of protecting those rights. What the natural rights actually are is a matter of dispute among liberals; indeed, each branch of liberalism has its own set of rights that it considers to be natural, and these rights are sometimes mutually exclusive with the rights supported by other liberals. As a result, there is some debate between natural rights theorists, ranging from modern writers such as Tibor Machan to Enlightenment thinkers such as Locke, Kant, or Jefferson.

Social Contract

One of the most influential theories of government in the past two hundred years has been the social contract, on which modern democracy and most forms of socialism are founded. The social contract theory holds that governments are created by the people in order to provide for collective needs (such as safety from crime, poverty, illiteracy) that cannot be properly satisfied using purely individual means. Governments thus exist for the purpose of serving the needs and wishes of the people, and their relationship with the people is clearly stipulated in a "social contract" (a constitution and a set of laws) which both the government and the people must abide by. If a majority is unhappy, it may change the social contract. If a minority is unhappy, it may persuade the majority to change the contract, or it may opt out of it by emigration or secession. This theory is based on the idea that all men live in a state of nature which is not ideal to perfect harmony. It is also an agreement among the members of an organized society or between the governed and the government defining and limiting the rights and duties of each. Thomas Hobbes, John Locke, Jean-Jacques Rousseau are three of the most famous philosophers of contractarianism. Today, natural rights are the basis for many issues involving the constitution and ones right to privacy under the government.

Governmental Operations

Governments concern themselves with regulating and administering many areas of human activity, such as trade, education, or medicine. Governments also employ different methods to maintain the established order, such as secrecy, police and military forces (particularly under despotism, see also police state), making agreements with other states, and maintaining support within the state. Typical methods of maintaining support and legitimacy include providing the infrastructure for administration, justice, transport, communication, social welfare, etc.; claiming support from deities; providing benefits to elites; providing shops for important posts within the state; limiting the power of the state through laws and constitutions; and appealing to nationalism. Different political ideologies hold different ideas on what the government should or should not do. The modern standard unit of territory is a country. In addition to the meaning used above, the word state can refer either to a government or to its territory. Within a territory, subnational entities may have local governments which do not have the full power of a national government (for example, they will generally lack the authority to declare war or carry out diplomacy).

Size of Government

The scale to which government should exist and operate in the world is a matter of debate. Government spending in developed countries varies considerably but generally makes up between about 30% and 70% of their GDP. One major exception is the United States, where central government spending takes up less than 20% of GDP. World Government: Some speculate that technological changes such as the Internet and the global English language would bring a World Government into existence. Some consider some governments such as the European Commission as trends towards such a system; however, others do not see this as possible.

Ownership

Ownership is the state or fact of exclusive possession or control of property, which may be an object, land/real estate, intellectual property or some other kind of property.

Ownership is the key building block in the development of the capitalist socioeconomic system. The concept of ownership has existed for thousands of years and in all cultures. Over the millennia, however, and across cultures what is considered eligible to be property and how that property is regarded culturally is very different. Ownership is the basis for many other concepts that form the foundations of ancient and modern societies such as money, trade, debt, bankruptcy, the criminality of theft and private vs. public property.

The process and mechanics of ownership are fairly complex since one can gain, transfer and lose ownership of property in a number of ways. To acquire property one can purchase it with money, trade it for other property, receive it as a gift, steal it, find it, make it or homestead it. One can transfer or lose ownership of property by selling it for money, exchanging it for other property, giving it as a gift, being robbed of it, misplacing it, or having it stripped from one's ownership through legal means such as eviction, foreclosure and seizure.

Ownership is self-propagating in that if an object is owned by someone, any additional goods produced by using that object will also be owned by the same person. If one finds an object, one can legitimately take ownership of that object as long as no one claims to have previously lost that object. Some jurisdictions place time restraints on finding lost property before that property becomes fair game for anyone to claim ownership of once found. Such is the case of the gold found in the sunken SS Republic. The SS Republic steamship sank off the coast of Georgia in 1865 and lost thousands of gold coins and bars to the ocean. In 2003 Odyssey Marine Exploration, Inc. discovered the ship and was awarded possession of the gold after the insurance company that had paid off damages to the original owners claimed they were the rightful owners of the gold.

What can You Own?

Personal Property (Objects)

Personal property is a type of property. In the common law systems personal property may also be called chattels. Under the common law, the only way to gain title to chattels was by writing one's name on them with a permanent marker. It is distinguished from real property, or real estate. In the civil law systems personal property is often called movable property or movables-any property that can be moved from one location or another. This term is in distinction with immovable property or immovables, such as land and buildings. Personal property may be classified in a variety of ways, such as goods, money, negotiable instruments, securities, and intangible assets including choses in action.

Land Ownership

Real estate or immovable property is a legal term (in some jurisdictions) that encompasses land along with anything permanently affixed to the land, such as buildings. Real estate (immovable property) is often considered synonymous with real property (also sometimes called realty), in contrast with personal property (also sometimes called chattel or personalty). However, for technical purposes, some people prefer to distinguish real estate, referring to the land and fixtures themselves, from real property, referring to ownership rights over real estate. The terms real estate and real property are used primarily in common law, while civil law jurisdictions refer instead to immovable property.

In law, the word real means relating to a thing (from Latin res, matter or thing), as distinguished from a person. Thus the law broadly distinguishes between [real property] (land and anything affixed to it) and [personal property] (everything else, e.g., clothing, furniture, money). The conceptual difference was between immovable property, which would transfer title along with the land, and movable property, which a person would retain title to. (The word is not derived from the notion of land having historically been "royal" property. The word royal - and its Spanish cognate real - come from the unrelated Latin word rex, meaning king.)

With the development of private property ownership, real estate has become a major area of business.

Corporations and Legal Entities

An individual or group of individuals can own corporations and other legal entities. A legal entity is a legal construct through which the law allows a group of natural persons to act as if it were an individual for certain purposes. Some companies and entities are owned privately by the individuals who registered them with the government while other companies are owned publicly.

A public company is a company owned by any member of the public who wishes to purchase stock in that company rather than by a relatively few individuals. A company that is owned by stockholders who are members of the general public and trade shares publicly, often through a listing on a stock exchange. Ownership is open to anyone who has the money and inclination to buy shares in the company. It is differentiated from privately held companies where the shares are held by a small group of individuals often members of one or a small group of families or otherwise related individuals (or other companies). For a discussion of the British and Irish variant of this type of company, see public limited company.

Intellectual Property: Intellectual (IP) property refers to a legal entitlement which sometimes attaches to the expressed form of an idea, or to some other intangible subject matter. This legal entitlement generally enables its holder to exercise exclusive rights of use in relation to the subject matter of the IP. The term intellectual property reflects the idea that this subject matter is the product of the mind or the intellect, and that IP rights may be protected at law in the same way as any other form of property.

Intellectual property laws confer a bundle of exclusive rights in relation to the particular form or manner in which ideas or information are expressed or manifested, and not in relation to the ideas or concepts themselves. It is therefore important to note that the term "intellectual property" denotes the specific legal rights which authors, inventors and other IP holders may hold and exercise, and not the intellectual work itself.

Intellectual property laws are designed to protect different forms of intangible subject matter, although in some cases there is a degree of overlap.

- copyright may subsist in creative and artistic works (e.g. books, movies, music, paintings, photographs and software), giving a copyright holder the exclusive right to control reproduction or adaptation of such works for a certain period of time.
- A patent may be granted in relation to an invention that is new, useful and not simply an obvious advancement over what exisited when the application was filed. A patent gives the holder an exclusive right to commercially exploit

the invention for a certain period of time (typically 20 years from the filing date of a patent application).

- o A trademark is a distinctive sign which is used to distinguish the products or services of one business from those of another business.
- o An industrial design right protects the form of appearance, style or design of an industrial object (e.g. spare parts, furniture or textiles).
- o A trade secret (also known as "confidential information") is an item of confidential information concerning the commercial practices or proprietary knowledge of a business.

Patents, trademarks and designs fall into a particular subset of intellectual property known as industrial property.

Like other forms of property, intellectual property (or rather the exclusive rights which subsist in the IP) can be transferred (with or without consideration) or licensed to third parties. In some jurisdictions it may also be possible to use intellectual property as security for a loan.

The basic public policy rationale for the protection of intellectual property is that IP laws facilitate and encourage disclosure of innovation into the public domain for the common good, by granting authors and inventors exclusive rights to exploit their works and invention for a limited period. However, various schools of thought are critical of the very concept of intellectual property, and some characterise IP as intellectual protectionism. There is ongoing debate as to whether IP laws truly operate to confer the stated public benefits, and whether the protection they are said to provide is appropriate in the context of innovation derived from such things as traditional knowledge and folklore, and patents for software and business methods. Manifestations of this controversy can be seen in the way different jurisdictions decide whether to grant intellectual property protection in relation to subject matter of this kind, and the North-South divide on issues of the role and scope of intellectual property laws.

Chattel Slavery: The living human body is, in most modern societies, considered something which cannot be the property of anyone but the person whose body it is. This is in contradistinction to chattel slavery. Chattel slavery is a type of slavery defined as the absolute legal ownership of a person or persons, including the legal right to buy and sell them. The slaves do not have the freedom to live life as they choose, but as they are instructed by their owners. In most countries, chattel slaves are considered as movable property. Slavery almost always occurs for the purpose of securing the labour of the slave.

Slavery is currently illegal in every country around the world, however, up until the 19th century slavery and ownership of people had existed in one form or another in nearly every society on earth.

Who Can Own Property?

Personal Ownership

In Western societies both men and women can own property, however, in some societies only adult men may own property. In other societies (such as the Haudenosaunee), property is matrilinear and passed on from mother to daughter.

Ownership by Corporations and Legal Entities

Legal entities, such as corporations, trusts, partnerships, religions, and nations (or governments) can own property in various societies past and present. Although corporations and other legal entities are owned or controlled by individuals or groups of individuals they are allowed to own their own property just as natural people are able to. The advantage in placing the ownership of an asset in the name of an entity is that the asset is protected from law suits against the owner of the entity. If the owner of the entity is personally sued the asset cannot be taken in the law suit.

When there is risk involved in the ownership of an asset as in the case of investment real estate the ownership of that asset is often made in the name of a corporate entity. Real estate property investors often form a corporation or other entity for the sole purpose of purchasing a single building. Rather than buying the building in the investor's personal name the investor will place the corporations' name on the deed. Since the corporation is a separate entity in the eyes of the law if a tenant is hurt on the premises and sues the owner of the building they are suing the corporation and not the investor. This protects the investor from losing many properties from one law suit.

Communal Ownership

Communal ownership of property occurs when a group of people share the ownership of property amongst each other. Any and every member of the group is free to use the property when they want but also those individuals agree to allow all others in the group to use the property when that person wants.

Although communal ownership of property is not as widespread as individual ownership of property both forms of ownership exist in most societies. In America, for example, national parks and publicly owned buildings such as libraries are communally owned by all Americans. In New York City a common form of real estate ownership is a cooperative (also cooperative or co-op). A co-op is a group of persons who join together, or cooperate, to own a building for mutual benefit. In an ideal communist nation the means of production of goods would be owned communally by all people of that nation.

One criticism of the concept of communal ownership is the Tragedy of the Commons where unrestricted access to a resource such as a pasture ultimately dooms the resource because of over-exploitation. This occurs because the benefits of exploitation accrue to individuals, while the costs of exploitation are distributed between all those exploiting the resource. This criticism has merit if the resource is permitted, by the community, to be exploited by the individual.

Social Stigmas

In modern Western popular culture some people (principally among the political left) believe that exclusive ownership of property underlies much social injustice, and facilitates tyranny and oppression on an individual and societal scale. Others consider the striving to achieve greater ownership of wealth as the driving factor behind human technological advancement and increasing standards of living.

Societies Without Ownership

A modern myth is that some societies, notably Native American ones, appeared to exist without the concept of personal ownership. Members of a society would feel free to take any objects they had need of, and expect them to be taken by others. Recently, however, researchers have started to question just how collectivist Native American societies really were. Citing earlier studies done by anthropologists and historians "who were able to interview tribal members who had lived in pre-reservation Indian society," they argue that in fact, "most if not all North American indigenous peoples had a strong belief in individual property rights and ownership."

These researchers further assert that Native American collectivism is a myth originating from the first encounters with tribes who, because of their hunting-orientation "did not view land as an important asset", and indeed, did not have a private property system with regards to land. The collectivist myth was initially propagated by reporters and politicians who never actually had contact with Native Americans and then made into a reality by the collectivist property rights system forced on Indians by the 1934 Indian Reorganization Act.

Ownership Society

Ownership society is a slogan for a model of society promoted by United States President George W. Bush. It takes as lead values personal responsibility, economic liberty, and the owning of property. The ownership society discussed by Bush also extends to certain proposals of specific models of health care and social security.

History

The term appears to have been used originally by President Bush (for example in a speech February 20, 2003 in Kennesaw, Georgia) as a phrase to rally support for his tax-cut proposals. From 2004 Bush supporters described the ownership society in much broader and more ambitious terms, including specific policy proposals concerning medicine, education and savings. The idea that the welfare of individuals is directly related to their ability to control their own lives and wealth, rather than relying on government transfer payments, is a long-standing one, particularly in British conservatism.

In a modern form its implementation was developed as a main plank of Thatcherism, and is traced back to David Howell, before 1970, with help from the phrase-maker Peter Drucker.

In political practice under Margaret Thatcher's administration, it was implemented by measures such as the sale at affordable prices of public housing to tenants, and privatization.

Ownership and Control: As formulated by the Cato Institute, the desiderata are that

- o patients have control of [decisions on] their personal health care,
- o parents control [i.e. have power over] their children's education, and
- o workers control [i.e. have some responsibility for the investment of, or explicit property rights in] their retirement savings.

Here the comments in brackets are an interpretation or paraphrase, consistent with a generalised idea of ownership. The conceptual link here is by means of the idea that private property, the most familiar and everyday form of ownership, is being extended. Control is closely associated with ownership in that sense.

This Cato Institute formulation is not, however, in terms of positive policies. It is more accurately a definition of ownership by taking the state out of the loop. So, for example, in health care ownership is not being defined just on the basis of informed consent.

There is no real originality, politically speaking, in the connection made between individual ownership of property and political stake-holding. This was an idea discussed in Europe and America in the eighteenth century. The novelty of the Cato Institute formulation would lie in the extrapolation. In the case of savings, for example, the extension would be an assertion of property rights in money held in savings or collected tax revenues.

Political Consequences and Unexpected Consequences

Consistently with the basic tenet, proponents of an ownership society usually support inherited wealth, and oppose inheritance taxes and wealth taxes. They are also likely to favour a pattern of property ownership based on the purchase, rather than rental, of accommodation.

The consequences for health and education are heavily dependent on details of implementation. For example, ownership in one's child's education, for a parent, might be in the form of an education voucher, a vote in the running of a school, influence on the school curriculum, or a generalised 'right' to have a child educated in line with one's own values.

One example from the UK of an unexpected or unintended consequence of government policy favouring direct share ownership, through some oversubscribed privatisation issues, was the holding of small parcels of shares by individuals numbered in millions. This broad-based ownership created an administrative overhead, for example in relation to every shareholder vote.

Quotations

We Conservatives have always passed our values from generation to generation. I believe that personal prosperity should follow the same course. I want to see wealth cascading down the generations. We do not see each generation starting out anew, with the past cut off and the future ignored. —John Major conference speech 1991.

...if you own something, you have a vital stake in the future of our country. The more ownership there is in America, the more vitality there is in America, and the more people have a vital stake in the future of this country.-President George W. Bush, June 17, 2004

Individuals are empowered by freeing them from dependence on government handouts and making them owners instead, in control of their own lives and destinies. In the ownership society, patients control their own health care, parents control their own children's education, and workers control their retirement savings. Cato Institute

"Many people don't have the time, inclination, or expertise necessary to take full responsibility for their own well-being in areas that are so complex as assuring they have sufficient income for retirement or choosing a health plan appropriate for their circumstances," says Robert Reischauer, president of the Urban Institute, a Washington think tank.

Government-owned Corporation

A government corporation or government-owned corporation is a legal entity created by a government to exercise some of the powers of the government. It may resemble a not-for-profit corporation as it has no need or goal of satisfying the shareholders with return on their investment through price increase or dividends.

In the United States, businesses that are government owned include Amtrak, Tennessee Valley Authority, Corporation for Public Broadcasting and the United States Postal Service. Many states have government owned businesses for operations as well. Generally speaking, a statute passed by a legislature specifically sets up a government owned company in order to undertake a specific public purpose with public funds or public property.

In the People's Republic of China, there are a number of different corporate forms which result in a mixture of public and private capital. In PRC terminology, a state owned enterprise refers to a particular corporate form, which is increasingly being replaced by the listed company.

In monarchical Commonwealth countries, particularly Canada, country-wide government corporations often use the style "Crown corporation". Equivalent terms include State-Owned Enterprises and the Crown entities in New Zealand. Examples of Crown corporations include the CBC in Canada and Air Canada before it underwent privatisation. Cabinet ministers (Ministers of the Crown) often control the shares in such public corporations. At the level of local government, territorial or other authorities may set up government corporations such as "Local Authority Trading Enterprises" (LATEs).

In Japan, Japan Post is currently partially owned by the government, but will soon be sold to the public. JR, NTT and

Japan Tobacco were formerly owned by the government. In most OPEC countries, the governments prefer to own the oil companies operating on their soil. A notable example is the Saudi national oil company, Saudi Aramco, which the Saudi government bought in 1988 and changed its name from Arabian American Oil Company to Saudi Arabian Oil Company. Saudi government also owns and operates Saudi Arabian Airlines, and owns 70% of SABIC, as well as many other companies. They are, however, being publicized gradually.

GOVERNMENT-LINKED COMPANIES

A Government Linked Company (GLC) is a corporate entity that may private or public (listed on a stock exchange) where an existing government owns a stake using a holding company. There are two main definitions of GLCs are dependent on the proportion of the corporate entity a government owns. One definition purports that a company is classified as a GLC if a government owns an effective controlling interest (>50%), while the second definition suggests that any corporate entity that has a government as a shareholder is a GLC.

PUBLIC COMPANY

A public company is a company owned by the public rather than by relatively few individuals. There are two different meanings for this term.

The first is a company that is owned by stockholders who are members of the general public and trade shares publicly, often through a listing on a stock exchange. The first company to issue shares is thought to be the Dutch East India Company in 1602. Ownership is open to anyone that has the money and inclination to buy shares in the company. It is differentiated from privately held companies where the shares are held by a small group of individuals, who are often members of one or a small group of families or otherwise related individuals, or other companies. The variant of this type of company in the United Kingdom and Ireland is known as a public limited company.

The second is a government-owned corporation. This meaning of a "public company" comes from the tradition of public ownership of assets and interests by and for the people as a whole, and is the less-common meaning in the United States.

"Publicly owned company" can also have either meaning, although in the United Kingdom it will usually refer to ownership by national, regional or local government.

Public versus Private Companies

A public company has several advantages. It is able to raise funds and capital through the sale of stock and convertible bonds. This is the reason why public corporations are so important, historically; prior to their existence, it was very difficult to obtain large amounts of capital for private enterprises. It has the ability to offer stock and stock options to directors, executives, and employees as part of compensation. This is much less advantageous if the company is required to treat stock options as an expense. Large stockholders, typically founders of the company, are able to sell off shares and get cash which they can put to other uses. In contrast, while ownership in a private corporation can also be sold, in part, determining a "fair value" that is acceptable to all parties can be difficult.

The goal of a public company is to enrich the owners of the company (the shareholders). The two ways that it does this is to distribute cash from the companies profits (known as dividends) and/or to reinvest the profits into the company to increase the intrinsic and share value of the company. In particular, since most investors are concerned about "buying low and selling high" the managers must in fact be constantly search for ways to make more money, in other words, constantly increasing profits. Besides simply increasing profits, another way to increase the stock price is to attempt to induce investors to pay more for a company's shares relative to the company's profits. Many have theorized that people will pay a higher premium for companies which have more stable profits, this theory has caused companies to diversify and form conglomerates.

A private company has several advantages. It has no requirement to publicly disclose much, if any financial information; such information could be useful to competitors. For example, Form 10-K is an annual report required by the SEC each year that is a comprehensive summary of a company's performance. Private companies do not file form 10-Ks. It is less pressured to "make the numbers"-to meet quarterly projections for sales and profits, and thus in theory able to make decisions that are best in the long-run. It spends less for certified public accountants and other bureaucratic paperwork required of public companies by government regulations. For example, the Sarbanes-Oxley Act in the United States does not apply to private companies. The wealth and income of the owners remains relatively unknown by the public. The norm is for new companies, which are typically small, to be privately owned. After a number of years, if a company has grown significantly and is profitable, or has promising prospects, there is often an initial public offering and the company becomes public. Less common, but not unknown, is for a public company to pay cash to its shareholders and become private. This is typically done through a leverage buyout. Public companies can also become private when purchased by a larger company that is private.

Trading and Valuation

The shares of a public company are traded on a stock exchange. The value or "size" of a public company is called its market capitalization, a term which is often shortened to "market cap". This is calculated as the number of shares outstanding (as opposed to authorized but not necessarily issued) times the price per share. For example, a company with two million shares outstanding and a price per share of $40 would have a market capitalization of $80 million.

PRIMARY MARKET

The primary market is that part of the capital markets that deals with the issuance of new securities. Companies, governments or public sector institutions can obtain funding through the sale of a new stock or bond issue. This is typically done through a syndicate of securities dealers. The process of selling new issues to investors is called underwriting. In the case of a new stock issue, this sale is called an initial public offering (IPO). Dealers earn a commission that is built into the price of the security offering, though it can be found in the prospectus.

PUBLIC BENEFIT CORPORATION

A public benefit corporation is a public corporation chartered by a state designed to perform some public service. A public authority is a type of public benefit corporation that takes on a more bureaucratic role, such as the maintenance of public infrastructure, that often has broad powers to regulate or maintain public property.

Authorities borrow from both municipal corporations law (that is, the laws responsible for the creation of cities, towns, and other forms of local government) and private corporations law. Other public benefit corporations resemble private non-profit organizations, and take on roles that private corporations might otherwise perform. These corporations often operate in heavily regulated industries, such as broadcasting and transportation.

Corporations such as these are often found in common law jurisdictions such as Commonwealth countries, including Canadian provinces and U.S. states.

Origins: Although many associate corporations, sometimes negatively, with private business, corporations in theory began as means to serve public purposes. Corporate theory has its roots in primarily government and religious institutions, where the institution itself is identifiable independently of its membership's mortality. For example, if the Pope dies, the Catholic Church continues to exist, just as it continues to exist as generations pass on and get replaced by new members.

Public benefit corporations likely have their direct roots in mercantile capitalism. In the early days of European exploration and colonization, a government or monarch would sometimes grant a charter to an entity allowing it to incorporate and make potentially risky investments. While certainly not public benefit corporations by today's standards, entities such as the Massachusetts Bay Company, Hudson Bay Company, and the Dutch East India Company arguably are early prototypes of publicly-chartered (in this case, crown-chartered) corporations successfully making risky investments.

The first public authority on record is the Port of London Authority, established 1908. According to the Port of London Acts

The Authority is a public trust established to "administer, preserve and improve the Port of London." The goal was to create an entity that would be run self-sufficiently like a private company yet remain under the control of the government. The name Authority is derived from the founding act of Parliament which repeatedly stated that "Authority is hereby given..."

Incorporation and Powers

Public benefit corporations are generally governed by boards of directors, which are appointed, rather than elected, and, internally, reflect bureaucratic forms. The corporation is government-owned and performs a specific, narrow function for the public good.

Public benefit corporations are most often created by statute. In many Commonwealth countries, public benefit corporations continue to receive charters from the British monarchy. In the United States, they receive their charters usually from states, but possibly from the federal government.

Public authorities are usually created with a specific mandate, such as the construction of bridges, mass transit, etc. Unlike departments or ministries of the state, these corporations usually are enabled by statute to raise revenues through bond issues.

Non-governmental Organization

The term non-governmental organization (NGO) is used in a variety of ways all over the world and, depending on the context in which it is used, can refer to many different types of organizations. In its broadest sense, a non-governmental organization is one that is not directly part of the structure of government. Anheier places the number of internationally operating NGOs at 40,000. National numbers are even higher: The United States has an estimated 2 million NGOs, most of them formed in the past 30 years. Russia has 4,000 NGOs. India is estimated to have between 1 and 2 million NGOs. In Kenya alone, some 240 NGOs come into existence every year.

International Red Cross and Red Crescent Movement is the world's largest group of humanitarian NGOs. Though voluntary associations of citizens have existed throughout history, NGOs along the lines seen today, especially on the international level, have developed in the past two centuries. One of the first such organizations, the International Committee of the Red Cross, was founded in 1863.

The phrase "non-governmental organization" came into use with the establishment of the United Nations Organization in 1945 with provisions in Article 71 of Chapter 10 of the United Nations Charter for a consultative role for organizations that are neither governments nor member states - see Consultative Status. The definition of "international NGO" (INGO) is first given in resolution 288 (X) of ECOSOC on February 27, 1950: it is defined as "any international organisation that is not founded by an international treaty".

The vital role of NGOs and other "major groups" in sustainable development was recognized in Chapter 27 of Agenda 21, leading to revised arrangements for consultative relationship between the United Nations and non-governmental organizations.

Globalization during the 20th century gave rise to the importance of NGOs. Many problems could not be solved within a nation. International treaties and international organizations such as the World Trade Organization were perceived as being too centred on the interests of capitalist enterprises. In an attempt to counterbalance this trend, NGOs have developed to emphasize humanitarian issues, developmental aid and sustainable development. A prominent example of this is the World Social Forum which is a rival convention to the World Economic Forum held annually in January in Davos, Switzerland. The fifth World Social Forum in Porto Alegre, Brazil, in January 2005 was attended by representatives from more than 1,000 NGOs.

Evolutionary Stages of Development NGOs

Three stages or generations of NGO evolution have been identified by Korten's (1990) Three Generations of Voluntary Development Action. First, the typical development NGO focuses on relief and welfare, and delivers relief services directly to beneficiaries. Examples are the distribution of food, shelter or health services. The NGO notices immediate needs and responds to them. NGOs in the second generation are oriented towards small-scale, self-reliant local development. At this evolutionary stage, NGOs build the capacities of local communities to meet their needs through 'self reliant local action'. Korten calls the third generation 'sustainable systems development'. At this stage, NGOs try to advance changes in policies and institutions at a local, national and international level; they move away from their operational service providing role towards a catalytic role. The NGO is starting to develop from a relief NGO to a development NGO.

Types of NGOs: Apart from 'NGO' oftentimes alternative terms are used as for example independent sector, volunteer sector, civic society, grassroots organizations, transnational social movement organizations, private voluntary organizations, self-help organizations and non-state actors (NSAs). Non-governmental organizations are an heterogeneous group. A long list of acronyms has developed around the term 'NGO'.

These include:

- o INGO stands for international NGO, such as CARE, Helvetas (Swiss Association for International Cooperation), RESPECT Refugiados, International Alert, ADFA-India ZOA Refugee Care, Medair and Mercy Corps;
- o BINGO is short for business-oriented international NGO;
- o RINGO is an abbreviation of religious international NGO such as Catholic Relief Services or stands for Research and Independent Non-governmental organization;
- o ENGO, short for environmental NGO, such as Global 2000;
- o CONGOs are government-operated NGOs, which may have been set up by governments to look like NGOs in order to qualify for outside aid or promote the interests of the government in question;
- o QUANGOs are quasi-autonomous non-governmental organisations, such as the W3C and the International Organization for Standardization (ISO), which is actually not purely an NGO, since its membership is by nation, and each nation is represented by what the ISO Council determines to be the 'most broadly representative' standardization body of a nation. Now, such a body might

in fact be a non-governmental organization-for example, the United States is represented in ISO by the American National Standards Institute, which is independent of the federal government. However, other countries can be represented by national governmental agencies-this is the trend in Europe.

There are also numerous classifications of NGOs. The typology the World Bank uses divides them into Operational and Advocacy : The primary purpose of an operational NGO is the design and implementation of development-related projects. One categorization that is frequently used is the division into 'relief-oriented' or 'development-oriented' organizations; they can also be classified according to whether they stress service delivery or participation; or whether they are religious and secular; and whether they are more public or private-oriented. Operational NGOs can be community-based, national or international.

The primary purpose of an Advocacy NGO is to defend or promote a specific cause. As opposed to operational project management, these organizations typically try to raise awareness, acceptance and knowledge by lobbying, press work and activist events.

USAID refers to NGOs as private voluntary organizations. However many scholars have argued that this definition is highly problematic as many NGOs are in fact state and corporate funded and managed projects with professional staff.

PURPOSES

NGOs exist for a variety of purposes, usually to further the political or social goals of their members or funders. Examples include improving the state of the natural environment, encouraging the observance of human rights, improving the welfare of the disadvantaged, or representing a corporate agenda. However, there are a huge number of such organizations and their goals cover a broad range of political and philosophical positions. This can also easily be applied to private schools and athletic organizations.

Methods: NGOs vary in their methods. Some act primarily as lobbyists, while others conduct programs and activities primarily.

For instance, such an NGO as Oxfam, concerned with poverty alleviation, might provide needy people with the equipment and skills they need to find food and clean drinking water. Another example of a NGO is Amnesty International, the largest Human rights organization in the world. It forms a global community of human rights defenders with more than 1.8 million members, supporters and subscribers in over 150 countries and territories.

Public Relations

Non-governmental organizations need healthy relationships with the public to meet their goals. Foundations and charities use sophisticated public relations campaigns to raise funds and employ standard lobbying techniques with governments. Interest groups may be of political importance because of their ability to influence social and political outcomes. At times NGOs seek to mobilize public support.

Consulting

Many international NGOs have a consultative status with United Nations agencies relevant to their area of work. As an example, the Third World Network has a consultative status with the UN Conference on Trade and Development (UNCTAD) and the UN Economic and Social Council (ECOSOC). While in 1946, only 41 NGOs had consultative status with the ECOSOC, by 2003 this number had risen to 2,350.

Project Management

There is an increasing awareness that management techniques are crucial to project success in non-governmental organizations. Generally, non-governmental organisations, which are private, have a community or environmental focus. They address varieties of issues such as religion, emergency aid, and humanitarian affairs. They mobilize public support and voluntary contributions for aid; they often have strong links with community groups in developing countries and they often work in areas where government-to-government aid is not possible. NGO's are accepted as a part of the international relations landscape, and while they influence national and multilateral policy-making, they are, increasingly, more directly involved in local action.

Management of NGOs

Two management trends are particularly relevant to NGOs: diversity management and participatory management. Diversity management deals with different cultures in an organization. Intercultural problems are prevalent in Northern NGOs that are engaged in developmental activities in the South. Personnel coming from a rich country are faced with a completely different approach of doing things in the target country. A participatory management style is said to be typical of NGOs. It is intricately tied to the concept of a learning organization: all people within the organization are perceived as sources for knowledge and skills. To develop the organization, individuals have to be able to contribute in the decision making process and they need to learn.

Staffing

Not all people working for non-governmental organizations are volunteers. Paid staff members typically receive lower pay than in the commercial private sector. Employees are highly committed to the aims and principles of the organization. The reasons why people volunteer are not necessarily purely altruistic, and can provide immediate benefits for themselves as well as those they serve, including skills, experience and contacts. There is some dispute as to whether expatriates should be sent to developing countries. Frequently this type of personnel is employed to satisfy a donor, who wants to see the supported project managed by someone from an industrialized country. However, the expertise these employees or volunteers may have can be counterbalanced by a number of factors: the cost of foreigners is typically higher, they have no grass-root connections in the country they are sent to and local expertise is often undervalued. The NGO-sector is an important employer in terms of numbers. For example, by the end of 1995, CONCERN worldwide, an international Northern NGO working against poverty, employed 174 expatriates and just over 5,000 national staff working in ten developing countries in Africa and Asia, and in Haiti.

Funding

Large NGOs may have annual budgets in the millions of dollars. For instance, the budget of the American Association of

Retired Persons (AARP) was over $540 million dollars in 1999. Human Rights Watch spent and received US$21.7 million in 2003. Funding such large budgets demands significant fundraising efforts on the part of most NGOs. Major sources of NGO funding include membership dues, the sale of goods and services, grants from international institutions or national governments, and private donations. Several EU-grants provide funds accessible to NGOs.

Even though the term 'non-governmental organization' implies independence of governments, some NGOs depend heavily on governments for their funding. A quarter of the US$162 million income in 1998 of the famine-relief organization Oxfam was donated by the British government and the EU. The Christian relief and development organization World Vision US collected US$55 million worth of goods in 1998 from the American government. Nobel Prize winner Medecins Sans Frontires (MSF) (known in English as 'Doctors Without Borders') gets 46 percent of its income from government sources.

Monitoring and Controlling NGOs

In March 2000 report on United Nations Reform priorities, U.N. Secretary General Kofi Annan wrote in favour of international humanitarian intervention, arguing that the international community has a 'right to protect' citizens of the world against ethnic cleansing, genocide and crimes against humanity. On the heels of the report, the Canadian government launched the Responsibility to Protect R2P project, outlining the issue of humanitarian intervention. While the R2P doctrine has wide applications, among the more controversial has been the Canadian government's use of R2P to justify its intervention and support of the coup in Haiti.

Years after R2P, the World Federalist Movement, an organization that supports "the creation of democratic global structures accountable to the citizens of the world and call for the division of international authority among separate agencies" has launched Responsibility to Protect-Engaging Civil Society R2PCS. The project, which is a collaboration of the WFM and Canadian government, aims to bring NGOs into lockstep with the principles outlined under the original R2P project. NGO Monitor is a conservative pro-Israel site that aims to promote "critical debate and accountability of human rights NGOs in the Arab-Israeli conflict." The organization has successfully conducted campaigns against Oxfam and the Ford Foundation-leading to formal apologies and changes in practice-on the grounds that these organizations are too anti-Israeli. NGOWatch is a project of the American Enterprise Institute that monitors NGOs. The project is primarily a negative analysis of NGOs that are generally considered to be on the progressive side of the political spectrum.

Indian NGOs is a portal of over 20,000 NGOs who work with the corporate sector in India. This portal offers insights into how the corporate sector is using NGOs to benefit their program. In recent years, many large corporations have beefed up their Corporate Social Responsibility departments in an attempt to preempt NGO campaigns against certain corporate practices. As the logic goes, if corporations work with NGOs, NGOs will not work against corporations.

Legal Status

NGOs are not legal entities under international law, like states are. An exception is the International Committee of the Red Cross which is considered a legal entity under international law, because it is based on the Geneva Convention.

It has been argued by various critics that NGOs are subversive in outcomes but well intentioned. It is suggested that imperialism and NGOs share a fine line. One of the first modern NGOs, for example, was the American Colonization Society. Another famous example includes various Christian missionaries throughout the Americas, Asia, and Africa during colonial times.

Criticism

In general, there is an overall positive view of NGOs across various literature sources in the North. However Southern scholars often take a more critical position. Some direct complaints target operational problems, inconsistencies, misuses of funds (some high-profile), dogmatic commitments to certain assumption about economic policy etc. Some have argued that power relations between NGOs and their 'target countries' are often highly racialised. Conceptually, there is a slowly growing body of work looking at the underside of the 'Aid Industry'. Although most complaint literature is against multilateral or bilateral agencies, there are occasional criticisms of NGO operational strategies and inadvertent adverse impacts. For example it is often argued that in poorer countries Northern funded and managed NGOs tend to substitute themselves for popular movements in fora like the World Social Forum with negative consequences for the development of local civil society. Critics like Issa Shivji and James Petras have argued that NGOs are often part of contemporary imperialism. In many Southern countries, e.g. South Africa, relations between popular movements of the poor and some NGOs have become very strained.

In many developing countries with dysfunctional economies, entry into the aid-industry is the most profitable professional career path for young college-graduates. As NGOs provide services in the community for free or at subsidized rates (such as training), the private-sector is unable to evolve and compete effectively as sustainable levels. Once an NGO begins offering products or services for a fee (handicrafts, evaluations, digging wells, counselling, etc.), they will over time inevitably compete with private-sector providers of these same services. But with their donation-funding support or access to voluntary labour, they have a significant competitive advantage.

Co-option (by political or other forces), mission-drift, changing core services based on an ever changing funding landscape, transparency, accountability, moving beyond a charismatic founding leader, and donor-driven rather than self-defined strategies are some additional areas for concern. New NGOs occasionally receive 'do-gooder' complaints of engaging in action to help, without understanding the full complexity and interplay of issues, resulting in doing more harm than good. But again, in general, NGOs are viewed as a beneficial complementary source filling gaps in society not provided by the public or for-profit sectors. NGOs have also played a crucial role in upholding International Law, especially United Nations treaties. Their work continues to be the leading factor in social, and political change.

PUBLIC GOOD

In economics, a public good is a good that is non-rival. This means: consumption of the good by one individual does not reduce the amount of the good available for consumption by others. Thus, if one individual eats a cake, there is no cake left for anyone else; but breathing air or drinking water from a stream does not significantly reduce the amount of air or water available to others. The term public good is often used to refer to goods that are non-excludable as well as non-rival. This means it is not possible to exclude individuals from the good's consumption. Fresh air may be considered a public good as it is not generally possible to prevent people from breathing it. However, technically speaking such goods should be called pure public goods. These are highly theoretical definitions: in the real world there may be no such thing as an absolutely non-rival or non-excludable good; but economists think that some goods in the real world approximate closely enough for these concepts to be meaningful.

Non-rivalness and non-excludability may cause problems for the production of such goods. Specifically, some economists have argued that they may lead to instances of market failure, where uncoordinated markets are unable to provide these goods in desired quantities. These issues are known as public goods problems, and there is a good deal of debate and literature on how significant they are, and on what their solutions might be. These debates can become important to political arguments about the role of markets in the economy. More technically, public goods problems are related to the broader issue of externalities.

Terminology, and Types of Public Goods

Paul A. Samuelson is usually credited as the first economist to develop the theory of public goods. In his classic 1954 paper The Pure Theory of Public Expenditure he defined a public good, or as he called it in the paper a "collective consumption good", as follows:

> ...[goods] which all enjoy in common in the sense that each individual's consumption of such a good leads to no subtractions from any other individual's consumption of that good...

This is the property that has become known as Non-rivalness. In addition a pure public good exhibits a second property called Non-excludability: that is, it is impossible to exclude any individuals from consuming the good.

The opposite of a public good is a private good, which does not possess these properties. A loaf of bread, for example, is a private good: its owner can exclude others from using it, and once it has been consumed, it cannot be used again.

A good which is rival but non-excludable is sometimes called a common pool resource. Such goods raise similar issues to public goods: the mirror to the public goods problem for this case is sometimes called the tragedy of the commons. For example, it is so difficult to police deep sea fishing that the world's fish stocks can be seen as a non-excludable resource, but one which is finite and diminishing.

It should be emphasised that these concepts are highly theoretical. For example, the definition of non-excludability states that it is impossible to exclude individuals from consumption. In reality, perhaps any good can become excludable: for example, radio or television broadcasts have in the past been used as a classic example of non-excludable goods. But as technology has developed, it is now possible to incorrupt these signals so that anyone without a special decoder is excluded from the broadcast.

Many forms of creative works have characteristics of public goods. For example, a poem can be read by many people without reducing the consumption of that good by others; in this sense, it is non-rival. Similarly, the information in most patents can be used by any party without reducing consumption of that good by others. Creative works may be excludable in some circumstances, however: the individual who wrote the poem may decline to share it with others by not publishing it. Copyrights and patents function to encourage the creation of such non-rival goods by providing temporary monopolies, or, in the terminology of public goods, providing a legal mechanism to enforce excludability for a limited period of time. Note that for public goods, the "lost revenue" of the producer of the good is not part of the definition: a public good is a good whose consumption does not reduce any other's consumption of that good.

Private and public goods

As well as public goods there can be public bads that have negative externality effects instead of positive ones. For example, pollution or political corruption may be bads that show some of the same non-excludability and non-rivalness properties. The economic concept of public goods should not be confused with the expression "the public good", which is usually an application of a collective ethical notion of "the good" in political decision-making. Another common confusion is that public goods are goods provided by the public sector. Although it is often the case that Government is involved in producing public goods, this is not necessarily the case. Public goods may be naturally available, they may be produced by private individuals and firms, by non-state collective action, or they may not be produced at all. The theoretical concept of public goods does not distinguish with regards to the geographical region in which a good may be produced or consumed. However some theorists use the term global public good to mean a public good which is non-rival and non-excludable throughout the whole world, as opposed to a public good which exists in just one national area. Knowledge is held to be an example of a global public good.

Collective Good

Collective goods (or social goods) are defined as public goods that could be delivered as private goods, but are usually delivered by the government for various reasons, including social policy, and financed from public funds like taxes.

Note: Some writers have used the term public good to refer only to non-excludable pure public goods. They may then call excludable public goods club goods.

Examples of Public Goods: Common examples of public goods include: defense and law enforcement (including the system of property rights), public fireworks, lighthouses, clean air and other environmental goods, and information goods, such as software development, authorship, and invention. Some goods-such as orphan drugs-require special governmental incentives to be produced, but can't be classified as public goods since they don't fulfil the above requirements (Non-excludable and non-rivalrous.)

The provision of a lighthouse has often been used as the standard example of a public good, since it is difficult to exclude ships from using its services and no ship's use detracts from that of others. However, since most of the benefit of a lighthouse accrues to ships using particular ports, lighthouse maintenance fees can often profitably be bundled with port fees (Ronald Coase, The Lighthouse in Economics 1974). This has been sufficient to fund actual lighthouses as club goods. A public good's status may change over time. Technological progress can significantly impact excludability of traditional public goods: encryption allows broadcasters to sell individual access to their programming. The costs for electronic road pricing have fallen dramatically, paving the way for detailed billing based on actual use. On the other hand, technological progress can also create new public goods. The simplest examples are street lights: they are relatively recent inventions (by historical standards), one person's enjoyment of them does not detract from other persons' enjoyment, and it is impossible to charge individuals separately for the amount of light they presumably use.

The Free Rider Problem

Public goods provide a very important example of market failure, in which market-like behaviour of individual gain-seeking does not produce efficient results. The production of public goods results in positive externalities which are not remunerated. Because no private organisation can reap all the benefits of a public good which they have produced, there will be insufficient incentives to produce it voluntarily. Consumers can take advantage of public goods without contributing sufficiently to their creation. This is called the free rider problem, or occasionally, the "easy rider problem" (because consumer's contributions will be small but non-zero).

For example, consider national defense, a standard example of a pure public good. A purely rational person (also known as homo economicus) is an individual who is extremely individualistic, considering only those benefits and costs that directly affect him or her. Public goods give such a person incentive to be a free rider.

Suppose this purely rational person thinks about exerting some extra effort to defend the nation. The benefits to the individual of this effort would be very low, since the benefits would be distributed among all of the millions of other people in the country. Further, there is a very high possibility that he could get injured or killed during the course of his or her military service.

On the other hand, the free rider knows that he or she cannot be excluded from the benefits of national defense, regardless of whether he or she contributes to it. There is also no way that these benefits can be split up and distributed as individual parcels to people. So the free rider would not voluntarily exert any extra effort, unless there is some inherent pleasure or material reward for doing so (such as, for example, money paid by the government, as with an all-volunteer army or mercenaries).

Possible Solutions to the Free Rider Problem

Dominant Assurance Contracts

Assurance contracts are contracts in which participants make a binding pledge to contribute to a contract for building a public good, contingent on a quorum of a predetermined size being reached. Otherwise their money is refunded. A dominant assurance contract is a variation in which an entrepreneur creates the contract and refunds the initial pledge plus an additional sum of money if the quorum is not reached. In game theory terms this makes pledging to build the public good a dominant strategy: the best move is to pledge to the contract regardless of the actions of others.

Coasian Solution

The coasian solution, named for the economist Ronald Coase and unrelated to the Coase theorem, proposes a mechanism by which potential beneficiaries of a public good band together and pool their resources based on their willingness to pay to create the public good. Coase (1960) argued that if the transaction costs between potential beneficiaries of a public good are sufficiently low, and it is therefore easy for beneficiaries to find each other and pool their money based on the public good's value to them, then an adequate level of public goods production can occur even under competitive free market conditions. However, Coase (1988) famously wrote: "The world of zero transaction costs has often been described as a Coasian world. Nothing could be further from the truth. It is the world of modern economic theory, one which I was hoping to persuade economists to leave."

A similar alternative for arranging funders of public goods production is to produce the public good but refuse to release it into the public until some form of payment to cover costs is met. Author Stephen King, for instance, authored chapters of a new novel downloadable for free on his website while threatening not to release subsequent chapters unless a certain amount of money was raised. Sometimes dubbed holding for ransom, this method of public goods production is a modern application of the street performer protocol for public goods production.

In some ways, the formation of governments and government-like communities such as homeowners associations can be thought of as applied instances of practicing the coasian solution by creating institutions to reduce the transaction costs.

Libertarians claim that these types of solutions are preferable to government provision in almost every case. Some even list defense, roads, law enforcement, and other areas traditionally reserved for the state as good candidates for market systems.

Government Provision

If voluntary provision of public goods will not work, then the obvious solution is making their provision involuntary. (Each of us is saved from our own individualistic short-sightedness, our tendency to be a free rider, while also being assured that no one else will be allowed to free ride.) One general solution to the problem is for governments or states to impose taxation to fund the production of public goods. The difficulty is to determine how much funding should be allocated to different public goods, and how the costs should be split.

Sometimes the government provides public goods using "unfunded mandates". An example is the requirement that every car be fit with a catalytic converter. This may be executed in the private sector, but the end result is predetermined by the state: the individually involuntary provision of the public good clean air. Unfunded mandates have also been imposed by the U.S. federal government on the state and local governments, as with the Americans with Disabilities Act, for example.

Subsidies

A government may subsidize production of a public good in the private sector. Unlike government provision, subsidies may result in some form of competitive market. The potential for cronyism (for example, an alliance between political insiders and the businesses receiving subsidies) can be limited with secret bidding for the subsidies or application of the subsidies following clear general principles. Depending on the nature of a public good and a related subsidy, principal agent problems can arise between the citizens and the government or between the government and the subsidized producers; this effect and counter-measures taken to address it can diminish the benefits of the subsidy.

Subsidies can also be used in areas with a potential for non-individualism: For instance, a state may subsidize devices to reduce air pollution and appeal to citizens to cover the remaining costs..

Privileged Group

The study of collective action shows that public goods are still produced when one individual benefits more from the public good than it costs him to produce it; examples include benefits from individual use, intrinsic motivation to produce, and business models based on selling complement goods. A group that contains such individuals is called a privileged group. A historical example could be a downtown entrepreneur who erects a street light in front of his shop to attract customers; even though there are positive external benefits to neighbouring businesses that aren't paying from the street light, the added customers to the paying shop provide enough revenue to cover the costs of the street light.

The existence of privileged groups is not a complete solution to the free rider problem, however, as underproduction of the public good can still result. The street light builder, for instance, would not consider the added benefit to neighbouring businesses when determining whether to erect his street light, making it possible that the street light isn't built when the cost of building is too high for the single entrepreneur even when the total benefit to all the businesses combined exceeds the cost.

An example of the privileged group solution could be the Linux community, assuming that users derive more benefit from contributing than it costs them to do it. For more discussion on this topic see also Coase's Penguin.

Merging of Free Riders

Another method of overcoming the free rider problem is to simply eliminate the profit incentive for free riding by buying out all the potential free riders. A property developer that owned an entire city street, for instance, would not need to worry about free riders when erecting street lights since he owns every business that could benefit from the street light without paying. Implicitly, then, the property developer would erect street lights until the marginal social benefit met the marginal social cost, since in this case they are equivalent to the private marginal benefits and costs.

While the purchase of all potential free riders may solve the problem of underproduction due to free riders in smaller markets, it may simultaneously introduce the problem of underproduction due to monopoly. Additionally, some markets are simply too large to make a buyout of all beneficiaries feasible-this is particularly visible with public goods that affect everyone in a country.

Legislated Exclusion

Another solution, which has evolved for information goods, is to create intellectual property laws, such as copyright or patents, covering the public goods. These laws attempt to remove the natural non-excludability by prohibiting reproduction of the good. Although they can solve the free rider problem, the downside of these laws is that they imply private monopoly power and thus are not Pareto-optimal. For example, in the United States, the patent rights given to pharmaceutical companies encourage them to charge high prices (above marginal cost), to advertise to convince patients to nag their doctors to prescribe the drugs, to sue even mild imitators in court, and to lobby for the extension of patent rights in a form of rent seeking.

This near-ubiquitous problem arises because the underlying marginal cost of giving the good to more people is low or zero, but, because of the limits of price discrimination (including both arbitrage and a lack of incentives to provide cheap, high quality copies to those with little ability to pay), those who are unwilling or unable to pay a profit-maximising price, do not get access to the good.

Joseph Schumpeter claimed that the "excess profits," or profits over normal profit, generated by the copyright or patent monopoly will attract competitors that will make technological innovations and thereby end the monopoly.

This is a continual process referred to as "Schumpeterian creative destruction", and its applicability to different types of public goods is a source of some controversy. The supporters of the theory point to the case of Microsoft, for example, which has been increasing its prices (or lowering its products' quality), and predict that these practices will make increased market shares for Linux and Apple largely inevitable.

Public Spirit

If enough people do not think like free-riders, the private and voluntary provision of public goods may be successful. A free rider might litter in a public park, but a more public-spirited individual would not do so, getting an inherent pleasure from helping the community. In fact, a public-spirited person might voluntarily pick up some of the existing litter. If enough people do so, the role of the state in using taxes to hire professional maintenance crews is reduced. This might imply that even someone typically inclined to free-riding would not litter, since their action would have such an obvious cost.

Public spirit may be encouraged by non-market solutions to the economic problem, such as tradition and social norms. For example, this kind of public spirit involving concepts such as nationalism and patriotism has been part of most successful war efforts, complementing the roles of taxation and conscription.

To some extent, public spiritedness of a more limited type is the basis for voluntary contributions that support public radio and television.

Government Debt

Government debt (also known as public debt or national debt) is money (or credit) owed by any level of government; either central government, federal government, municipal government or local government. As the government represents the people, government debt can be seen as an indirect debt of the taxpayers.

Government debt can be categorized as internal debt, owed to lenders within the country, and external debt, owed to foreign lenders. Governments usually borrow by issuing securities such as government bonds and bills. Less credit worthy countries sometimes borrow directly from commercial banks or supranational institutions. Some people consider all government liabilities, including future pension payments and payments for goods and services the government has contracted for but not yet paid, as government debt.

Another common division of government debt is by duration. Short term debt is generally considered to be one year or less, long term is more than ten years. Medium term debt falls in the middle.

Government and Sovereign Bonds

A government bond is a bond issued by a national government denominated in the country's domestic currency. Bonds issued by national governments in foreign currencies are normally referred to as sovereign bonds. Government bonds are usually considered risk-free bonds, because the government can raise taxes, reduce spending, or simply print more money to redeem the bond at maturity. Investors in sovereign bonds have the additional risk that the issuer is unable to obtain foreign currency to redeem the bonds.

Municipal, Provincial or State Bonds

Municipal bonds or "munis" in the United States are debt securities issued by local governments (municipalities).

Denominated in Reserve Currencies

Governments borrow money in a currency for which the demand is strongest. The advantage of issuing bonds in a currency such as the euro or the US dollar, is that the universe of investors for the bonds is very large. Countries such as the United States, France and Germany have only issued in their domestic currency. Relatively few investors are willing to invest in currencies that do not have a long track-record of stability. The disadvantage for a government issuing bonds in a foreign currency, is that there is a risk that they will not be able to obtain the foreign currency to pay the interest or redeem the bonds. In 1997/1998, during the Asian financial crisis this became a serious problem when many countries were unable to keep their exchange rate fixed due to speculative attacks.

Risk

Lendings to a national government in the country's own sovereign currency are often considered "risk free" and are made at a so-called "risk-free interest rate". This is because the debt and interest can be repaid by raising taxes, a reduction in spending, or failing that by simply printing more money. Some economists argue that, in an economy near the full employment, this would increase inflation and reduce the value of the invested capital. An extreme example of this is provided by Weimar Germany of 1920s which suffered from hyperinflation due to its government's inability to pay the national debt.

A politically unstable state is anything but risk-free as it may, being sovereign, cease its payments with impunity. Famous examples of this phenomenon are the Spain of eighteenth century which nullified its government debt seven times during a century and revolutionary Russia of 1917 which refused to accept the responsibility for Imperial Russian debt. Another political risk is caused by external threats. It is most uncommon for invaders to accept responsibility for the national debt of the annexed state or that of an organization it considered a rebellion. For example, all debts taken by Confederate States of America were left unpaid after the American Civil War.

U.S. Treasury bonds denominated in U.S. dollars are often considered "risk free" in the U.S. but this ignores the risk to foreign purchasers of currency exchange rate movements. In addition, this implicitly accepts the stability of the US government and its ability to continue repayments in a difficult financial crisis.

Lendings to a national government in a currency other than its own does not allow for the same confidence in the ability to repay but this is offset somewhat by reducing the exchange rate risk to foreign lenders. On the other hand, national debt in foreign currency cannot be disposed of by starting a hyperinflation, which increases the credibility of the debtor. Usually small states with volatile economies have most of their national debt in foreign currency. For countries in the Eurozone, the euro is the local currency, although no single state can trigger inflation by printing more money.

Lendings to a local or municipal government can be just as risky as a loan to a private company, unless the local or municipal government has the power to tax. In this case, the local government can escape its debts by increasing the taxes, or reduce spending, just as a national one. Local government loans are sometimes guaranteed by the national government and this reduces the risk. In some jurisdictions, interest earned on local or municipal bonds is tax-exempt income, which can be an important consideration for the wealthy.

Clearing and Defaults

Public debt clearing standards are set by the Bank for International Settlements, but defaults are governed by extremely complex laws which vary from jurisdiction to jurisdiction. Globally, the International Monetary Fund has the power to intervene to prevent anticipated defaults. It has been very heavily criticized for the measures it advises nations to take, which often involve cutting back essential services as part of an economic austerity regime. In triple bottom line analysis, this can be seen as degrading capital on which the nation's economy ultimately depends.

Private debt, by contrast, has a relatively simple and far less controversial model: credit risk (or the consumer credit rating) determines interest rate, more or less, and entities go bankrupt if they fail to repay. Governments cannot really go bankrupt (and suddenly stop providing services to citizens), thus a far more complex way of managing defaults is required.

Smaller jurisdictions, such as cities, are usually guaranteed by their regional or national levels of government. When New York

City over the 1960s declined into what would have been a bankrupt status (had it been a private entity) by the early 1970s, a "bailout" was required from New York State and the United States. In general such measures amount to merging the smaller entity's debt into that of the larger entity and thereby gaining it access to the lower interest rates the large one enjoys. The larger entity may then assume some agreed-upon oversight in order to prevent recurrence of the problem.

Structure

In the dominant economic policy generally ascribed to theories of John Maynard Keynes, sometimes called Keynesian economics, there is tolerance for fairly high levels of public debt to pay for public investment in lean times, which can be paid back with tax revenues that rise in the boom times.

As this theory gained popularity in the 1930s globally, many nations took on public debt to finance large infrastructural capital projects - such as highways or large hydroelectric dams. It was thought that this could start a virtuous cycle and a rising business confidence since there would be more workers with money to spend. However, it was only the military spending of World War II that really ended the Great Depression.

Nonetheless, the Keynesian scheme remained dominant, thanks in part to Keynes' own pamphlet How to Pay for the War, published in his native United Kingdom in 1940. Since the war was being paid for, and being won, Keynes and Harry D. White, Assistant Secretary of the United States Department of the Treasury, were, according to John Kenneth Galbraith, the dominating influences on the Bretton Woods agreements. These agreements set the policies for the BIS, IMF, and World Bank, the so-called Bretton Woods Institutions, launched in the late 1940s.

These are the dominant economic entities setting policies regarding public debt. Due to their role in setting policies for trade disputes, the GATT and World Trade Organization also have immense power to affect foreign exchange relations, as many nations are dependent on specific commodity markets for the balance of payments they require to repay debt. Understanding the structure of public debt and analysing its risk requires one to:

- o Assess the expected value of any public asset being constructed, at least in future tax terms if not in direct revenues. A choice must be made about its status as a public good - some public "assets" end up as public bads, such as nuclear power plants which are extremely expensive to decommission - these costs must also be worked in to asset values.
- o Determine whether any public debt is being used to finance consumption, which includes all social assistance and all military spending.
- o Determine whether triple bottom line issues are likely to lead to failure or defaults of governments - say due to being overthrown
- o Determine whether any of the debt being undertaken may be held to be odious debt, which permits it to be disavowed without any effect to a country's credit status. This includes any loans to purchase "assets" such as leaders' palaces, or the people's suppression or extermination. International law does not permit people to be held responsible for such debts - as they did not benefit in any way from the spending and had no control over it.
- o Determine if any future entitlements are being created by expenditures - financing a public swimming pool for instance may create some right to recreation where it did not previously exist, by precedent and expectations.

Scale

Global debt is of great concern since, very often, social capital is depleted (such as cases of pestilence or welfare services on families or friends), and natural capital is ravaged for "natural resources" to make interest payments.

This has led to calls for universal debt relief for poorer countries. A less extreme measure is to permit civil society groups in every nation to buy the debt in exchange for minority equity positions in community organizations. Even in dictatorships, the combination of banks and civil society power could force land reform and overthrow unaccountable governments, since the people and banks would be aligned against the oppressive government. Creditary economics and Islamic economics argue that any level of debt by any party simply represents a violent and coercive relationship that must end. As the existing system of public debt finance based on Bretton Woods is critical to the financial architecture, significant monetary reform would be required to realize this.

Most analysts consider the current U.S. budget deficit of over US$500 billion per year to represent a problem that must be addressed quickly. Recently, the U.S. public debt has grown to over US$8 trillion. Meanwhile, Canada's national debt has begun to shrink (as of 2005, Canada's net debt as a fraction of GDP was half its peak, and was the lowest among the G8 nations).

Japan's national debt has increased rapidly since 1993 to more than 170% of GDP, sometimes the world's largest, depending on exchange rate, over $700 billion is added yearly to the total of over US$8 trillion, testing the world financial system. However, almost all of it is financed domestically, but still manages to severely cripple the national government.

Using a debt to GDP ratio is one of the most accepted measures of assessing a nation's debt. For example, one of the criteria of admission to the European Union's Euro currency is that a country's debt does not exceed 60% of that country's GDP. In contrast, per capita measures are often inappropriate, particularly in developing nations, which have far more people than capital. One billion people live on under US$1/day; two billion more on under US$5/day. This totals almost one half of the world's population.

Problems

Sovereign debt problems have been a major public policy issue since World War II, including the treatment of debt related to that war, the developing country "debt crisis" in the 1980s, and the shocks of the Russian financial crisis in 1998 and Argentina's default in 2001. For a comprehensive discussion of the procedures that have evolved for resolving the problems of governments that have defaulted on their contractual debt obligations, see: Restructuring Sovereign Debt: the Case for Ad Hoc Machinery, by Lex Rieffel, Brookings Institution Press, 2003.

Implicit Debt

Government "implicit" debt is the "promise" by a government of future payments from the state. Usually long term promises of social payments such as pensions and health expenditure are what is referred to by this term; not promises of other expenditure such as education or defence (which are largely paid on a "quid pro quo" basis to government employees and contractors, rather than as "social welfare", including welfare per se, to the general population).

The problem with the implicit government insurance liabilities is that it's very hard to make any accurate assumptions about these liabilities, since the scale of future payments depends on so many factors.

First of all, the social security claims are not any "open" bonds or debt papers with a stated time frame, "time to maturity", "nominal value", or "net present value".

In the United States there is no money in the governments coffers for social insurance payments, or for any payments, more than what's required to run day-to-day business. This insurance system is called PAYGO (pay-as-you-go) as opposed to save and invest.

The fear is that when the "baby boomers" start to retire the working population in the United States will be a smaller percentage of the population than it is now, for a perhaps incalculable time into the future.

This will make the government expenditures a "burden" on the country-larger than the 35% of GDP that it is now. Remember that the "burden" of the government is what it spends, since it can only pay its bills through taxes, debt, and inflation of the currency (government spending = tax revenues + change in government debt held by public + change in monetary base held by the public). "Government social benefits" paid by the United States government during 2003 totalled $1.3 trillion.

Public Finance

Public finance (government finance) is the field of economics that deals with budgeting the revenues and expenditures of a public sector entity, usually government. Governments, like any other legal entity, can take out loans, issue bonds and invest. Based on the taxing authority of the entity, they issue bonds such as tax increment bonds or revenue bonds. A bond issued by a public sector entity may give tax advantages to its owners.

The Economic Basis of Government Activity

Efficiency:

- o A model of efficient resource use
- o Equity vs efficiency
- o Market efficiency conditions
- o Market failures
- o Pareto efficiency
- o Government efficiency-how efficient are governments at obtaining their objectives? How much of their expenditure actually goes to where it is intended? What types of waste exist?
- o Scope of government activities-what do governments spend money on? What should governments spend money on? what can be left to markets? Why governments should be concerned with externalities, public goods.

Externalities and government policy:

- o Internalization of externalities
- o The Coase Theorem. The Coase theorem is the idea that government, with the power to establish the rights to use resources, can internalize externalities when transaction costs of bargaining are zero.

Public goods:

- o The characteristics of
- o The demand for pure public goods
- o Efficient output of a pure public good
- o The free rider problem

Public choice and the political process:

- o Arrow's impossibility theorem

Government Expenditures

Income distribution:

- o Income distribution-How will these government expenditures influence the incomes of one group relative to another group? Government programs like ?disaster relief? Transfer wealth to people that have suffered a loss due to natural disaster. Social security transfers wealth from the young to the old. Engaging in a war transfers wealth to certain sectors of society. Public education transfers wealth to families with children in these schools. Public road construction transfers wealth from people that do not use the roads to those people that do (and to those that build the roads).
- o Income Security
- o Employment insurance
- o Health Care

Financing:

- o Income redistribution effects of the various types of taxes and types of borrowing
- o Taxation, Prices and Efficiency
- o Impact of taxes on market prices and efficiency

Taxes:

- o The various types of taxes
- o Taxation efficiency
- o Taxation fairness
- o User fees

Debt:

- o Government debt-the effect of previous years borrowing-the cost of servicing the debt-intergenerational consequences
- o Types of government bonds
- o Effects on the bond market

Private Sector

The private sector of a nation's economy consists of all that is outside the state. It includes a variety of entities such as for-profit and non-profit enterprises, corporations, banks (other than central banks), any other non-governmental organizations, as well as individuals not employed by the state.

Capitalism revolves primarily around the private sector controlling industry.

Social Sector

Social sector is one of several terms created as alternatives to non-profit sector and non-governmental sector. The latter are seen as putting an emphasis on what this sector is not, rather than calling attention to its focus on a social mission.

Other terms that have been proposed are voluntary sector, third sector, independent sector and mission-based sector.

Consumer Debt

Consumer debt is consumer credit which is outstanding. In macroeconomic terms, it is debt which is used to fund consumption rather than investment.

Some consider all debt incurred for anything else other than investments unwise, while others believe that consumer credit is beneficial in growing the economy. The difference between perspectives is often a matter of personal values, which can be attributed to widespread social biases. Historically, across many cultures, being in personal debt was considered almost immoral. More recently, an alternative analysis might view consumer debt as a way to increase domestic production. If credit is easily available, the increased demand for consumer goods should cause an increase of overall domestic production. Both domestic and international economists have supported a recent upsurge in South Korean consumer debt, which has helped fuel economic expansion. On the other hand, credit card debt is almost unknown just across the sea in Japan and China, one because of long standing historical biases against personal debt, the other because the economy is still underdeveloped. Theoretical underpinnings aside, personal debt is on the rise, particularly in the United States.

The most common form of consumer debt is credit card debt, payday loans, and other consumer finance, which are often at higher interest rates than long term secured loans, such as mortgages. Interests rates vary, of course, depending on current economic situation and the financial status of the individual, but 12-15% per annum is not unusual.

Long-term consumer debt is often considered fiscally suboptimal. While some consumer items may be useful investments that justify debt (such as automobiles, which are usually but not always exempted in discussions of consumer debt, and business suits), most consumer goods are not. For example, incurring high-interest consumer debt through buying a big-screen television "now", rather than saving for it, can not usually be financially justified by the subjective benefits of having the television early. On the other hand, personal finance advisors like Robert Kiyosaki encourage a more liberal attitude towards taking on debt if it can be leverage into a small business or real estate. This higher-risk, possibly high-outcome, "personal-finances-as-a-game" attitude runs counter to the traditional mores of rising slowly through the ranks of a company through discipline and hard work, but may have increasingly validity in an age of globalization.

In many countries, the ease with which individuals can accumulate consumer debt beyond their means to repay has paradoxically preciptated a growth industry in debt consolidation and credit counselling.

COOPERATIVE

A cooperative (also cooperative or cooperative or co-op) has been defined in the International Cooperative Alliance (ICA) Statement on the Cooperative Identity as "an autonomous association of persons united voluntarily to meet their common economic, social, and cultural needs and aspirations through a jointly-owned and democratically-controlled enterprise." They "are based on the values of self-help, self-responsibility, democracy, equality, equity and solidarity. In the tradition of their founders, cooperative members believe in the ethical values of honesty, openness, social responsibility and caring for others." Such enterprises are the focus of study in the field of Cooperative economics.

Cooperative Identity: Such legal entities have a range of unique social characteristics. Membership is open, meaning that anyone who satisfies certain non-discriminatory conditions may join. Unlike a union, in some jurisdictions a cooperative may assign different numbers of votes to different members. However most cooperatives are governed on a strict "one member, one vote" basis, to avoid the concentration of control in an elite. Economic benefits are distributed proportionally according to each member's level of economic interest in the cooperative, for instance by a dividend on sales or purchases. Cooperatives may be generally classified as either consumer or producer cooperatives, depending largely on the mutual interest that their membership shares. Classification is also often based on their function.

TYPES OF COOPERATIVES

Housing Cooperative

A housing cooperative is a legal mechanism for ownership of housing where residents either own shares (share capital co-op) reflecting their equity in the cooperative's real estate, or have membership and occupancy rights in a not-for-profit cooperative (non-share capital co-op), and they underwrite their housing through paying subscriptions or rent.

Housing cooperatives come in three basic equity structures. In market-rate housing co-ops, members can sell their shares in the co-op whenever they like for whatever price the market will bear, much like any other residential property. Market-rate co-ops are very common in New York City. Limited Equity co-ops, which are often used by affordable housing developers, allow members to own some equity in their home, but limit the sale price of their membership share to that which they bought in for. Provisions are often made for inflation, or improvements made on the building.

The purpose of this is to prevent co-op members from using their share in the co-op to speculate on rising real estate prices, and to keep the price of a membership share affordable to future members. In the third structure, called zero-equity or "Group Equity" by the North American Students of Cooperation (NASCO), one of the proponents of this model, individual members do not build up equity in the co-op-the co-op is not owned by its members, but by itself.

Housing cooperatives may occupy various types of physical structure. Co-ops can be structured as individual housing units grouped together, such as in an apartment building, or they can be groups of people living together in one housing unit, as an alternative to the traditional family structure.

Building Cooperative

Members of a building cooperative-in Britain known as a self-build housing co-operative-pool resources to build housing, normally using a high proportion of their own labour. When the building is finished, each member is the sole owner of a homestead, and the cooperative may be dissolved.

This collective effort was at the origin of many of Britain's building societies, which however developed into "permanent" mutual savings and loan organisations, a term which persisted in some of their names (such as the former Leeds Permanent). Nowadays such self-building may be financed using a step-by-step mortgage which is released in stages as the building is completed.

The term also refers to workers' co-operatives in the building trade.

Retailers' Cooperative

A retailers' cooperative (often known as a secondary or marketing cooperative in the UK) is an organization which employs economies of scale on behalf of its members to get discounts from manufacturers and to pool marketing. It is common for locally-owned grocery stores, hardware stores and pharmacies. In this case the members of the cooperative are businesses rather than individuals. The well-known Best Western hotel chain is actually a giant cooperative, although it now prefers to call itself a "non-profit membership association." It gave up on the "cooperative" label after the courts kept insisting on calling it a franchis or despite its non-profit status.

Utility Cooperative

A utility cooperative is a public utility that is owned by its customers. It is a type of consumer cooperative. In the US, many such cooperatives were formed to provide rural electrical and telephone service as part of the New Deal.

Worker Cooperative

A worker cooperative or producer cooperative is a cooperative that is wholly owned and democratically controlled by its "worker-owners". There are no outside, or consumer owners, in a worker's cooperative-only the workers own shares of the business. Membership is not compulsory for employees, and only employees can become members.

Social Cooperative

A particularly successful form of multi-stakeholder cooperative is the Italian "social cooperative", of which some 7,000 exist. A "type A" social cooperative brings together providers and beneficiaries of a social service as members. A "type B" social cooperative brings together permanent workers and previously unemployed people who wish to integrate into the labour market.

Social co-operatives are legally defined as follows:

- o the objective is the general benefit of the community and the social integration of citizens
- o type A co-operatives provide health, social or educational services
- o those of type B integrate disadvantaged people into the labour market. The categories of disadvantage they target may include physical and mental disability, drug and alcohol addiction, developmental disorders and problems with the law. They do not include other factors of disadvantage such as race, sexual orientation or abuse
- o various categories of stakeholder may become members, including paid employees, beneficiaries, volunteers (up to 50% of members), financial investors and public institutions. In type B co-operatives at least 30% of the members must be from the disadvantaged target groups
- o the cooperative has legal personality and limited liability
- o voting is one person one vote
- o no more than 80% of profits may be distributed, interest

is limited to the bond rate and dissolution is altruistic (assets may not be distributed)

A good estimate of the current size of the social cooperative sector in Italy is given by updating the official ISTAT figures from the end of 2001 by an annual growth rate of 10% (assumed by the Direzione Generale per gli Ente Cooperativi). This gives totals of 7,100 social cooperatives, with 267,000 members, 223,000 paid employees, 31,000 volunteers and 24,000 disadvantaged people undergoing integration. Combined turnover is around 5 billion euro. The cooperatives break into three types: 59% type A (social and health services), 33% type B (work integration) and 8% mixed. The average size is 30 workers.

Consumers' Cooperative

The term cooperative also applies to businesses owned by their customers: a Consumers' Cooperative. Employees can also generally become members. Members vote on major decisions, and elect the board of directors from amongst their own number. A well known example in the US is the REI (Recreational Equipment Incorporated) co-op. The world's largest consumer cooperative is the Cooperative Group in the United Kingdom, which has a variety of retail and financial services. There are also a number of other, independent consumer cooperative societies in the UK, such as the East of England Cooperative Society and Midcounties Cooperative. In fact the Cooperative Group is actually something of a hybrid, having both corporate (other consumer cooperatives) and individual members. Japan has a very large and well developed consumer cooperative movement with over 14 million members; retail co-ops alone had a combined turnover of 2.519 trillion Yen (21.184 billion U.S. Dollars [market exchange rates as of 11/15/2005]) in 2003/4. (Japanese Consumers' Cooperative Union., 2003). As well as retail co-ops there are medical, housing, insurance co-ops alongside institutional (workplace based) co-ops, co-ops for school teachers and university based co-ops.

Around 1 in 5 of all Japanese households belongs to a local retail co-op and 90% of all co-op members are women. (Takamura, 1995). Nearly 6 million households belong to one of the 1,788,000

Han groups (Japanese Consumers' Cooperative Union., 2003). These consist of a group of five to ten members in a neighbourhood who place a combined weekly order which is then delivered by truck the following week. A particular strength of Japanese consumer co-ops in recent years has been the growth of community supported agriculture where fresh produce is sent direct to consumers from producers without going through the market.

AGRICULTURAL COOPERATIVE: AGRICULTURAL COOPERATIVES ARE WIDESPREAD IN RURAL AREAS.

In the United States, there are both marketing and supply cooperatives. Agricultural marketing cooperatives, some of which are government-sponsored, promote and may actually distribute specific commodities. There are also agricultural supply cooperatives, which provide inputs into the agricultural process.

In Europe, there are strong agricultural / agribusiness cooperatives, and agricultural cooperative banks. Most emerging countries are developing agricultural cooperatives. Where it is legal, medical marijuana is generally produced by cooperatives.

Cooperative Banking (Credit Unions and Cooperative Savings Banks): The Cooperative Bank's head office, 1 Balloon Street, Manchester. The statue in front is of Robert Owen, a pioneer in the Cooperative movement.

Credit Unions provide a form of cooperative banking.

In North America, the caisse populaire movement started by Alphonse Desjardins in Quebec, Canada pioneered credit unions. Desjardins wanted to bring desperately needed financial protection to working people. In 1900, from his home in Levis, Quebec, he opened North America's first credit union, marking the beginning of the Movement Desjardins.

While they have not taken root so deeply as in Ireland or the USA, credit unions are also established in the UK. The largest are work-based, but many are now offering services in the wider community. The Association of British Credit Unions Ltd-ABCUL-represents the majority of British Credit Unions. British Building Societies developed into general-purpose savings & banking institutions with "one member, one vote" ownership and can be seen as a form of financial cooperative (although many 'de-mutualised' into conventionally-owned banks in the 1980s & 1990s). The UK Cooperative Group includes both an insurance provider CIS and the Cooperative Bank, both noted for promoting ethical investment.

Other important European banking cooperatives include the Credit Agricole in France, Migros and Coop Bank in Switzerland and the Raiffeisen system in many Central and Eastern European countries. The Netherlands, Spain, Italy and various European countries also have strong cooperative banks. They play an important part in mortgage credit and professional (i.e. farming) credit.

Cooperative banking networks, which were nationalized in Eastern Europe, work now as real cooperative institutions. A remarkable development has taken place in Poland, where the SKOK network has grown to serve over 1 million members via 13,000 branches, and is larger than the country's largest conventional bank. In Scandinavia, there is a clear distinction between mutual savings banks (Sparbank) and true credit unions (Andelsbank).

Car-Sharing: Car-sharing is an arrangement by which individuals and groups share vehicles, which are stored in convenient common locations. It may be thought of as a very short-term, locally-based car hire, run on a members-only basis. It is most prevalent in Switzerland (where the Mobility

Car-Sharing cooperative has more than 50,000 clients), but is also common in Germany, Austria, and the Netherlands, and is fast growing in popularity in other European countries, Asia and North America. Car sharing operations may be for-profit or non-profit organizations. Zipcar and Flexcar are examples.

In Britain, where the term 'car sharing' has also been used for carpools or ride-sharing, some people prefer the term 'car clubs'.

Federal or Secondary Cooperatives: In some cases, Cooperative societies find it advantageous to form Federal or Secondary Cooperatives in which all members are themselves Cooperatives. Historically, these have predominantly come in the form of Cooperative Wholesale Societies, and Cooperative Unions.

Cooperative Federations are a means through which Cooperative Societies can fulfil the sixth Rochdale Principle, Cooperation amongst Cooperatives, with the ICA noting that "Co-operatives serve their members most effectively and strengthen the cooperative movement by working together through local, national, regional and international structures."

Cooperative Wholesale Society: According to Cooperative economist Charles Gide, the aim of a Cooperative wholesale society is to arrange "bulk purchases, and, if possible, organise production." The best historical example of this were the English CWS and the Scottish CWS, which were the forerunners to the modern Cooperative Group.

Cooperative Union

A second common form of Cooperative Federation is a Cooperative Union, whose objective (according to Gide) is "to develop the spirit of solidarity among societies and... in a word, to exercise the functions of a government whose authority, it is needless to say, is purely moral." Cooperatives UK and the International Cooperative Alliance are examples of such arrangements.

Cooperative Party: In some countries with a strong Cooperative sector, such as the UK, Cooperatives may find it advantageous to form a Parliamentary Political party to represent their interests. The British Cooperative Party is a prime example of such an arrangement.

HOUSING COOPERATIVE

A housing cooperative is a legal entity, usually a corporation, that owns real estate, one or more residential buildings. Each shareholder in the legal entity is granted the right to occupy one housing unit, sometimes subject to an Occupancy Agreement, which is similar to a lease. The Occupancy agreement specifies the co-op's rules.

LEGAL STATUS

As a legal entity, a co-op can contract with other companies or hire individuals to provide it with services, such as a maintenance contractor or a building manager. It can also hire employees, such as a manager or a caretaker, to deal with specific things that volunteers may prefer not to do or may not be good at doing, such as electrical maintenance. However, as many housing cooperatives strive to run self-sufficiently (and recognize the economical efficiency of doing so), as much work as possible is completed by its members.

A shareholder in a co-op does not own real estate, but a share of the legal entity that does own real estate. Cooperative ownership is quite distinct from condominiums where people "own" individual units and have little say in who moves into the other units. Because of this, most jurisdictions have developed separate legislation, similar to laws that regulate companies, to regulate how co-ops are operated and the rights and obligations of shareholders.

Ownership

Each resident or resident household has membership in the cooperative association. Members have occupancy rights to a specific suite within the housing cooperative as outlined in their "occupancy agreement", or "proprietary lease" which is essentially a lease. In some cases, the co-op follows Rochdale rules where each shareholder has only one vote. Most cooperatives are incorporated as limited stock companies where the number of votes an owner has is tied to the number of shares owned by the person. Whichever form of voting is employed it is necessary to conduct an election among shareholders to determine who will represent them on the board of directors (if one exists), the governing body of the cooperative. The board of directors is generally responsible for the business decisions including the financial requirements and sustainability of the cooperative. Although politics vary from co-op to co-op and depend largely on the wishes of its members, it is a general rule that a majority vote of the board is necessary to make business decisions.

Management

In larger co-ops, members of a co-op typically elect a board of directors from amongst the shareholders at a general meeting, usually the annual general meeting. In smaller co-ops, all members sit on the board.

The board typically elects its own officers, such as a president, vice-president and so on. Usually, the directors are volunteers, or are paid an honorarium. The board may then establish standing committees from among the shareholders, who usually also volunteer their time, to either handle the business affairs of the co-op or make recommendations to the full board on such issues as its finance, membership and maintenance of its housing units.

FINANCE

A housing co-op is normally de facto non-profit, since usually most of its income comes from the rents paid by its residents, who are invariably its members. There is no point in creating a deliberate surplus-except for operational requirements such as setting aside funds for replacement of assets-since that simply means that the rents paid by members are set higher than the expenses.

It is relatively difficult to start a housing co-op because if the idea is, for instance, to build a building or group of buildings to house the members, this usually takes a significant mortgage for which a financial institution will want assurances of responsibility. It may also take a year or more for the members to organize the design and construction, as well as time and foresight to establish even basic organizational policies. It is rare that these kinds of skills of organization are available in a random group of people who often have pressures on their existing housing. It may be somewhat easier to organize a group of closely related housing units. This opportunity may arise, for example, if an existing apartment building's owner is thinking about selling it.

There are housing co-ops of the rich and famous-John Lennon, for instance, lived in a housing cooperative, and most apartments in New York City that are owned rather than rented are held through a cooperative rather than via a condominium arrangement.

There are two main types of housing cooperative financing methods, market rate and limited equity. With market rate, the share price is allowed to rise on the open market and shareholders may sell at whatever price the market will bear when they want to move out. In many ways market rate is thus similar financially to owning a condominium, with the difference being that often the co-op carries a mortgage, resulting in a much higher monthly fee paid to the co-op than would be so in a condominium. The purchase price of a comparable unit in the co-op is typically much lower, however.

With limited equity, the co-op has rules regarding pricing of shares when sold. The idea behind limited equity is to maintain affordable housing. A sub-set of the limited equity model is the no-equity model, which looks very much like renting, with a very low purchase price (comparable to a rental security deposit) and a monthly fee in lieu of rent. When selling, all that is recouped is that very low purchase price.

Building Cooperatives

Building cooperatives are cooperative housing corporations where individuals or families work together to directly construct their own homes on a co-op basis.

Members of this type of cooperative purchase building materials in bulk and cooperate with other members of the co-op during the construction phase of the cooperative. When the housing has been completed the members usually own their own homes directly. In some cases, roads, parkland and community facilities continue to be owned by the cooperative.

Building co-ops were extremely popular in many parts of Canada from the 1930s to the 1960s. Father James (Jimmy) Tompkins and Dr. Moses Coady were key organizers in Nova Scotia of the first building co-ops. Through active local study groups they began research on cooperatives and developed a concept of how a building co-op could work.

Father Tompkins helped the start-up in 1936 of the first self-help, building co-op in North America near Glace Bay (Reserve Mines), Nova Scotia, Canada. A group of coal miners formed the Housing cooperative with a housing loan of CAN $22,000. The housing loan was used to pay for building materials. Each miner's personal contribution was his labour-"sweat equity". They worked together to build eleven homes. The miners moved into the first houses in 1938. These homes continue to be occupied today at Tompkinsville.

Retailers' Cooperative

A retailers' cooperative is a business entity which employs economies of scale on behalf of its retailer-members to get discounts from manufacturers and to pool marketing. It is common for locally-owned grocery stores, hardware stores and pharmacies. It should be distinguished from a consumers' cooperative, in which the consumers own and manage the store itself. It is a form of purchasing cooperative for retailers.

Worker Cooperative

A worker cooperative is a cooperative owned and operated by its "worker-owners". There are no outside or consumer owners in a worker cooperative-only the workers own shares of the business. Only one membership share may be issued to a member. One membership share is the equivalent of one vote. Membership is not compulsory for employees, but only employees can become members.

One of the world's best known example of worker cooperation is the Mondragon Cooperative Corporation (MCC) in the Basque Country.

History of Worker Cooperatives

Since there is no coherent legislation across the United States, much less Federal laws, most worker cooperatives make use of traditional consumer cooperative law and try to fine-tune it for their purposes. In some cases the members (workers) of the cooperative in fact "own" the enterprise by buying a share that represents a fraction of the market value of the cooperative. But this is seldom the case in most modern day worker cooperatives. This system of "buying-in" has proven unworkable because as the value of the cooperative increases, new members cannot afford to buy a share and are reduced to purchasing over a long-term, which means going into debt to the cooperative, maybe for years. Worker cooperatives organized this way mostly became traditional businesses with the original coop members hiring employees.

When the current cooperative movement resurfaced in the 1960s it developed mostly on a new system of "collective ownership" where par value shares were issued as symbolic of egalitarian voting rights. Once brought in as a member, after a period of time on probation usually so the new candidate can be evaluated, he or she was given power to manage the coop, without "ownership" in the traditional sense. In the UK this system is known as common ownership.

Some of these early cooperatives still exist and most new worker cooperatives follow their lead and develop a relationship to capital that is more radical than the previous system of equity share ownership.

In Britain this type of cooperative was traditionally known as a producer cooperative, and, while it was overshadowed by the consumer and agricultural types, made up a small section of its own within the national apex body, the Cooperative Union. The 'new wave' of worker cooperatives that took off in Britain in the mid-1970s created the Industrial Common Ownership Movement (ICOM) as a separate federation. Buoyed up by the alternative and ecological movements and by the political drive to create jobs, the sector peaked at around 2,000 enterprises. However the growth rate slowed, the sector contracted, and in 2001 ICOM merged with the Cooperative Union (which was the federal body for consumer cooperatives) to create Cooperatives UK, thus reunifying the cooperative sector.

Trade Unions

Unions are often unnecessary in worker cooperatives because the workers have direct control over the management and ownership of the business-they are negotiating with themselves. Some worker cooperatives still choose to become members of local unions to demonstrate their support for the labour movement and to working conditions that have resulted from years of struggle. While an unusual situation, there is no contradiction in doing so. Worker cooperatives that join unions often benefit from the trade that comes their way from the community of union members and those who support unions for political reasons. The labour contract negotiated becomes the baseline of benefits due to the membership and guarantees to the community that the working conditions are not those of a "sweatshop". Union membership also guarantees that the worker cooperative will not operate on the basis of typical small business sacrifice, where the owner(s) sometimes work day and night to keep their business afloat and expect similar sacrifices of their workers. Union membership for worker cooperatives gives the enterprise a legitimate standard of operations.

Internal Structure

Worker cooperatives can have a wide variety of internal structures. Probably the majority of co-ops use a hierarchical structure based on that of a conventional business, with the exception that the board of directors is elected. Some co-ops, however, use a structure based on left-wing activist collectives, with all members allowed and expected to play a managerial role- and sometimes using consensus decision-making. Such unconventional structures tend to be associated with more radical political aims such as anarchism and parecon.

SOCIAL COOPERATIVE

An Italian social cooperative is a particularly successful form of multi-stakeholder cooperative, of which some 7,000 exist. A "type A" social cooperative brings together providers and beneficiaries of a social service as members. A "type B" social cooperative brings together permanent workers and previously unemployed people who wish to integrate into the labour market.

Social cooperatives are legally defined as follows:

- o the objective is the general benefit of the community and the social integration of citizens
- o type A cooperatives provide health, social or educational services
- o those of type B integrate disadvantaged people into the labour market. The categories of disadvantage they target may include physical and mental disability, drug and alcohol addiction, developmental disorders and problems with the law. They do not include other factors of disadvantage such as race, sexual orientation or abuse
- o various categories of stakeholder may become members, including paid employees, beneficiaries, volunteers (up to 50% of members), financial investors and public

institutions. In type B cooperatives at least 30% of the members must be from the disadvantaged target groups

- o the cooperative has legal personality and limited liability
- o voting is one person one vote
- o no more than 80% of profits may be distributed, interest is limited to the bond rate and dissolution is altruistic (assets may not be distributed)

A good estimate of the current size of the social cooperative sector in Italy is given by updating the official ISTAT figures from the end of 2001 by an annual growth rate of 10% (assumed by the Direzione Generale per gli Ente Cooperativi). This gives totals of 7,100 social cooperatives, with 267,000 members, 223,000 paid employees, 31,000 volunteers and 24,000 disadvantaged people undergoing integration. Combined turnover is around 5 billion euro. The cooperatives break into three types: 59% type A (social and health services), 33% type B (work integration) and 8% mixed. The average size is 30 workers.

CONSUMERS' COOPERATIVE

A consumers' cooperative is a business owned by its customers for their mutual gain. It is a form of free enterprise that is oriented toward service rather than pecuniary profit. The customers or consumers of the goods and/or services the business provides are also the individuals who have provided the capital required to launch or purchase that enterprise. (Although a consumers' co-op is sometimes called a retail cooperative, it should be distinguished from a retailers' cooperative, whose members are the stores or chains themselves, rather than the individual consumers.)

A consumers' cooperative may comprise supermarkets, convenience stores, and other businesses owned by independently-owned, and run Cooperative societies, which benefit from joint coordination and cooperation in managing their businesses. As mutually-owned businesses, each member of a society has a shareholding equal to the sum they paid in when they joined.

Consumers Cooperatives may, in turn, form Cooperative Federations. These may come in the form of cooperative wholesale societies, through which Consumers' Cooperatives collectively purchase goods at wholesale prices and, in some cases, own factories. Alternatively, they may be members of Cooperative Unions.

PRIVATIZATION

Privatization (alternately "denationalization" or "disinvestment") is the transfer of property or responsibility from the public sector (government) to the private sector (business). The term can refer to partial or complete transfer of any property or responsibility held by government. A similar transfer in the opposite direction could be referred to the nationalization or municipalization of some property or responsibility.

The term also has been used to describe an unrelated, non-governmental interaction involving the buyout, by the majority owner, of all shares of a holding company's stock-privatizing a publicly traded stock.

Types of Privatization

There are three main methods of privatization:

- o Share Issue privatization (SIP)-selling shares on the stock market
- o Asset Sale privatization-selling the entire firm or part of it to a strategic investor, usually by auction or using Treuhand model
- o Voucher privatization-shares of ownership are distributed to all citizens, usually for free or at a very low price.

Share issue privatization is the most common type.

Share issue can broaden and deepen domestic capital markets, boosting liquidity and potentially economic growth, but if the capital markets are insufficiently developed it may be difficult to find enough buyers, and transaction costs (e.g. underpricing required) may be higher.

For this reason, many some governments elect for listings in the more developed and liquid markets such as Euronext, the London, New York or Hong Kong Stock Exchanges are popular because they are highly developed and sophisticated.

As a result of higher political and currency risk deterring foreign investors, asset sales are more common in developing countries.

Voucher privatization has mainly been used in the transition economies of Central and Eastern Europe-countries such as Russia, Poland and Czechoslovakia (Czech Republic and Slovakia)

Pro-Privatization and Anti-Privatization Arguments

Pro-Privatization: Proponents of privatization believe that private market actors can more efficiently deliver many goods or service than government due to free market competition. In general, over time this will lead to lower prices, improved quality, more choices, less corruption, less red tape, and quicker delivery. Many proponents do not argue that everything should be privatized; the existence of problems such as market failures and natural monopolies may limit this. However, a small minority thinks that everything can be privatized, including the state itself.

The basic economic argument given for privatization is that governments have few incentives to ensure that the enterprises they own are well run. Governments have the de facto monopoly to raise money by taxation should revenues be insufficient. As Governments may borrow money more cheaply from the debt markets than private enterprises, they will squeeze out more efficient private companies through this misallocation of resources. Where governments lack it, it is said that private owners do have profit motive. The theory holds that, not only will the enterprise's clients see benefits, but as the privatized enterprise becomes more efficient, the whole economy will benefit. Ideally, privatization propels the establishment of social, organizational and legal infrastructures and institutions that are essential for an effective market economy.

Privatizing a non-profitable company which was state-owned may force the company to raise prices in order to become profitable. However, this would remove the need for the state to provide tax money in order to cover the losses.

A very substantial benefit to share or asset sale privatizations is that bidders compete to offer the state the highest price, creating revenues for the state to redistribute in addition to new tax revenue. Voucher privatisations, on the other hand, would be a genuine return of the assets into the hands of the general population, and create a real sense of participation and inclusion. Vouchers, like all other private property, could then be sold on if preferred.

- o Performance: State-run industries tend to be bureaucratic. A political government may only be motivated to improve a function when its poor performance becomes politically sensitive, and such an improvement is easily reversed by another regime.
- o Improvements: Conversely, the government may put off improvements due to political sensitivity and special interests - even in cases of companies that are run well and better serve their customers' needs.
- o Corruption: A monopolized function is prone to corruption; decisions are made primarily for political reasons, personal gain of the decision-maker (i.e. "graft"), rather than economic ones.
- o Accountability: Managers of privately owned companies are accountable to their owners/shareholders and to the consumer, and can only exist and thrive where needs are met.
- o Civil Liberty Concerns: A company controlled by the State may have access to information or assets which may be used against dissidents or any individuals who disagree with their policies.
- o Goals: A political government tends to run an industry or company for political goals rather than economic ones.
- o Capital: Privately held companies can more easily raise investment capital in the financial markets, investment decisions are governed by market interest rates. State-owned industries have to compete with demands from other government departments and special interests.
- o Security: Governments have had the tendency to "bail out" poorly run businesses when, economically, it may be better to let the business fold, often due to the sensitivity of job losses.

- o Lack of Market Discipline: Poorly managed state companies are insulated from the same discipline as private companies, which could go bankrupt, have their management removed, or be taken over by competitors.
- o Natural Monopolies: The existence of natural monopolies do not mean that these sectors must be state owned. Governments can enact or are armed with anti-trust legislation and bodies to deal with anti-competitive behaviour of all companies public or private.
- o Concentration of Wealth: Ownership of and profits from successful enterprises tend to be dispersed and diversified. The availability of more investment vehicles stimulates to capital markets and promotes job creation.
- o Political Influence: Nationalized industries are prone to interference from politicians for political or populist reasons. Examples include making an industry buy supplies from local producers (when that may be more expensive than buying from abroad), forcing an industry to freeze its prices/fares to satisfy the electorate or control inflation, increasing its staffing to reduce unemployment, or moving its operations to marginal constituencies.
- o Profits: Private companies make a profit by enticing consumers to buy their products in preference to their competitors'. Private corporations exist to serve exactly the needs of their clients; their clients' propensity to pay is usually correlated with how well they serve the needs. Corporations of different sizes may target different market niches in order to focus on marginal groups and satisfy their demand.

ANTI-PRIVATIZATION

Opponents of privatization dispute the claims concerning the alleged lack of incentive for governments to ensure that the enterprises they own are well run, on the basis of the idea that governments are proxy owners answerable to the people. It is argued that a government which runs nationalized enterprises poorly will lose public support and votes, while a government which runs those enterprises well will gain public support and votes. Thus, democratic governments do have an incentive to maximize efficiency in nationalized companies, due to the pressure of future elections.

Opponents of certain privatizations believe certain parts of the social terrain should remain closed to market forces in order to protect them from the unpredictability and ruthlessness of the market (such as private prisons, basic health care, and basic education). Another view is that some of the utilities which government provides benefit society at large and are indirect and difficult to measure or unable to produce a profit, such as defense. Still another is that natural monopolies are by definition not subject to competition and better administrated by the state.

The controlling ethical issue in the anti-privatization perspective is the need for responsible stewardship of social support missions. Market interactions are all guided by self-interest, and successful actors in a healthy market must be committed to charging the maximum price that the market will bear. Privatization opponents believe that this model is not compatible with government missions for social support, whose primary aim is delivering affordability and quality of service to society.

Many privatization opponents also warn against the practice's inherent tendency toward corruption. As many areas which the government could provide are essentially profitless, the only way private companies could, to any degree, operate them would be through contracts or block payments. In these cases, the private firm's performance in a particular project would be removed from their performance, and embezzlement and dangerous cost cutting measures might be taken to maximize profits.

Some would also point out that privatizing certain functions of government might hamper coordination, and charge firms with specialized and limited capabilities to perform functions which they are not suited for. In rebuilding a war torn nation's infrastructure, for example, a private firm would, in order to provide security, either have to hire security, which would be both necessarily limited and complicate their functions, or coordinate with government, which, due to a lack of command structure shared between firm and government, might be difficult. A government agency, on the other hand, would have the entire military of a nation to draw upon for security, whose chain of command is clearly defined. Opponents would say that this is a false assertion: numerous books refer to poor organisation between government departments (for example the Hurricane Katrina incident).

Furthermore, opponents of privatization argue that it is undesirable to transfer state-owned assets into private hands for the following reasons:

- o Performance: A democratically elected government is accountable to the people through a legislature, Congress or Parliament, and is motivated to safeguarding the assets of the nation. The profit motive may be subordinated to social objectives.
- o Improvements: the government is motivated to performance improvements as well run businesses contribute to the State's revenues.
- o Corruption: Government ministers and Civil servants are bound to uphold the highest ethical standards, and standards of probity are guaranteed through codes of conduct and declarations of interest. However, the selling process could lack transparency, allowing the purchaser and civil servants controlling the sale to gain personally.
- o Accountability: The public does not have any control or oversight of private companies.
- o Civil Liberty Concerns: A democratically elected government is accountable to the people through Parliament, and can intervene when civil liberties are threatened.
- o Goals: The government may seek use state companies as instruments to further social goals for the benefit of the nation as a whole.
- o Capital: Governments can raise money in the financial markets most cheaply to re-lend to State-owned enterprises.
- o Lack of Market Discipline: Governments have chosen to keep certain companies/industries under public ownership because of their strategic importance or sensitive nature.

- o Cuts in Essential Services: If a government-owned company providing an essential service (such as water supply) to all citizens is privatized, its new owner(s) could lead to the abandoning of the social obligation to those who are less able to pay, or to regions where this service is unprofitable.
- o Natural Monopolies: Privatization will not result in true competition if a natural monopoly exists.
- o Concentration of Wealth: Profits from successful enterprises end up in private, often foreign, hands instead of being available for the common good.
- o Political Influence: Governments may more easily exert pressure on state-owned firms to help implementing Government policy.
- o Downsizing: Private companies often face a conflict between profitability and service levels, and could over-react to short-term events. A state-owned company might have a longer-term view, and thus be less likely to cut back on maintenance or staff costs, training etc., to stem short term losses.
- o Profiteering: Private companies do not have any goal other than to maximize profits. A private company will serve the needs of those who are most willing (and able) to pay, as opposed to the needs of the majority, and are thus anti-democratic.

Outcomes

Nellis and Kikeri have shown that in competitive industries with well-informed consumers, privatization consistently improves efficiency. Such efficiency gains mean a one-off increase in GDP, but through improved incentives to innovate and reduce costs also tend to raise the rate of economic growth. The type of industries to which this generally applies include manufacturing and retailing. Although typically there are social costs associated with these efficiency gains, many economists argue that these can be dealt with by appropriate government support through redistribution and perhaps retraining.

In sectors that are natural monopolies or public services, the results of privatization are much more mixed, as a private monopoly behaves much the same as a public one in liberal economic theory. In general, if the performance of an existing public sector operation is sufficiently bad, privatization (or threat thereof) has been known to improve matters. Indeed, Megginson & Netter showed that the greatest gains from privatization are achieved in the pre-privatization period as reforms are made to prepare for the transfer to private hands. Changes may include, inter alia, the imposition of related reforms such as greater transparency and accountability of management, improved internal controls, regulatory systems, and better financing, rather than privatization itself. Regarding political corruption, it is a controversial issue whether the size of the public sector per se results in corruption. The Nordic countries have low corruption but large public sectors. However, these countries score high on the Ease of Doing Business Index, due to good and often simple regulations, and for political rights and civil liberites, showing high government accountability and transparency.

Also regarding corruption, the sales themselves give a large opportunity for grand corruption. Privatizations in Russia and Latin America were accompanied by large scale corruption during the sale of the state owned companies. Those with political connections unfairly gained large wealth, which has discredited privatization in these regions. While media have reported widely the grand corruption that accompanied the sales, studies have argued that in addition to increased operating efficiency, daily petty corruption is, or would be, larger without privatization, and that corruption is more prevalent in non-privatized sectors. Furthermore, there is evidence to suggest that extralegal and unofficial activities are more prevalent in countries that privatized less.

ALTERNATIVES TO PRIVATIZATION

MUNICIPALIZATION

Transferring control of a nationalized business to municipal government is an alternative sometimes proposed to privatization.

Sub-contracting

It is possible that national services may sub-contract or out-source functions to private enterprises. A notable example of this is in the United Kingdom, where many municipalities have contracted out their garbage collection or administration of parking fines by tender to private companies.

In addition, the British government is debating the possibility of involving the private sector more in the workings of the NHS, principally by referring patients to private surgeries to ease the load on existing NHS human resources, and covering the cost of this.

Part Ownership

An enterprise may be privatized, with a number of shares in the company being retained by the state. This is a particularly notable phenomenon in Germany, where the state owns around a third of Deutsche Telekom. As of 2005, the state of North Rhine-Westphalia is also planning to buy shares in the energy company EON in an attempt to control spiralling costs.

Whilst partial privatization could be an alternative, it is more often a stepping stone to full privatization. It can offer the business a smoother transition period during which it can gradually adjust to market competition. Some state-owned companies are so large that there is the risk of sucking liquidity from the rest of the market, even in the most liquid marketplaces, and thus must be sold off bit by bit. The first tranche of a multi-step privatization would also in the first instance establish a valuation for the enterprise to mitigate complaints of under-pricing.

Notable Privatizations

Privatization programmes have been undertaken in many countries across the world, falling into three major groups. The first is privatization programmes conducted by transition economies in Central and Eastern Europe after 1989 in the process of instituting a market economy. The second is privatization programmes carried out in developing countries under the influence of international financial institutions such as the World Bank and IMF. The third is privatization programmes carried out by developed country governments, the most comprehensive probably being those of New Zealand and the United Kingdom in the 1980s and 1990s.

Privatization has been notably successful in telecommunications in Europe because genuine competition has arisen: the former state-owned enterprises lost their monopolies due to legislation and technological change, competitors entered the market, and prices for broadband access and telephone calls fell dramatically.

Some examples of failed privatizations of natural monopolies may be the rail privatization in the UK and in telecommunications in Mexico; in both countries, public disaffection has led to government intervention. Another notable example of this is Thames Water.

British Rail is an example of privatization program that has been deemed a failure. The track-owning company has been effectively repossessed by the British government, and many of the train-running companies are at risk of having their concession removed on the grounds that they fail to provide adequate services. One of them, Connex, actually had its franchise cut short in June 2003 by the government for what the Strategic Rail Authority called "poor financial management." In this case Stephen Byers (then Secretary of State for Transport) decided to call in administrators with regard to Railtrack (the infrastructure company created in 1993 and privatised in 1996) and transferring the infrastructure to the new Private Company Limited by Guarantee, Network Rail (a not for profit private company with no shareholders), Train Operation remains in the hands of private operators with franchises awarded by the Department for Transport (except for Merseyrail the franchise of which is awarded by Merseyside Passenger Transport Executive).

There are various precedents in history which some would claim as examples in which improper privatization, or the failure of government to conduct certain functions, caused various complications.

1. In the 18th Century, military functions such as maintaining forts and garrisons along the African coast were, in effect,

privatized to the East India Company, with parliament obliged to pay 13,000 pounds a year to support the East India Company in this end. However, this being somewhat of a government monopoly itself, it cannot said to be a perfect counter to privatization. The East India Company proceeded to shirk various expenses, most notably in the maintenance of fortifications. In one case, a shipment of inferior bricks sent to repair the walls of one fortification were of such low quality that it became necessary to rebuild the entire wall from its foundation.

2. Prior to the great depression, various state governments and the Hoover administration attempted to provide relief through private firms like the Red Cross. However, due to their limited capabilities, the firms were often unable to provide for the various functions that people required, and could only provide them in specific areas besides. Also, because they depended on limited resources (even with occasional payments from the government) they would usually be unable to provide them for very long.
3. During World War Two, the Truman Commission uncovered various instances in which contracts given out to various private firms to provide various military materials fostered considerable profiteering which often resulted in inadequate weapons and equipment being sent to the front.
4. In the reconstruction of Iraq, the government decided to contract out many different reconstruction functions to private firms. Shortly thereafter, those firms have been accused of cutting corners and being generally ineffective in reconstructing the country. Halliburton, in particular, was accused of, among other things, skimping on the cost of providing meals to soldiers. Various other complaints include the lagging reconstruction of water and electricity utilities, and providing defective equipment to soldiers.
5. Many, such as Dick Polman of The Philadelphia Inquirer, noted that prior to Hurricane Katrina, the government had "privatized many of FEMA's basic functions". The uncoordinated action between private emergency relief

agencies, as well as the military (which would often turn back relief trucks) resulting in the poor response to the storm that many would claim was a result of this privatization.

NATIONALIZATION

Nationalization is the act of transferring assets into public ownership. It usually refers to the transfer of private assets, but may also mean assets owned by other levels of government, such as municipalities. The opposite of nationalization is usually privatization, but may also be municipalization. A renationalization occurs when assets are nationalized after a previous privatization. Nationalizations are distinguished from property redistributions in that in the former case, the government retains control of the property after acquisition.

Some nationalizations take place when a government seizes criminal property. For example, the French government seized Renault because its owners had collaborated with Nazi Germany.

Compensation

A key issue in nationalization is whether the private owner is properly compensated for the value of the institution. The most controversial nationalizations are those where no compensation or an amount unreasonably below the likely market value of the nationalized assets is paid, and are known as expropriations. Many nationalizations through expropriation have come after revolutions.

The traditional Western stance on compensation was expressed by United States Secretary of State Cordell Hull, during the 1938 Mexican nationalization of the petroleum industry, that compensation should be "prompt, effective and adequate." According to this view, the nationalizing state is obligated under international law to pay the deprived party the full value of the property taken. The opposing position has been taken mainly by developing countries, claiming that the question of compensation should be left entirely up to the sovereign state, in line with the Calvo Doctrine. Communist states have held that no compensation is due, based on communist notions of private property.

In 1962, the United Nations General Assembly adopted Resolution 1803, "Permanent Sovereignty over National Resources," which states that in the event of nationalization, the owner "shall be paid appropriate compensation in accordance with international law."

In doing so, the UN rejected both the traditional Calvo-doctrinist view and the Communist view. The term "appropriate compensation" represents a compromise between the traditional views, taking into account the need of developing countries to pursue reform even without the ability to pay full compensation, and the Western concern for protection of private property.

When nationalizing a large business, the cost of compensation is so great that many legal nationalizations have happened when firms of national importance run close to bankruptcy and can be acquired by the government for little or no money. A classic example is the UK nationalization of the British Leyland Motor Corporation.

At other times, governments have considered it important to gain control of institutions of strategic economic importance, such as banks or railways, or of important industries struggling economically.

The case of Rolls-Royce plc, nationalized in 1971, is an interesting blend of these two arguments. This policy was sometimes known as ensuring government control of the "commanding heights" of the economy, to enable it to manage the economy better in terms of long-term development and medium-term stability.

The extent of this policy declined in the 1980s and 1990s as governments increasingly privatized industries that had been nationalized, replacing their strategic economic influence with use of the tax system and of interest rates.

Nonetheless, national and local governments have seen the advantage of keeping key strategic assets in institutions that are not strongly profit-driven and can raise funds outside the public-sector constraints, but still retain some public accountability. Examples from the last five years in the United Kingdom include the vesting of the British railway infrastructure firm Railtrack in the not-for-profit company Network Rail, and the divestment of much council housing stock to "arms-length management companies," often with mutual status.

MUNICIPALIZATION

Municipalization is the transfer of corporations or other assets to municipal ownership. The transfer may be from private ownership (usually by purchase) or from other levels of government. It is the opposite of privatization and is different from nationalization.

Services

There have been two main waves of municipalization in developed countries. The first took place in the late nineteenth and early twentieth century, when municipalities in many developed countries acquired local private providers of a range of public services.

The driving reason in most cases was the failure of private providers to sufficiently expand service provision outside wealthy parts of urban areas. The second wave took place in the early 1990s, when after the end of the communist states in eastern Europe state-owned companies in many public service sectors were broken up and transferred to municipal control. This was typical in sectors such as water, waste management and public transport, although not in electricity and natural gas.

Such regional companies either remained under municipal control, or were privatized. Privatization was done variously: by selling them to investors, by giving a concession or a management contract. Examples include the water sector in the Czech Republic, over half of which has been privatized.

Governments

In the U.S., municipalization often refers to incorporation of an entire county into its municipalities, leaving no unincorporated areas. This generally ends de facto the county's own home rule, which in most states allows it to act as the municipal service provider in those unincorporated areas. The county is left offering only those services mandated of it by the state constitution, which are generally only extensions of state government like courts and sheriff departments.

As with utilities, the county's assets usually end up being distributed among the cities, though this is less likely if the process is gradual rather than all at once.

One example of municipalization is the Sacramento Municipal Utilities District, or SMUD, of Sacramento, California. In another, larger example, Fulton County, Georgia, which includes the city of Atlanta, is currently undergoing full municipalization.

REGULATION

A regulation is a legal restriction promulgated by government administrative agencies through rulemaking supported by a threat of sanction or a fine.

This administrative law or regulatory law is in contrast to statutory or case law. Regulation mandated by the government or state attempts to produce outcomes which might not otherwise occur, produce or prevent outcomes in different places to what might otherwise occur, or produce or prevent outcomes in different timescales than would otherwise occur.

Common examples of regulation include attempts to control market entries, prices, wages, pollution effects, employment for certain people in certain industries, standards of production for certain goods and services. The economics of imposing or removing regulations relating to markets is analysed in regulatory economics.

Regulation as a Legal Term

A regulation as a legal term is a rule created by an administration or administrative agency or body that interprets the statutes setting out the agency's purpose and powers, or the circumstances of applying the statute.

A regulation is a form of secondary legislation which is used to implement a primary piece of legislation appropriately, or to take account of particular circumstances or factors emerging during the gradual implementation of, or during the period of, a primary piece of legislation.

Other forms of secondary legislation are statutory instruments, statutory orders, by-laws and rules. Some of these (but not all of them) need to be referred back before being implemented, to the primary legislative process.

Types of Regulation

Regulations, like any other coercive action, have costs for some and benefits for others. Efficient regulations may only be said to exist where the total benefits to some people exceed the total costs to others.

Regulation are justified using various reasons and therefore can be classified in several broad categories:

- o Market failures-regulation due to inefficiency. Intervention due to a classical economics argument to market failure.
- o Risk of monopoly
- o Collective action, or public good
- o Inadequate information
- o Unseen externalities
- o Collective desires-regulation about collective desires or considered judgements on the part of a significant segments of society
- o Diverse experiences-regulation with a view of eliminating or enhancing opportunities for the formation of diverse preferences and beliefs
- o Social subordination-regulation aimed to increase or reduce social subordination of various social groups
- o Endogenous preferences-regulation's purpose is to affect the development of certain preferences on an aggregate level
- o Irreversibility-regulation that deals with the problem of irreversibility - the problem in which a certain type of conduct from current generations results in outcomes from which future generations may not recover from at all.

- o Interest group transfers-regulation that results from efforts by self-interest groups to redistribute wealth in their favour, which may disguise itself as one or more of the justifications above.

PUBLIC BROADCASTING

Public broadcasting is a form of public service broadcasting (PSB) intended to serve the diverse needs of the listening public. Except for the United States, it has traditionally been the dominant form of broadcasting in much of the world.

It is a system in which radio, television, and potentially other electronic media outlets receive some or all of their funding from the public.

The broadcasters' funds can come directly from individuals through voluntary donations, licence fees, or indirectly as state subsidies that originated as taxes. Many public broadcasters supplement this with contributions from corporations, in return for underwriting spots. While these announcements resemble traditional advertisements on commercial broadcasting stations, there are usually limitations, such as a prohibition of making product claims, stating prices, or providing an incentive to buy.

Commercial broadcasting now occurs in many countries around the world, and the number of countries with only public broadcasting has declined substantially. The mass media marketplace is tremendously competitive, and as such, it can be difficult for a public service broadcaster to survive amongst commercial interests. This may become even more of an issue with the increased number of channels that digital broadcasting provides.

Defining Public Broadcasting

There is no standard definition of what public broadcasting is exactly, although a number of official bodies have attempted to pick out the key characteristics. Public service broadcasters generally transmit programming that aims to improve society by informing viewers. In contrast, the aim of commercial outlets is to provide popular shows that attract an audience-therefore leading to higher prices when advertising is sold. For this reason, the ideals of public broadcasting are often incompatible with commercial goals. Of course, public broadcasters also strive to entertain their viewers, but they can still come across as being overly paternalistic in nature.

The Broadcasting Research Unit lists the following as major goals or characteristics of a public broadcaster: 1 Geographic universality - The stations' broadcasts are available nationwide, with no exception.

This criterion is failed by Five in the UK, which a substantial minority of the population cannot receive. Generally, the "nationwide" criterion is satisfied by either having member stations across the country (as is the case with PBS in the United States) or, as is the case with most other public broadcasters around the world, the broadcaster owning sufficient transmitters to broadcast nationwide.

Some of these definition points may not be acceptable everywhere. For example in the United States public broadcasting may see part of its mission to bring in foreign shows, e.g. shows from the CBC/Radio-Canada or the BBC.

An alternative model for implementing public service media exists, known as Citizen Media. As it relates to broadcasting, this generally means a radio or television outlet which has some sort of public access, that is, most or much of the programming is created by members of the public which receives the programming. This can be in the form of community radio, campus radio, and public access television, although the latter is not a form of over-the-air broadcasting, as it is only available on cable television systems.

Advantages and Disadvantages: Public broadcasters receive all or a substantial part of their funding from government sources, either from the general tax revenues or from licence fees. Since public broadcasters do not rely on advertising as a source of revenue to the same degree as commercial broadcasters, this allows public broadcasters to air programs that are less saleable to the mass market, such as public affairs shows, documentaries, and educational programs. The fact that public broadcasters do not chase ratings in the same way as commercial broadcasters often leads to the criticism that they are unresponsive to what their viewers want.

Additionally, public broadcasting facilitates the implementation of cultural policy (an industrial policy and investment policy for culture). Some examples include:

- o The Canadian government is committed to official bilingualism (English and French). As a result, the public broadcaster, the CBC employs translators and journalists who speak both official languages and it encourages production of cross-cultural material. Quebec separatists argue that this is also a policy of cultural imperialism and assimilation.
- o In the UK, the BBC supports multiculturalism and diversity, in part by using on-screen commentators and hosts of different ethnic origins.
- o In New Zealand, the public broadcasting system provides support to Aboriginal (Maori) broadcasting, as a way to improve the opportunities and maintain the cultural heritage of these New Zealanders.

Critics of public broadcasting systems argue that this implementation of cultural policy imposes the values of the public broadcaster on the populace. However, it can also be argued that commercial broadcasting has a bias for certain values or cultural forms, such as pop culture, militarism, culture bias, and consumerism.

Public broadcasting, and also some pirate broadcasting, provides a counterweight to the commercial media. Advocates of deliberative democracy, argue that public broadcasting helps to maintain modern technological democracies. At the same time, public broadcasting systems have also been used by dictators and totalitarian governments to spread hatred and incite genocide. However, in theory in "western democracies" public broadcasting is not beholden to political parties, or the government of the day.

This is especially true where the broadcaster is funded by television licence fees and so, theoretically, not dependent on the government for any of its funding.

Implementation of Public Broadcasting around the World: The model, established in the 1920s, of the British Broadcasting Corporation - an organization widely trusted, even by citizens of the Axis Powers during World War II - was widely emulated throughout Europe, the British Empire, and later the Commonwealth. The public broadcasters in a number of countries are basically an application of the model used in Britain.

Modern public broadcasting is often a mixed commercial model. For example, the CBC has always relied on a subsidy from general revenues of the government. However, more recently CBC television has started taking advertising. This means they must compete with commercial broadcasting. Some argue that this dilutes their mandate as truly public broadcasters, who have no commercial bias to distort their presentation.

The rest of this section looks at some specific implementations of public broadcasting around the world.

8

Information Systems for Public Sector Management

As in many countries, public sector reform in India has consisted of five main components: increased efficiency, decentralisation, increased accountability, improved resource management, and marketisation. 'Information age reform' means delivering these ongoing reform components with a more overt role for information and with greater use of information technology. A review of global experience suggests that information age reform has great potential to improve public administration and other components of the public sector. However, the Indian reality - like that for many developing countries - has been more problematic, with many failures of such reform; failures that can be described as total, partial or failures of sustainability and replication.

The explanation for such failure lies partly in the approach to reform adopted by senior public officials. A 'four Is' model of approaches is described: the pre-information age approach of 'ignore', and the information age approaches of 'isolate', 'idolise' and 'integrate'. Analysis of Indian cases suggests it is the last approach that is most likely to deliver reform objectives; yet it remains the least commonly-adopted. Changes are therefore required in current strategies for public administration training and the management of change. Such findings will hold true for many other developing countries.

Reform Agenda

Public sector reform is, if generally defined, change within public sector organisations that seeks to improve their performance.

As such, reform can be seen as an ongoing process in India since the inception several centuries ago of institutions that we now label 'public sector'. However, reform is typically defined more narrowly. It is often associated with the ideology of the 'New Right' towards the public sector; an ideology that grew up especially from the 1970s and which sought particular types of change in the way the public sector was run. This ideology has, albeit slowly and by 'fits and starts', increasingly begun to shape the agenda for change in the Indian public sector.

What constitutes the public sector reform agenda in India? There has been no consistent menu of elements but typical components - driven by the global agenda of new public management - include those listed below.

- Increased Efficiency: Improving the input-output ratio within the public sector. The rationale of such reforms is to address the large size of public sector expenditure and/or the inefficiency of many of its processes.
- Decentralisation: The transfer of decision making to lower, more localised levels of the public sector. The rationale of such reforms is to reduce the costs of centralised decision making, and to create more flexible and responsive decision making.
- Increased Accountability: Making public sector staff more accountable for their decisions and actions. The rationale of such reforms is to increase the pressure on staff to perform well, to make them more responsive to recipient groups, and to reduce inefficient or corrupt practices.
- Improved Resource Management: Increasing the effective use of human, financial and other resources. The rationale of such reforms is clear from their definition. It often includes a refocusing of the way the performance of these resources is planned, measured and managed.
- Marketisation: Increasing the use of market forces to cover relationships within the public sector, relationships between citizens ('consumers') and the public sector, and relationships and boundaries between public and private sector. The rationale of such reforms is that market relations

will drive costs down and increase efficiency and/or effectiveness of service delivery.

There has been much criticism of the components listed: of what they seek to achieve in theory, and of what they do and do not achieve in practice.

In this paper, we are not going to participate in that particular debate because that is not our purpose. These components will be taken as a given; as initiatives that are being evermore widely undertaken or imposed. For increasing numbers of Indian public servants, the issue is not the rights and wrongs of reform, but how best to implement reform initiatives in which they find themselves involved.

INFORMATION AGE IN INDIA

Almost simultaneous with the development of a reform agenda, there has been a growing sense in India of a real or impending 'information age'.

The roots of ideas about a new 'information age' - treated here as synonymous with emergence of an 'information economy', 'information society' or 'post-industrial society' - are invariably traced back to the work of writers such as Daniel Bell, Fritz Machlup, Yuji Masuda and Alvin Toffler (e.g. Bell, 1974; Machlup, 1962; Masuda, 1983; Toffler, 1980). Through analysis of extant trends, they described a vision of a new world paradigm that was already coming into existence and that would increasingly develop. General features of this new paradigm include a domination of services over other economic sectors, niche instead of mass markets, and the emergence of a 'post-bureaucratic' form of organisation. The early, and optimistic, writings about the information age have been much criticised. Critics argue:

- o That things have not changed as much as predicted. Peasant farmers - who, with their families, form a major proportion of the world's population - continue to live and work much as they have ever done. They have yet to appreciate the pleasures of surfing the Net or teleworking. Even in the high citadels of the new world, shifts in working patterns and social life may be tangible and important, but they are not yet revolutionary. A modified criticism is therefore that change has been, and will be, a very uneven process that creates inequalities.

- o That, when things do change, there will be problems as well as benefits. The information age may be marked by higher living standards but also by unemployment, insecurity, electronic surveillance and alienation.
- o That the technology focus of information age writing distracts us from the human, social and political factors which explain - and therefore ultimately determine - what happens in our world.

There is a great deal of validity in these criticisms, but what they do not deny is that- albeit slowly and unevenly, for better or worse - there are identifiable information age trends. Thus, while the concept of an information age retains a large measure of hyperbole, it does serve to highlight important trends that are shaping the world in which we live.

It is certain that they have begun to shape the economic and political context in India.

Whilst many see the 1970s as something of a 'lost decade' for India in computing terms, the country more than made up in the 1980s. The 1984-87 period in office of 'Rajiv and his computer boys' marked a defining moment during which India's image and activity as a global software player really began to take off, and during which a clear link was made between computing and reform of Indian public administration.

Although information technology (IT) has never since been so heavily-championed at such a high level in government, the catalytic actions of the mid-1980s set loose two specific, related and seemingly unstoppable information age trends in India:

- o The increasing importance of information, including the increasing visibility and value of information systems.
- o The increasing use of information technology.

Defining IT and IS: Information technology can be defined as computing and telecommunications technologies that provide automatic means of handling information. IT is therefore taken here to represent equipment: both the tangible hardware and the intangible software. A computer linked to other computers on a local area network represents one example of IT.

Information systems (IS) can be defined as systems of human and technical components that accept, store, process, output and transmit information. They may be based on any combination of human endeavours, paper-based methods and IT. A financial information system of staff and computers that gathers data and processes it into reports used for managerial decision making represents one example of an IS.

Thus:

- o IT on its own does not do anything useful; in order to do anything, it must become part of an information system.
- o Information systems do not necessarily involve computers and telecommunications equipment.
- o Even when they do, information systems are much more than just IT because they involve people and their actions.

For the public sector in India, this means that one can therefore see a trend of 'information age reform' that combines the existing reform agenda with the promise of the information age. Indeed, from humble beginnings in the Indian Statistical Institute in 1956, government expenditure on IT has grown to average more than US$350m per annum by the late 1990s (Dataquest, 1998).

Information age reform is therefore a growing reality for India which means two things that are different from traditional reform:

- o First, a much greater (i.e. more overt) role for information and information systems in the processes of change in the public sector.
- o Second, a much greater (i.e. more widely employed) role for information technology in the processes of change in the public sector.

PROMISE OF INFORMATION AGE

Reform: There is great potential for these trends of information age reform to bring significant benefits to India because government has been, and still remains, the single largest collector, user, holder and producer of information. Information is a central resource for all staff levels and for all activities: 'In pursuing the democratic/political processes, in managing resources, executing functions, measuring performance and in service delivery, information is the basic ingredient' (Isaac-Henry, 1997, p.132) The work of government is thus very information-intensive, and four main types of formal information are identifiable:

- o Information to Support Internal Management: This includes information about staff for personnel management, and information about budgets and accounts for financial management. Like the other three types of information, it can be used for everything from day-to-day operational implementation up to long-term policy analysis and planning.
- o Information to Support Public Administration and Regulation: This includes information that records the details of the main 'entities' in India: people, business enterprises, buildings, land plots, imports/exports, etc. It is used for a variety of purposes such as legal, judicial and fiscal.
- o Information to Support Public Services: Examples include education (e.g. school staff records), health (e.g. patient records), transport (e.g. passenger reservation information) and public utilities (e.g. customer billing information).
- o Information made Publicly Available: This includes:
  - Information government wishes to disseminate such as press releases, consultation papers, details of policies, laws and regulations, and details of benefits and entitlements.
  - Information government collects that it may make available, such as demographic or economic statistics.
  - Information government is required to supply such as audited accounts, internal policy documents and correspondence, and responses to requests from politicians or journalists or citizens.

Given this information-intensity, changes in information systems must be an essential part of all reform initiatives in India, and changes in information technology will also have a great potential. In theory, everything that IT can do could be done by some other means. In practice, its ability to increase the speed and/or reduce the cost of information tasks mean it can do things that would not otherwise be contemplated. IT therefore can bring change and has three basic change potentials within reform:

- o Supplant: Automate existing human-executed processes which involve accepting, storing, processing, outputting or transmitting information. For example, the automation of existing clerical functions.
- o Support: Assist existing human-executed processes. For example, assisting existing processes of government decision making, communication, and decision implementation. (This can also be seen as a potential to empower if IT assists the activity of citizens outside government.)
- o Innovate: Create new IT-executed processes or support new human-executed processes. For example, creating new methods of public service delivery. IT can bring five main benefits to the reform process. In practice, these are not neatly differentiated but they can be summarised as:
- o Cheaper: Producing the same outputs at lower total cost.
- o More: Producing more outputs at the same total cost.
- o Quicker: Producing the same outputs at the same total cost in less time.
- o Better: Producing the same outputs at the same total cost in the same time, but to a higher quality standard.
- o For the First Time: Producing new outputs.

The first three represent efficiency gains for the public sector; the last two represent effectiveness gains. Of course, these are the direct and objective benefits. IT can bring many others such as better staff motivation, greater political control, or an improved public image for the organisation (with Indian Railways being a case in point for all three of these indirect benefits).

IT is therefore seen to have a great potential to contribute to reform (Traunmuller and Lenk 1996), with this potential being illustrated by the following examples from around the world:

- o Increased Efficiency: IT's role in increasing efficiency has been described above, mainly relating to its 'supplant' role. In the US, the Lawrence Livermore National Laboratory developed a World Wide Web-based system to reduce the cost and increase the speed of parts procurement (Gebauer and Schad, 1998).
- o Decentralisation: IT can provide support for more efficient and effective decision making at decentralised locations and create new information flows that incorporate those locations. In Ireland, the Department of Social Welfare created more than a dozen computerised applications in order to support the decentralisation of responsibilities from Dublin to outlying offices (Cooney and O'Flaherty, 1996).
- o Increased Accountability: IT can create new accountability information and can deliver accountability information to new recipients, providing for more efficient or effective accountability. In the US, 'collusion detection software' was developed and applied to root out impropriety in bids and contract awards for supply of public school milk (Anthes, 1993).
- o Improved Resource Management: IT can create new performance information and deliver it to decision makers, providing more effective managerial control over government resources. In Malaysia, government development authorities collaborated to develop a computerised system to facilitate land resource management (Raman and Yap, 1996).
- o Marketisation: IT can supply the new information necessary for the establishment of market relations, and can also form the conduit for delivery of new forms of public service. 'In Spain and Portugal, smart cards are issued to people to claim unemployment benefit at kiosks, and to check on job vacancies and training opportunities.' (Gosling, 1997, p.69).

Bibliography

AUCOIN, Peter, and Mark D. JARVIS. Modernizing Government Accountability: A Framework for Reform. Ottawa: Canada School of Public Service, 2005.

CHRISTOPH, James B. Canadian Public Administration, J. E. Hodgetts and D.C. Corbett. Toronto: MacMillan, 1960.

DAWSON, Robert MacGregor: The Civil Service of Canada. London: Oxford University Press, 1929.

DUNN, Christopher: The Handbook of Canadian Public Administration. Toronto: Oxford University Press, 2002.

FORSEY, Eugene: Freedom and Order: Collected Essays. Toronto: McClelland and Stewart, 1974.

GRIFFITH, Wyn: The British Civil Service 1854-1954. London: Her Majesty's Stationery Office, 1954.

HODGETTS, J.E. : The Canadian Public Service: A Physiology of Government 1867-1970. Toronto: University of Toronto Press, 1973.

HOGG, Peter W.: Constitutional Law of Canada, Student Edition 2004. Toronto: Thomson Canada Limited, 2004.

HURLEY, James Ross: Amending Canada's Constitution. Ottawa: Ministry of Supply and Services Canada, 1996.

MURRAY, Sir George: Report on the Organization of the Public Service of Canada. Ottawa: 1910.

NORTHCOTE, Stafford H. and C.E. Trevelyan: Report on the Organisation of the Permanent Civil Service, London: 1854.

SAVOIE, Donald J. Breaking the Bargain: Public Servants, Ministers and Parliament. Toronto: University of Toronto Press, 2003.

SIMPSON, Jeffrey. Spoils of Power: The Politics of Patronage. Toronto: Collins Publishers, 1988.

THOMAS, Paul: Optimum Online: The Journal of Public Sector Management, volume 38, Issue 2, May 2008.

Index

♦♦♦